The Sounds of Aguante

Luis Achondo

THE SOUNDS OF AGUANTE

Politics of Fandom in South American Football

Wesleyan University Press Middletown, Connecticut

Wesleyan University Press
Middletown CT 06459
www.wesleyan.edu/wespress

Manufactured in the United States of America
Designed by Mindy Basinger Hill / Typeset in Minion Pro

We gratefully acknowledge that this publication has been made possible, in part, by funding provided by the Iberian and Latin American Music Fund of the American Musicological Society (AMS).

Library of Congress Cataloging-in-Publication Data
available at https://catalog.loc.gov/
cloth ISBN 978-08195-0192-9
paper ISBN 978-08195-0193-6
ebook ISBN 978-08195-0194-3

5 4 3 2 1

FOR WHITNEY AND CAMILA

CONTENTS

ACKNOWLEDGMENTS

This book has been written during transnational movements between the Global North and South—journeys marked by violence, cultural friction, migratory instability, and a once-in-a-lifetime pandemic. Amid these challenges, several individuals and institutions have provided invaluable support and stability. These acknowledgments are a humble and limited way to express my deep appreciation for their help and encouragement.

I would like to begin by expressing my gratitude to the series of grants and institutions that funded the fieldwork and writing of this book: Fulbright, the Institute for International Education, the Tinker Foundation, and Brown University's Graduate School, Cogut Institute for the Humanities, and Center for Latin American and Caribbean Studies (CLACS). Additionally, the Fondecyt Postdoctorado 3220114 grant from Chile's Agencia Nacional de Investigación y Desarrollo (ANID) was instrumental in completing this book.

During my doctoral studies at Brown University, I had the privilege of interacting with many wonderful individuals. In the Department of Music, I am especially grateful to Emily Dolan, Dana Gooley, Kiri Miller, and Marc Perlman. I owe a special thanks to Marc and Kiri, whose expertise and experience were offered with humility, enthusiasm, and care as mentors and later as committee members. My doctoral journey was guided by Joshua Tucker, to whom I am immensely grateful for his guidance, patience, and perspective. It is difficult to quantify how much of his wisdom and ideas are woven into this book. I also deeply appreciate my fellow graduate students for their friendship and intellectual curiosity: Byrd McDaniel, Louis Wenger, Jamie Corbett, Esther Kurtz, Dave Fossum, Melody Chapin, Michael Deck, Alexander Hardan, Violet Cavicchi, and Jay Loomis. Faculty members in the Department of Anthropology, particularly Paja Faudree and Jessaca Leinaweaver, were a constant source of support, helping me think anthropologically about sound and music. Brown was everything I hoped for when I decided to migrate to the United States.

After completing my doctoral studies, I spent a year as a HILLS Postdoctoral Scholar in the Humanities at Case Western Reserve University. During this time, I began transforming my dissertation into a book manuscript and had the good fortune of engaging in stimulating conversations with graduate students and faculty members, including George Blake, Francesca Brittan, Georgia Cowart, Daniel Goldmark, Susan McClary, AJ Kluth, and David Rothenberg. Presenting at their colloquium series significantly influenced my ideas on music.

At Memorial University, I have been warmly welcomed by administrators, faculty, staff, and students. I am especially grateful to Harris Berger and Meghan Forsyth for their support. It is truly an honor to be part of this vibrant community.

I spent three years as a postdoctoral fellow at the Pontificia Universidad Católica de Chile, where doctoral candidates and undergraduate students in musicology provided fresh perspectives on music and culture. Conversations with José Manuel Izquierdo, Malucha Subiabre, Alejandro Vera, and especially Daniel Party greatly enriched my views on pedagogy and scholarship.

I am also grateful to the Centro de Culturas Musicales y Sonoras (CMUS), funded by ANID's Millennium Science Initiative Program NCS2022_016. At CMUS, I had the privilege of engaging in interdisciplinary conversations with Natalia Bieletto, Andrea Chamorro, Leonardo Díaz, Daniel Domingo, Daniela Fugellie, Laura Jordán, Eileen Karmy, Martín Liut, Sebastián Muñoz, Carla Pinochet, Javier Rodríguez, Javier Silva, Ignacio Soto, and Christian Spencer. Their insights significantly enriched my theoretical approaches to sound and music.

Presentations at the Society for Ethnomusicology, the Latin American Studies Association, and the Sociedad Chilena de Musicología provided valuable opportunities to develop my ideas and engage with scholars from both the Global North and South. A keynote presentation at ICTMD-Chile at the Universidad de Tarapacá, along with invited presentations at the Simposio de Violencias Acústicas and the roundtable Problemas en Torno a la Voz y la Escucha (both organized by Natalia Bieletto) at Universidad Mayor, were instrumental in refining my ideas as I neared the completion of this manuscript.

Beyond my institutional affiliations, I have been incredibly fortunate to receive the support and encouragement of many remarkable scholars. I would like to extend my deepest gratitude to Jacky Avila, Christina Azahar, Sean Bellaviti, Luis Campos, Ian Copeland, Ana María Díaz, Shannon Garland, Kaleb Goldschmitt, Paula Harper, Max Jack, Jan Koplow, Myrta Leslie Santana, Mike Levine, Alejandro Madrid, Amanda Minks, Marysol Quevedo, Michael O'Brien, Javier Osorio, Tony Rasmussen, Jacob Rekedal, Fernando Rios, Hannah Snavely, Susan Thomas, Sergio Ospina, Lydia Wagenknecht, Juan Eduardo Wolf, Katerine Zamora, and Eduardo Herrera, who served as a committee member and has become a selfless mentor. The collective insights, guidance, and encouragement of these scholars have profoundly informed and enriched this book. I sincerely apologize if I have inadvertently omitted anyone.

At Wesleyan University Press, I am deeply grateful to Suzanna Tamminen, Hannah Krasikov, Natalie Jones, the editorial and production teams, and the editors of the Music/Culture Series—Deborah Wong, Sherrie Tucker, and Jeremy Wallach—for their immense support and encouragement throughout the entire process. I also extend my thanks to the anonymous reviewers, whose thought-provoking questions, insightful clarifications, and suggestions for new analytical areas pushed me to elevate the book to the highest intellectual standards.

I also want to extend my heartfelt gratitude to all the fans who took the time to speak with me. Each individual who contributed to this project opened a door for me, and I am profoundly grateful for your trust, even when our views on moral and political matters may have differed. Your insights and experiences have enriched this work in ways I cannot fully express. Any mistakes in this book are entirely my own.

I could not have written this book without the unwavering support of my friends and family. Friends have been a constant source of support and reflection, especially Lucas, Tomás, Nicolás, Álvaro, and Alejandro. My parents, Luis and Zunilda, have steadfastly supported me from the moment I decided to become a musician and later a scholar, continuing their support while I lived abroad, even during the two years we could not see each other due to the COVID-19 pandemic. My sister, Mayarí, has provided invaluable emotional support, unique philosophical insights, and suggestions to improve my writing. Gracias por todo, familia. Gary, Gretchen, and Morgan have welcomed me into their lives with love and care, with Gretchen also generously contributing clear writing suggestions. Whitney has become the bedrock of my existence, offering boundless love, support, care, and intellectual curiosity. Her insights, humor, strength, and singing voice are woven throughout these pages. Finally, nothing would make sense without Camila, the engine of my world. Every laugh, every word, every gesture, and every song she shares has made this writing meaningful. Has sido un soplo de energía formidable en un mar de incertidumbre. Este libro es tuyo.

NOTE ON THE COMPANION WEBSITE

Video examples of some of the cases discussed in this book are available on the accompanying Reader's Companion: https://www.weslpress.org/readers-companions/. Access using the password: SA01936. In text, references to audio-visual materials are marked . Readers are encouraged to consult the website as they read through this book.

VIDEOS AVAILABLE ON THE COMPANION SITE

Introduction

VIDEO 0.1 Los de Abajo: "El Bulla va caminando para Pedreros"

(Trans)local Feedbacks

VIDEO 1.1 Hinchas playing murga porteña
VIDEO 1.2 Los Fabulosos Cadillacs: "Matador"
VIDEO 1.3 La Guardia Imperial: "Muchachos, traigan vino juega la Acade"
VIDEO 1.4 La 12: "Nosotros Alentamos"
VIDEO 1.5 Los Borrachos del Tablón: "Todos los domingos a la tarde, yo vengo a alentarte"
VIDEO 1.6 Los Borrachos del Tablón: "Qué feo ser bostero y boliviano"
VIDEO 1.7 La Gloriosa Butteler: "Saltando Paredes"
VIDEO 1.8 Héctor Maure: "Marcha Peronista"
VIDEO 1.9 Los Borrachos del Tablón: "Dale campeón"
VIDEO 1.10 La 12: "Sí, sí, señores, yo soy de Boca"
VIDEO 1.11 Los Borrachos del Tablón: "Quiero la Libertadores"

Attribution and Creativity

Affect and Labor

Vocal Damage

Epilogue

The Sounds of Aguante

Introduction

I had been waiting for nearly ten minutes when Miguel arrived at Vicente Valdés. A critical intersection in southern Santiago de Chile, the luminous subway station was overflowing with people, as usual. We decided to move away from the crowd while we waited for the other *hinchas* (pronounced "eencha"; fans or supporters) of Universidad de Chile.[1] Known as La U and founded by the nation's premier public university, U. de Chile stands as one of the most popular and successful teams in the country's professional soccer, or football.[2] I asked Miguel if he had caught the 2018 World Cup's opening match, only to receive a terse response indicating his infrequent engagement with both national and foreign club matches. "Well, I do watch games of [Argentina's] Racing Club sometimes," he added, trying to qualify his assertion.[3] He did not seem wholly invested in the conversation, constantly checking his phone and nervously observing the passersby around us. He became aware of his rudeness and told me that "the *barra* is tense."

A barra denotes an organized group of hinchas within an *hinchada* (pronounced "eenchada"; essentially, a club's fanbase) that is known for its continuous chanting, musical performances, choreographed displays, and involvement in violent and criminal activity.[4] Miguel was specifically referring to Los de Abajo (The Underdogs), a group of primarily working-class hinchas who, since the late 1980s, have supported U. de Chile using fan practices initially borrowed from the Argentine football fandom. A clique known as Ferroazul had stolen a cloth banner from the violent cabal Los Suicidas (The Suicidals) the previous night—a frontline faction of Garra Blanca (White Claw), the barra of archrivals Colo-Colo. Miguel explained to me: "It's like if Garra Blanca had stolen a banner from Los de Abajo's leading factions. Los Suicidas are going crazy looking for revenge." Earlier that day, I had come across a Facebook post showing a stolen banner turned upside down, but I had failed to grasp the theft's relevance at that moment.

Stealing banners from opposing groups constitutes a fundamental mechanism for gaining notoriety within the violent conflicts that shape the culture of *aguante*—a term that, roughly translatable as "endurance" or "stamina," signifies the transnational football fandom of Latin America's Southern Cone. In a bid to exert social control and bolster the status, influence, and assets of their respective barras, hinchas constantly engage in confrontations with their rivals. These struggles encompass a spectrum of actions ranging from vocal performance to acts as extreme as torture and homicide. Due to the symbolic value attached to banners—synecdoches of factions—these thefts frequently escalate into physical clashes. In the past, physical brawls acted as mediators in these robberies, but the radicalization of fan hostilities has normalized the utilization of firearms and other lethal weapons. This necropolitical reality set the stage for the theft of Los Suicidas' banner.

The radicalization of the symbolic conflict inherent in football is a phenomenon that spans the entire Southern Cone. Chilean, Argentine, and Uruguayan hinchas discuss and compete, both domestically and internationally, over which hinchada is the most musically creative, dominantly assertive, unwaveringly loyal, and sonically intense in South America. For many hinchas throughout the region, these rivalries transcend the symbolic realm, escalating into intense enmities that spill over into other aspects of their daily lives. Many of these conflicts are transnational in nature, evident in the large-scale brawls that frequently erupt before and after international matches. That said, the (trans)local dimension of aguante extends beyond conflict, encompassing a dense web of affinities and exchanges. Circulating throughout Chile, Argentina, and Uruguay via international matches, television broadcasts, streaming services, migratory movements, and both analog and digital media, these practices socialize geographically distant subalterns, create transnational channels of communication, and disseminate alternative cosmopolitan imaginaries (Achondo 2021, 2023).

Recognizing these dynamics, a wealth of publications has aimed to emphasize the central role of football in Latin American cultures and societies (Buarque de Hollanda and Busset 2023; Campomar 2014; Gaffney 2008; Galeano 1998; Mason 1995; Orton 2023). Supporting the idea that "the imagined community of millions seems more real as a team of eleven named people" (Hobsbawm 1990,

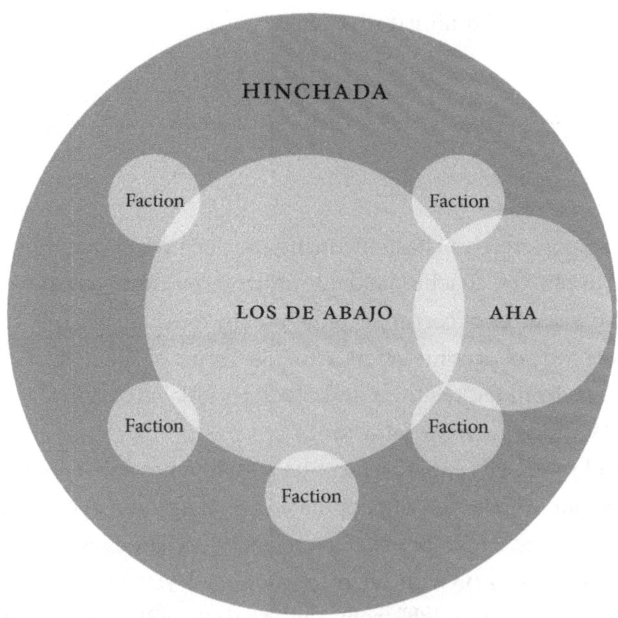

FIGURE 0.1 U. de Chile's fanbase.

143), this body of literature has shed light on how the sport serves as a conduit for the expression of nationalism (Archetti 1999; Sibaja and Parrish 2014), the exertion of state control (Alabarces and Rodríguez 1996; Moreira et al. 2018; Nadel 2014), and the reinforcement of national narratives for both domestic and international purposes (Alabarces 2007; Brown 2014; Elsey 2011; Karush 2003; Rein 2014; Snyder 2022). Beyond the confines of the nation-state, football permeates many aspects of everyday life, influencing the region's social movements, geopolitical relations, and economic trends. More than mere spaces of obsessive leisure, football clubs have evolved into pivotal mediators of the social, cultural, economic, and political life in the region (Elsey 2011; Frydenberg 2011; Nadel 2014; Rein 2014). Intertwined with neighborhood relations, these institutions have historically provided avenues for civic and democratic engagement for hinchas, who have been afforded the opportunity to elect administrators, influence club policies, and partake in activities and services spanning from utilizing multisport facilities to engaging in adult education (Forment 2007; Rein 2015).

TABLE 1 U. de Chile's Administrative History

PERIOD	1934–1978	1978–2006	2007–PRESENT
Administrative Entity	Universidad de Chile	Corfuch	Azul Azul

Clubs have empowered hinchas, nurturing the perception that they bear equal significance to players, coaches, and administrators. However, this perspective has also led to instances of corrupt exploitation by hinchas, all while enabling the elites to assert control over members, cultivate forms of clientelism, and extract economic value from fan relations and practices (Alabarces 2012, 2018; Garriga 2007, 2010; Hawkins 2017; Moreira 2008).

Miguel and I were en route to a meeting with hinchas and community members from Puente Alto, a densely populated working-class district in southern Santiago. Miguel was a member of the Asociación de Hinchas Azules (Association of Blue Hinchas, AHA), an organization that crystallized in 2014 with the purpose of "recovering the club" from Azul Azul (Blue Blue)—the public limited sports company that transformed U. de Chile into a profit-oriented, sports advertisement corporation. In 2007, influential right-wing businessmen and politicians acquired the club's rights after the nonprofit Corfuch faced bankruptcy due to a contentious reinterpretation of the law governing football clubs' taxation.[5] Corfuch had been created in the 1980s by the Universidad de Chile to administer the club after decades of university management. In addition to regaining agency within the club, AHA also aimed to "reconstruct the club's social fabric," which had been eroded by the discontinuation of Corfuch's democratic assemblies, educational initiatives, sports programs, and other community-oriented activities. In fact, the gathering in Puente Alto marked the third meeting focused on establishing an alternative educational space where local youth could absorb the values of camaraderie, loyalty, and direct democracy that AHA believes define the ethos of U. de Chile.

Because I was wearing a blue U. de Chile sweatshirt, Miguel advised me to conceal it with my coat as we got off the train. I asked him worriedly if Los Suicidas hailed from Puente Alto. He answered that they originated from La Pintana, a deprived district also located in the southern part of the city. Miguel was visibly tense, especially considering that the flyer for the meeting had gained significant traction on social media. His concerns were amplified by the presence of Chalo, the head of Ferroazul, at previous gatherings. "They've burned and shot up houses." Miguel added grimly, "They don't want to recover the banner, they want to kill someone." As AHA members eventually arrived at Vicente Valdés, Miguel once again voiced his apprehensions.

Despite the relatively mild temperature for a June night, I zipped up my coat as we exited the subway in Puente Alto. Around twenty hinchas were gathered in a chilly white room. Concerned about potential gunshots, I chose a spot away from the windows. The room was tense, somewhat alleviated by the absence of Chalo. Riva entered shortly after the meeting began, wearing loose-fitting U. de Chile clothes, a pendant featuring an owl emblem (symbolic of the club and the university), and an ample amount of hair gel. Taking a seat to my right, he told me that he had asked neighbors to stay watchful for any suspicious activities. In a composed manner, he mentioned that he would receive a phone call if Garra Blanca were to come. Observing my unease, he encouraged me to calm down. "This is a blue neighborhood," and gesturing toward the hincha on his right, he added, "Rodri and I are part of Los de Abajo's *piño de choque* [fighting group]." He went on to explain that they had secured their territory through fighting, revealing his scars and U. de Chile tattoos on his chest and arms. "La Pintana is a war zone right now," he continued, "everything is going crazy over there, [U. de Chile hinchas] are fighting [with Colo-Colo hinchas] over every meter." Generally structured around neighborhood associations, the factions within barras are perpetually entangled in territorial disputes with rival groups. The theft of Los Suicidas' banner exacerbated preexisting neighborhood hostilities.

After an hour of tense anticipation, it became evident that Los Suicidas would not be making an appearance, so we delved into a discussion about the project. As the meeting concluded, Riva emphasized the importance of caution in the days ahead, stating, "Garra Blanca are shooting up people's houses. We shouldn't wear La U clothes and be careful when going to the stadium." Although Miguel concurred, he also valued that the hinchada was still establishing fresh "horizontal, participatory, and democratic spaces—*haciendo club* [roughly, 'bringing the club to life']."

These thefts and retaliations have become cyclical, plunging hinchas into an ongoing state of violent conflict—a necropolitical radicalization that has coincided with both the expansion of the Chilean neoliberal model (Ganti 2014) and the global hyper-commodification of football (Giulianotti 2002). Chile, functioning as the global test case for neoliberal policy since the 1970s, has systematically privatized state-owned firms, reduced government power, embraced open markets, imposed more flexible labor relations, and dismantled welfare programs (Ahumada 2019; Han 2012; Moulian 1997; Paley 2001; Pérez 2022; Richards 1997). Drawing inspiration from the English model (Giulianotti and Robertson 2009), authorities have also implemented a series of laws that have managed to fully privatize and commercialize football. Supported by the Law 20620, which targets stadium violence, the Law 20019 forced clubs to become publicly traded companies in the mid-2000s, turning stock ownership into the main mode of administration and participation. Companies such as Azul Azul banned hinchas from club spaces, reframing them as consumers while criminalizing those who deviate from market-based relations.

These asymmetries, intersecting with broader conditions of violence and precarity, have ignited both internal and external conflicts. Within the U. de Chile hinchada, various factions have criticized the market-driven model, contesting what they refer to as "fútbol de mercado" (roughly, "corporate football") through actions ranging from sonic modes of dissent to material acts of violent disruption. Amid club marginalization and unequal societal resources, conflicts have also erupted within the hinchada itself, as factions vie for internal social control, the hierarchical accumulation of symbolic and material capital, and the domination of other peer collectives, regardless of their actual involvement in these power struggles.

These hostilities have intersected with contingent necropolitics. With the expansion of organized crime in impoverished areas, barras and criminal cartels have become increasingly intertwined. Recognizing the sentiments of dispossession stemming from asymmetries and inequalities in football and society at large, drug-trafficking syndicates have expanded and capitalized on their preexisting connections with barras, garnering influence and acceptance within their ranks. The resonance between the value of violence within aguante and narco culture has heightened and intensified existing conflicts within the fandom, leading to an entanglement of the two realms. Indeed, both Ferroazul and Los Suicidas have connections to the world of drug trafficking. These radicalized groups see rival hinchas as radical enemies whom they are willing to fight, torture, and assassinate.

The following night, I attended a friendly match between U. de Chile and Unión Española at the latter's Santa Laura Stadium. As I jotted down notes about the stadium's basic facilities, a WhatsApp message from Riva popped up on my phone: "Bro, a guy from Los Suicidas has died. Things are going to get nasty. Don't tell anyone, just be careful." Los de Abajo had shot and injured many hinchas when they ambushed Los Suicidas. One of them was rumored to have died. I checked news websites on my phone, but no information about the incident was available. This did not surprise me, given that the recurring deaths of hinchas rarely garner attention in the public domain. Nevertheless, Los Suicidas had shared the following on Facebook: "Bullets will be fired, coffins will be prepared, you will die."

U. de Chile hinchas began to trickle into the stadium, hanging their banners on the barbed-wire fence that demarcated the field from the audience. The iconography embraced by older factions drew inspiration from metal culture, which held substantial sway among the proletariat during the late 1980s and early 1990s. The banners of younger groups integrated elements of narco culture, amalgamating U. de Chile motifs with depictions of weaponry and other symbols celebrating criminality. Fifteen minutes before the kick-off, the fence became engulfed by banners, obscuring the view of the field.

The connections between football fandom and other areas of popular culture extends beyond the realms of metal and narco aesthetics. While their musical repertoire encompasses contrafacta renditions of diverse forms of popular music, the influence of carnival culture is deeply ingrained within hinchadas. Barras have adopted the *bombo con platillo* (a double-headed bass drum with a mounted cymbal) and the rhythms of *murga porteña*—a genre linked to the Buenos Aires carnival—as accompaniments to their chants.

The U. de Chile hinchas maintained a continuous flow of singing and movement throughout the entire game. Positioned on *para-avalanchas* (anti-stampede metal bars) with their backs turned to the field, the frontline of Los de Abajo prompted additional singing from their peers through a combination of insults and assertive hand gestures. Jumps and rhythmic fist bumps accompanied their vocalizations. Concurrently, two hinchas captured the performance on their phones—videos that they that would later share across Los de Abajo's social media channels.

Eventually, over the melody of "The Battle Hymn of the Republic," Los de Abajo erupted with the chant "Les robamos la bandera, que la vengan a buscar" (We Stole Your Flag, Come and Get It Back). The defiant declaration was accompanied by ecstatic jumps and intense vocalizations, leading into one of their most cherished chants against Garra Blanca (video 0.1):

El Bulla va caminando para Pedreros (¡Culiando zorras!)	The Noise is walking to Pedrero (fucking zorras!)[6]
El indio pide custodia porque es cagón (¡Cagón!)	The Indian asks for police custody because he's a pussy (pussy!)[7]
Vamos a romper los baños y el alambrado (¡Al indio culia'o!)	We'll destroy the bathrooms and the fences (the Indian fucker!)
Para ver cuál hinchada es la mejor (¡La del León!)	To show which hinchada is the best (the Lion's one!)
Oh, porque el Bulla es un sentimiento	Oh, because El Bulla is a sentiment
Oh, a balazos se van a tirar	Oh, they'll shoot at us
Oh, Indio, sapo y la conch'e tu ma're	Oh, Indian, motherfucking snitch
A balazos se van a tirar	Oh, they'll shoot at us

Following the amplification of the necropolitical landscape of hinchadas, the chant transitioned into a new segment, accompanied by a change in the drum from quarter to half notes. The hinchas stopped jumping, raised their arms into the air, and stretched them out while rhythmically clapping along. This shift infused the atmosphere with a slower yet intensely charged pathos:

Porque soy de abajo	Because I'm an underdog
Y tenemos aguante	And I have endurance
A ese indio hueco	That Indian hueco [homophobic slur]
Lo vamos a reventar	Will be destroyed
Somos de la brava	We're the bravest one
Siempre te acompaño	I'm always there
A ese indio hueco	That Indian hueco
Lo vamos a reventar	Will be destroyed

Set to the melody of "Verano del '92" (Summer of '92) by the Argentine rock band Los Piojos, the lyrics pitted Los de Abajo against Garra Blanca, employing sexist and homophobic slurs as they vowed their utter obliteration. Los de Abajo continued to sing the same chant for several minutes, audibly reasserting their proclaimed dominance over Garra Blanca. The stadium reverberated with the hinchada's collective voice.

As the game neared its conclusion, a young hincha approached the crowd nervously, requesting Los de Abajo's blue flags. Tension spread through the stands, but I struggled to understand the situation. Eventually, I overheard a man informing a woman that "the zorras are outside." I panicked, torn between leaving the stadium and waiting until the brewing combat subsided. Opting for the former, I made my way out just as families around me hurriedly departed.

Stepping out of the stands, I was met with a cacophony of shouts and chants as Garra Blanca erupted into rioting outside the stadium. The soundscape was tumultuous: The cries and chants collided with the echoes of police gunfire and blaring sirens. A guard stationed at the gate yelled, "Run to your right—it's a mess on the other side!" Following the crowd, I began running as well. The parallel street reverberated with the sounds of Garra Blanca also sprinting in the same direction. Upon reaching the corner, I encountered a firetruck moving against the traffic. Its destination was the car that Garra Blanca had set ablaze—an automobile that I later learned Chalo utilized for stealing ATMs as part of his everyday job. I kept running until I reached a bus stop. Although I missed one, another promptly arrived, affording me a safe exit from the area.

AGUANTE

The aguante discourse underpins the scenes of violence depicted in the preceding ethnographic vignette (Alabarces 2005, 2012, 2014; Améstica 2017; Garriga 2007, 2010; Moreira 2007, 2008). *Aguantar* (aguante in its infinitive form) means to endure, resist, or support something or someone, encompassing actions ranging from vocalizing intensely to enduring torture. Accruable and deployable, aguante functions as a symbolic capital that, operating within a necropolitical regime of value, can be transacted with directors, police, and politicians for economic, social, and political goods. Enduring pain and performing arduous embodied practices mark hinchas as *aguantadores* (men embodying aguante), engendering internal asymmetries and facilitating the hierarchical distribution of resources within the football universe.[8] While the accumulation and expression of aguante can manifest through displays of loyalty and passion, its fundamental acquisition and exertion transpire through immediate and meditated, overt and aestheticized, forms of violence. This necropolitical reality has positioned death as an everyday component of hinchas' lives—a consistent yet unquantifiable toll that rarely breaches the public sphere.[9]

Mediating ethics and aesthetics, aguante is, in the words of hinchas, "una forma de vida" (a way of living)—a framework that, orbiting around a positive interpretation of violence, informs how hinchas perceive, think, and behave in the world. Aguante presents football as an all-encompassing, radicalized competition wherein adversaries must be subjugated, if not obliterated, not only on the field but also in the stands and beyond (Achondo 2021). Rooted in working-class values, hinchas pit aguante's expressions, social norms, regimes of value, and modes of interaction against the liberal democratic values and markers of respectability favored by the region's elites (Achondo 2023).[10] As hinchas conceptualize violence as the central mediator of social life, they extend aguante's framework of enmity to encompass not only rival fans but also the police, club administrators, football's governing bodies, and society at large. Valuing violent action as a means to compete, exert social control, forge dominant personae, and configure hierarchical asymmetries, this way of thinking and being in the world is organized around an array of insurmountable conflicts, with resolution attainable only through force, if not death.

Tied to socioeconomic precarity, aguante is intertwined with neoliberalism (Alabarces 2012). During the brutal military regimes of the 1970s and 1980s, the Southern Cone served as the testing ground for neoliberal policies (Ganti 2014), aiming to prove the mantra that "human well-being can best be advanced by liberating individual entrepreneurial freedom and skills within an institutional framework characterized by strong private property rights, free markets, and free trade" (Harvey 2005, 2). David Harvey (2007) argues that neoliberalism has reinforced the dominance of the upper class by diverting wealth and dismantling preexisting institutions advocating for a more equitable distribution of resources. The global hegemony of neoliberalism has not only inflicted precarity upon vulnerable populations but has also facilitated the emergence of criminally exploitative behaviors within its legal and market frameworks (Schneider and Schneider 2008). The thanatopolitical implementations of neoliberalism—characterized by the deregulation of moral schemes, economic relations, and use of violence—have created the conditions for the emergence of barras. These collectives have served as alternative spaces for social control, production of value, accumulation of capital, and, paradoxically, insurrectional politics against neoliberal asymmetries.

The development of aguante's ambivalent relationship with neoliberalism has coincided with the global hyper-commodification of football (Giulianotti 2002; Giulianotti and Robertson 2009). Since the 1980s, substantial amounts of capital have been poured into the sport from media corporations, clothing companies, public relations firms, and the stock market through club shares, among others. The solidification of football's political economy has also run parallel to the emergence of new sociocultural dynamics, including increased labor migration, the proliferation of continental and global competitions, and novel modes of representation facilitated by the rise of football-focused media outlets. Barras have responded to the hyper-commodification of the sport in an ambiguous, if not paradoxical, manner. While their transactional methods have found resonance within the profit-driven operations of these sports corporations, their significance within the clubs' social fabric has diminished, prompting them to rebel against the disparities enacted by football's structures and value production processes.

Conflict serves as a fundamental driving force in aguante, weaving through the competitive essence of the sport, the antagonistic relations with governing bodies, and the hostile dynamics between and within hinchadas. Social theorists emphasize that conflict serves as a stabilizing force within social worlds—an "unequal relationship" between competing entities, aimed "not of liquidating an adversary, and the relationship itself, but of modifying the relationship, or at least strengthening their relative position" (Wieviorka 2009, 10). Conflicts operate as structuring phenomena, lending stability to conflicting relationships by institutionalizing them, establishing norms for negotiation, and developing modes of interaction that uphold both relational bonds and divisive distinctions. It is when hostilities are not sublimated through "conflictual consensus" that conflicts can "explode into violence" (Mouffe 2013, 122). Within this framework, while conflict holds the potential for violence, the two should not be equated as the latter entails a rupture of the former.

In adeptly untangling these concepts, however, this approach to conflict has inadvertently portrayed violent acts as exceptional disruptions of "the basic parameters of social life" (Žižek 2008, 207), falling to explain realities where violence serves as a normative, creative, and generative mediator. Such is the case with aguante, where the expansion and radicalization of the football conflict have positioned violence as its central social articulator. As Pedro Marra (2021) observes, in contexts "where social and economic networks deteriorate or are unevenly distributed," such as within *torcidas organizadas* (Brazilian fan organizations), "violence is especially salient in the articulation of social relations" (40). Aguante thus emerges as an arena where violence emerges as an immediate and mediated catalyst of social relations and political action. Mediated by necropolitics, aguante has evolved into a sonorous death-world.

VIOLENCE

Inherently unstable, violence can be applied to a multitude of phenomena (Das 2008). Operating along a multidimensional continuum (Scheper-Hughes and Bourgois 2003), violent acts extend through political (Bourgois 2001; Nordstrom 2004), structural (Farmer 2004), symbolic (Bourdieu 1999), mediated (Meintjes 2017), everyday (Scheper-Hughes 1992), and intimate domains (Das 2007). Far from existing as an isolated social anomaly, violence is interwoven into the engine and social fabric of every society, propelling not only destructive but also creative transformations. It informs the actions of the state and legal frameworks of liberal democracies (Benjamin 2021), serves as a deterrent against the rise of social inequalities (Clastres 1994), sparks processes of decolonization (Fanon 2004), and governs official and alternative administrations of necrotic worlds (Emerson 2019; Esposito 2008; Mbembe 2019).

Violence emerges as the driving force behind aguante, mediating the political action, creative expression, and social relations of barras. Omnidirectional and omnipresent, immediate and mediated, violence functions atmospherically within the fandom. It manifests through a range of aestheticized expressions, from necrotic lyrics to actual acts of murder. In the realm of fan governance, violence catalyzes asymmetries, appropriates spaces, enforces norms, allocates resources, controls bodies, and mediates hostilities. Within the broader domains of football and society, it becomes an instigator of insurrection—a tool to counteract violences and inequalities perpetrated by states, law enforcement, and football's governing bodies.

The role of violent action in exerting social control finds parallels in Pierre Clastres's (1994) work on the generative potential of violence among certain Amerindian societies. Comparing Indigenous social structures and modern liberal states, he presents violence as a positive and productive societal force. While democratic states maintain a monopoly on legitimate violence to uphold an order rooted in the unequal distribution of resources, some Indigenous groups employ violence not as a consequence of unsuccessful exchanges but as a mechanism to prevent the emergence of internal and external hierarchies, divisions, and inequalities. Immediate and inherent, violence serves as "the principal means of maintaining this society's non-division, of maintaining each community's autonomy as *single totality*, free and independent of others" (Clastres 1994, 169; emphasis in the original). As the core operational mode of social organization, violence functions as a mode of governance and resource allocation among certain Amerindian groups, safeguarding Indigenous integrity by maintaining communities segmented, nonhierarchical, and immune to the encroachment of the state.

Walter Benjamin (2021) foregrounds the foundational role of violence in shaping the very essence of the modern state. Examining violent acts in relation to justice and law, he argues that causality lies at the core of violence's inherent ambiguity, suggesting that its manifestations function as interventions in the realm of moral relations. Violence is historically and inexorably intertwined with and monopolized by the functions of the state and the legal system. Indeed, violent acts aim to either preserve or replace existing laws, with the state attaining hegemony not by annihilating opposition but by securing the authority to devise rules—regulations that it subsequently upholds through the use and implicit threat of violent action. Violence thus assumes a pivotal role in both the creation and maintenance of the law itself—a dual function that operates within an unceasing dialectical interplay between violent generation and preservation. Benjamin concludes that, as long as law-preserving violence endures, the potency of law-positing violence wanes, thereby enabling the perpetuation of state power, the encroachment of the law, and the suppression of counterforces within society.

The insurrectional annulment of law and state violence thus becomes a moral imperative for Benjamin. He advocates for a "pure violence" (2021, 58), a violence that stands as a means in itself, detached from justification, and indifferent to ends. This violence finds human expression in revolutionary acts like the proletarian general strike, where workers collectively halt their labor not to present specific demands but to dismantle the core of labor relations under capitalism. It is neither law-positing nor law-preserving but law-destroying violence—pure means with no regard for outcomes or repercussions. Nonetheless, Benjamin acknowledges that human violence carries the risk of not only momentary brutality but also structural injustice. And yet, in an enigmatic stance, Benjamin posits that the profane order can pave the way for an impending "divine violence" (57), an annihilating yet redeeming superior force that, by manifesting divinity in humanity, foreshadows a world deposed of state and law violence.

Franz Fanon (2004) similarly regards violence as a means of insurrection. Informed by the pervasiveness of violence in colonial formations, his writing becomes an affective tool to underscore the impact of colonial brutality on colonized bodies and minds. Violence, as the central mode of controlling and structuring the colony, becomes atmospheric—a ubiquitous and pervasive force of domination. This atmosphere of violence materializes itself not only in brutal exertions over individuals and communities but also in self-destructive forms of alienation, "internecine feuds" that ultimately reinforce "the colonist's existence and domination" (17–18). Fanon argues that, given that colonialism is not a rational but a purely violent machine, it can only be confronted with violent action. This impending "greater violence" (23) is inherent in colonial violence itself, as those immersed in this atmospheric violence can seize and harness it as a "cleansing force" for decolonization (51).

These writings demonstrate that violence, far from solely destructive, can also be socially and politically productive. Violence, inherent in every social structure, is a tool accessible to all members of society, albeit unevenly distributed. As a social and political instrument, it can either create or dismantle communities, establish or overthrow norms, enforce or contest control, distribute or accumulate resources, and uphold or ignite insurrection against prevailing orders. Production and destruction thus form a double-blade sword—a Möbius strip of endless ruination and generation. Simultaneously productive and destructive, violence is not an exception but rather a crucial mediator of social and political organization.

Violence structures aguante, mediating its modes of relation and organization. Violent action empowers hinchas to govern their own communities, allowing them to wrest power from dominant forces and mold their own structures, relations, and organizations. The centrality of violence emplaces hinchas in perpetual struggles over the control and direction of aguante, the football business, and sports administration. Neither divine nor decolonial, however, the violent disruption of sports and societal asymmetries frequently leads to the emergence of necrotic conflicts within and between hinchadas. Indeed, while the violent upheaval brought about by aguante might, whether consciously or not, represent a reclamation of the power wrested from them by the hyper-commodification of football and society, aguante does not necessarily transform inequity into equality. Violence disrupts prevailing hegemonic systems while simultaneously configuring imbalanced and unjust structures and relations. Immersed in an atmosphere polluted by extreme forms of domination such as torture and murder, aguante functions as a necropolitical social formation.

Coined by Achille Mbembe (2003, 2019), *necropolitics* underscores the insufficiency of *biopolitics*—the political administration of life (Foucault 1990)—in explaining social formations where life is governed by the power of death and violence. Necropolitics demonstrates that, in contexts of radical enmity, subjects, groups, and institutions deploy necropower to materially destroy human bodies and configure death-worlds—forms of social existence where "populations are subjected to conditions of life conferring upon them the status of *living dead*" (Mbembe 2003, 40; emphasis in the original). While Mbembe's original analysis primarily focused on the state of exception and the stage of siege (Mbembe 2003), he later illustrated that necropolitics does not solely pertain to hegemonic exercises of necropower but also to subaltern formations where violence emerges as the prevalent mode of relationality (Mbembe 2019).

Necropolitics thus points to alternative formations within a larger thanatopolitical world. Following Guy Emerson (2019), I understand necropolitics as a subaltern reclamation of control over life and death through the exercise of necropower, seizing power from official entities and institutions. In line with Roberto Esposito (2008), I categorize the hegemonic politics and administration of death as *thanatopolitics*. Whereas biopolitics focuses on policies aimed at safeguarding physical bodies for society's well-being (Foucault 1990), thanatopolitics centers on official deployments of power to eradicate the body politic, both physically and symbolically. A response to the Southern Cone's military regimes, neoliberal governments, and corporate entities, aguante has emerged as an extreme struggle over governance—a conflict concerning the social and political administration of death and violence.

Aguante necropolitics has served as a culture-making phenomenon. Far from being solely destructive, violence has nurtured a distinct aesthetic framework. This necropolitical formation has produced and been reproduced through artistic creations, sonic practices, literary forms, and media content. These expressions, symbolic and material, mediated and immediate, have progressively intensified and overwhelmed subjectivities over the course of decades.

By reconceptualizing aguante necropolitics as a culture-making phenomenon, I aim to complement interpretations that tie football violence to transient states of deindividuation (Herrera 2018; Marra 2021). While I acknowledge that violent atmospheres can momentarily push individuals into mental states conducive to disorderly acts, I argue that violence also serves as a subject-making force within aguante. For those who comprehend aguante as "a way of living," violence holds positive moral value, informing their way of thinking and being in the world. Aguante generates an "excess of meaning," burdening subjectivities "with a discourse that can, in extreme cases, come to look like a plethora of meaning" (Wieviorka 2009, 151). This underscores the subject-making potential of necropolitical formations, spaces where individuals are saturated with radicalized meanings and sensations. Aguante, with its culture-making necropolitics, has also given rise to a distinct acoustemology.

NECROPOLITICAL ACOUSTEMOLOGY

This book provides an approach to the intersection of sound and violence "*in* and *from* the South" (Steingo and Sykes 2019, 4), arguing that aguante has nurtured a necropolitical acoustemology. Through drumming, whistling, launching pyrotechnics, and singing contrafacta of popular music, hinchas not only offer their support to their teams but also engage in social relations and political struggles. Hinchadas deploy sound as a representation of, or even in addition to, material violence, serving as a means to incite insurrection against neoliberal and sports-related asymmetries. As it aurally overwhelms subjectivities and fuels deadly conflicts within and between fanbases, sonic aguante simultaneously allows hinchas to exert social control, impose internal hierarchies, and navigate hostilities where force has evolved into the sole method of resolution. Treating sound as an object with fluid analytical boundaries, this book asserts that violence, with its culture-making potential, can function as a creative, transformative force capable of generating vibrant soundworlds.

While music studies has overwhelmingly presented sound as an inherently positive force (Teitelbaum 2022), some scholars have heard more sinister resonances. These writings have amplified troubling uses of music in detention centers (Chornik 2013; Cloonan and Johnson 2009; Cusick 2006, 2008, 2013; Ochoa Gautier 2017), wartime contexts and their aftermaths (Daughtry 2015; Goodman 2010; Pieslak 2009; Pilzer 2022; Pettan 1998), spaces afflicted by terror (Araujo 1988; Birenbaum Quintero 2006; Daughtry and Ritter 2007; Fast and Pegley 2012; Meintjes 2017; Ritter 2002; Simonett 2001; Sneed 2007), nationalistic conflicts (McDonald 2013; Millar 2020), and even within football stadiums (Herrera 2018; Jack 2021b). This scholarship has shed light on the nexus of sound and violence, offering a significant counterpoint to research underscoring the social benefits of music. While some of these studies tend to associate violent acts with destruction, others have underscored their capacity to create, transform, and reproduce acoustic frameworks, accentuating the socially, politically, and culturally constructive dimensions of violence.

J. Martin Daughtry (2015) discusses how listening can situate subjects within warfare, exposing their bodies and psyches to pain. Building upon Steve Goodman's (2010) conceptualization of sound as a vibrational force that encompasses non-, pre-, and para-sonic materials and events, Daughtry argues that sonic vibration facilitates the expansiveness of violence. He writes, "Like sound, and in part through sound, *violent acts are immersive and omnidirectional*, enveloping perpetrators, bystanders, and targets into a single, expansive field of variegated and unpredictable effects" (175; emphasis in the original). Daughtry leans toward presenting sound's vibrational ontology as inherently destructive, suggesting that warfare constrains acoustemological explorations. He argues that violence destroys culture and subjectivity in its pursuit of controlling or eradicating political will: "Culture, both in the anthropological sense of a 'historically transmitted pattern of meanings embodied in symbols' and in the vernacular sense of highly valued artistic works and behavioral practices . . . is eroded under the caustic power of violent acts" (19).

Ana María Ochoa Gautier (2006a) offers a contrasting perspective. While Daughtry argues that stable acoustemologies are unattainable amid the cultural instability of war, Ochoa Gautier suggests that, in social formations where violence saturates everyday life, the acoustic realm can undergo stable and enduring epistemological transformations. She challenges the view of violence as an anticultural phenomenon, asserting that violence is a historically grounded force capable of redefining sonic practices and knowledges. Ochoa Gautier explains that violent atmospheres can structurally transform practices of voicing, sounding, musicking, listening, and silencing, as they become shaped by, responsive to, and exertions of violence.

Studies conducted within zones of conflict affirm the idea that musical performance can be simultaneously violent and culturally productive. Louis Meintjes (2017) demonstrates that Zulu dancing, situated in a conspicuously precarious reality, mediates violence through performance. Dancers imagine and reflect upon violence through performance, integrating it "into the entertainment industry through recordings and professional performances" (146). David McDonald (2013) observes that musical performance provides Palestinians with a platform to enact symbolic acts of violence. In the context of violent occupation, performance becomes an arena for dissent, resignification, and national affirmation, producing acts that function as "legitimate forms of martyrdom and resistance" (2). In his study of political violence among Irish republicans, Stephen Millar (2020) also presents music as a tool for performative productivity. He illustrates that rebel songs have been reperformed throughout history, emphasizing a sense of continuity and situating experiences within a well-defined, historically rooted culture of conflict.

Aguante's necropolitical acoustemology is a culturally situated and historically grounded framework that regards the production and perception of sound as a way of social and political orientation amid atmospheric violence. In Steven

Feld's acoustemological theory (1996, 2003, 2012, 2015), sound acts as a vibrational force that, emanating, penetrating, and resonating in different bodies and surfaces, positions agents in historically concrete, socially contingent, and culturally reciprocal relations between hearing and speaking, listening and sounding. Within necropolitical formations, however, this "relational ontology" (Feld 2015, 12–13) becomes entangled with an "ontology of vibrational force" (Goodman 2010, xix). Sound practice thus emerges as a manifestation of violent ways of thought and existence. Aurally immersed in cross-generational expressions of deadly violence, hinchas become sensorially overwhelmed and subjectively attuned to necropolitics.

Aguante's soundworld encompasses various forms of mediated and immediate violence. Practices of fandom sometimes emerge as symbolic reflections of necropolitics, taking on aestheticized forms in the digital and visceral realms. Yet sound can also function as a source and expression of necropower in its own right. In weaponized manifestations, it operates as a viscerally felt, subject-disorienting force—a phenomenon of "contact and displays" that modulates "the physical, affective, and libidinal dynamics of populations, of bodies, of crowds" (Goodman 2010, 10). Radicalized barras deploy sound not only to subjugate rival players and hinchadas but also to silence their peers, exert social control, create asymmetries, occupy and claim spaces, and distribute resources unevenly. In addition to immersing hinchas in aggressive sonorities and necrotic lyrics, these sonic struggles often lead to physical confrontations, protracted hostilities, and even the disappearance of certain groups, all while reinforcing the dominance of specific factions.

AGUANTE'S TRANSNATIONAL ASSEMBLY

The book also illustrates that the aguante world is constituted not only by visceral crowds but also by mediated gatherings. It reveals how the remediation of aguante has configured an oppositional assembly that engages in (trans)local encounters and conflicts in digital, analog, and physical domains. In addition to foregrounding the resonances between sports and music media, this transnational public forum has amplified the voice of hinchas, enabling them to present themselves as central constituents of the sport's spectacle and social fabric. By challenging neoliberal definitions of football clubs as for-profit companies and fans as mere consumers, aguante's public assembly has simultaneously made audible silenced realities in the Southern Cone.

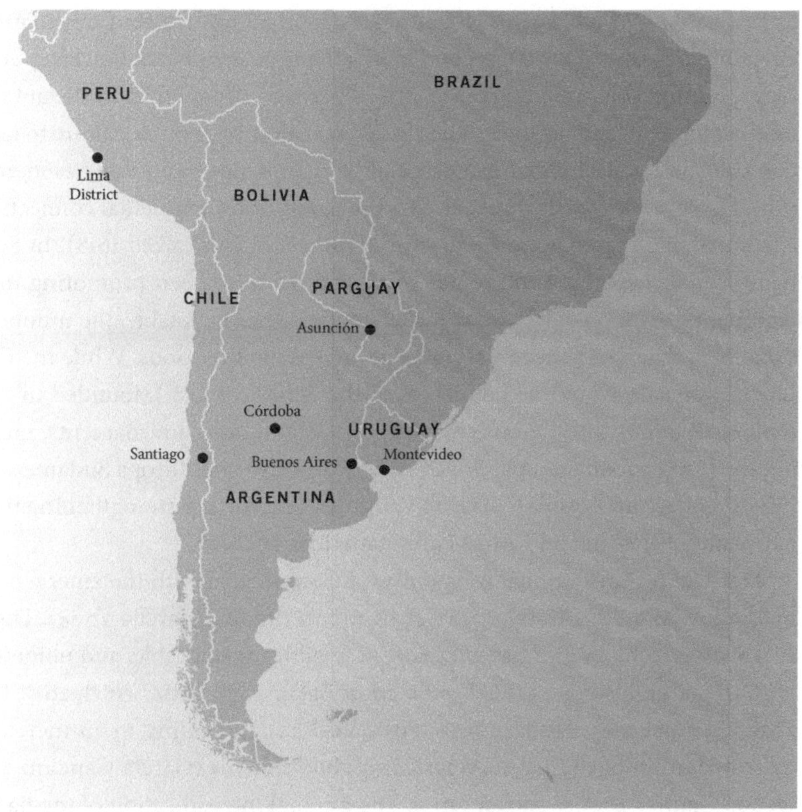

FIGURE 0.2 Map of the Southern Cone.

While Paraguay and Brazil's southern states are occasionally included in the Southern Cone, insiders typically use this term to denote the transnational space constituted by Chile, Argentina, and Uruguay.[11] Nevertheless, even though the region has experienced transborder flows of people and artifacts since before its colonization, these countries remain highly diverse and heterogeneous. Alejandro Grimson (2005) notes that regionalization and globalization have altered the function and meaning of the Southern Cone's territorial borders, resulting in material and symbolic exchanges that have contributed to the formation of transnational imaginaries. In the context of aguante, a feedback loop involving face-to-face interactions, in-game relations, analog circuits, and digital networks has connected hinchas and facilitated dialogue and friction both within and across national borders.

Reflecting and advancing globalization, football has fostered transnational encounters at least since the second half of the nineteenth century (Elsey 2017). By promoting alliances and conversations between geographically distant fans, football has emerged as "one of the strongest realms in popular culture to facilitate transnational kinds of proto-sociality" (Giulianotti and Robertson 2009, 160). However, football's impact extends beyond transcontinental connections, encompassing regional modes of transnationalism (Alabarces 2018). In South America, specifically, continental competitions have been promoting intraregional integration since the 1930s (Palomino 2020). Notably, the number of such tournaments has seen a significant increase in the 2000s. While the Copa Libertadores de América (Liberators of the Americas Cup), founded in 1960, remains the most prestigious competition, several other tournaments, including the Copa Sudamericana (South American Cup) and Recopa Sudamericana (South American Recopa), have been introduced, further strengthening transnationality between and within Latin American spaces.

The rise in transnational interactions has coincided with the emergence of mediation as a constitutive process in urban life (Mazzarella 2004). Digital and analog technologies have become accessible, manageable, and ubiquitous even in marginal contexts (Achondo 2022; Baker 2015; Butterworth 2017; Dent 2020; Manuel 1993; Stobart 2010, 2011; Veal 2007), leading to an increasing intermediation of the Latin American public spheres (García Canclini 2001; Ochoa Gautier 2006a; Tucker 2013). The gradual intensification of media networks has provided disenfranchised subalterns with the resources to forge oppositional publics (Warner 2002). The transmedia feedback loops that have digitally densified the Southern Cone are particularly noticeable in the realm of football, where radio broadcasts, transnational cable networks, cassettes, compact discs, digital streaming services, and social media platforms have created frictions that transcend national borders. In fact, since the 2010s, the growing "dissemination of aguante logics throughout the continent" has raised "concerns among those who perceive a trend toward the 'Argentinization' of violent phenomena" (Alabarces 2012, 11).

While digital technologies have reshaped how football fans communicate and develop a sense of groupness, aguante's (trans)locality has also been significantly influenced by in-person encounters. Migration resulting from the economic and thanatopolitical crises that marred the Southern Cone in the 1970s and 1980s led to substantial cross-border movement, revealing the existence of transnational similarities among immigrants. In conjunction with the continental competitions mentioned earlier, these exchanges challenge narratives that deterministically tie aguante's transnationality solely to digitality.

These visceral, analog, and digital feedback loops have decentered aguante from Argentine stadiums. Today, hinchas outside Argentina not only consume but also adapt, alter, and repurpose practices of fandom, sometimes bypassing or influencing Argentine hinchadas in the process (Achondo 2021, 2022, 2023).[12] While Argentina remains a crucial node, hinchas throughout the Southern Cone now engage in "transformative cycles of feedback" (Novak 2013, 17). Enacting friction with local fan traditions, aguante circulation should not be understood as "something that takes place between cultures" (17) but rather as "a culture-making process" (18).

This is thus a story of *remediation.* Building from media theories exploring the representation of one medium in another (Bolter and Grusin 1999), David Novak (2010) defines remediation as the process "of repurposing media for new contexts of use" (41). It is a creative practice that "feeds circulating media into new expressions and performances," ultimately shaping "contemporary cosmopolitan subjects" (41–42). The feedback loops generated by aguante have created shared media nodes among geographically distant cosmopolitans, fostering transnational encounters and deliberations (Turino 2000). In enacting necropolitical loops, remediation has given rise to cosmopolitan imaginaries and relationalities mediated by violence. However, far from promoting homogeneity, the circulation of aguante has enacted "disjuncture and difference" (Appadurai 1996, 27), creating friction on the local, national, and transnational levels. Music has been a protagonist in this process of (trans)local friction, as the reflexive circulation of chants via photocopies, cassettes, compact discs, live streams, and digital audios and videos has significantly mediated aguante's culture-making process, producing (trans)local affinities and enmities within the Southern Cone. The remediation of aguante has thus forged an alternative cosmopolitan formation—a public assembly performatively configured through the convergence of speech, sonic, and bodily acts (Butler 2015).

Aguante's public assembly has enabled geographically distant subalterns to engage in oppositional forms of action, deliberation, and remediation. Within stadiums and mediated spaces, hinchas have constructed a transnational imaginary where they emerge as the central constituency of the sport. By (re)mediating game experiences, shaping match narratives, and producing value, they position themselves as the ultimate custodians of club identity, sociality, and morality, thus challenging neoliberal conceptualizations of hinchas as mere consumers or delinquents. The (trans)local dissemination of aguante has interlinked disparate subalterns into a larger, affirmative cosmopolitan assembly that, while diverse, collectively challenges the ideology and governance of political elites, sports media, and football authorities. Hinchadas perceive aguante's deviant feistiness as an expression of anti-bourgeois sentiment, utilizing it to critique, whether consciously or not, liberal democracy while making audible the deteriorating conditions of urban life in the region.

Aguante does not correspond with Michael Hardt and Antonio Negri's (2000, 2004, 2009, 2017) framework for understanding alternative public formations within late capitalism. According to them, the contemporary world is characterized by a universalizing yet decentralized market regime—an ensemble of political, corporate, and nongovernmental entities that derive profit not only from labor power but also from social life itself. The Multitude, as they articulate, represents an interconnected immaterial formation emerging from this Empire, embodying a unified collective political subject capable of fostering alternative forms of radical democracy within neoliberalism. The Multitude is pure biopolitical production—an all-encompassing, inherently positive force of liberation. Aguante offers an alternative perspective on the political potential of public formation, challenging the notion that circulation is inherently biopolitical. Interconnection can be as much necropolitical as biopolitical. The friction and fragmentation of the global world can give rise to "damaged forms of publicness" (Warner 2002, 63). Indeed, radical barras heavily rely on controlling, hierarchizing, and even eroding the group identity of those who also participate in aguante. While football serves as a platform for political expression both in the realm of sports and society, it simultaneously perpetuates asymmetries and injustices, illustrating that certain publics harbor "both empowering and disempowering potential for those participating in them" (Papacharissi 2015, 132). Aguante operates as a transnational assembly that allows hinchas to navigate the inequality, precarity, and thanatopolitics of global capitalism, while also engaging in unjust and asymmetrical modes of politics and governance.

FIELDWORK

This book draws on thirty-six months of ethnographic fieldwork conducted from June 2016 to December 2023 in Argentina, Chile, and Uruguay. It builds its arguments on conversations and interviews with hinchas and participant observation in matches, protests, assemblies, meetings, rehearsals, and other spaces of fan socialization. In addition to data collected through archival work in Buenos Aires, the book also incorporates material gathered through virtual ethnography, including media analysis and remote interviews with hinchas.

The project initially aimed to explore how sound mediates aguante in Buenos Aires, a city I knew fairly well as I had lived there for two years as a child. My plan was to focus on a specific team, which I intended to choose based on the contacts I would develop during my preliminary fieldwork in June 2016. However, in January of that year, I met Lucas, an Argentine political scientist who came for a semester-long internship at Brown University, where I was pursuing my doctoral studies. Lucas and I quickly became close friends, largely due to his passion for football, especially for Club Atlético San Lorenzo de Almagro (henceforth, San Lorenzo), one of the big five of Argentine football.[13] When I shared my project with Lucas, he became determined to make San Lorenzo the focus of my ethnography. He presented three arguments. First, he asserted that San Lorenzo has the most loyal fanbase in Argentina, a highly esteemed trait in the football world. Second, he highlighted San Lorenzo's unique relationship with place. The team's connection with the iconic Boedo neighborhood was severed during the last military regime (1976–1983), a bond that San Lorenzo hinchas are actively striving to revive. Third, Lucas argued that the San Lorenzo fanbase is the most creative in Argentina, responsible for creating many of the chants that other hinchadas sing. These connections between creativity, place, and politics intrigued me and ultimately led me to focus on developing connections with San Lorenzo hinchas during my preliminary fieldwork.

Upon arriving in Buenos Aires, I quickly realized that my fieldwork was going to be challenging. The trip from Ezeiza International Airport to my Airbnb in the affluent Belgrano neighborhood was long, so I opted for a taxi. "Chilean?" the driver eventually asked me, "Why did you come to Buenos Aires?" After explaining my research to him, he expressed concern: "It's very dangerous. Barras are dangerous. They don't care about anything. I go with my kid [to the stadium], but I'm always afraid of getting caught in a fight. There are so many internal conflicts. These guys are involved in drug dealing, prostitution, robberies. They are bad people." After a moment, he offered to introduce me to hinchas: "If you don't have the right connections, they will kick your ass. You will need to get them gifts. And you will have to pay me too, of course. I can introduce you to Bebote Álvarez. Let me call my friend."

As I googled information on Bebote Álvarez, a notorious leader of a prominent barra, he made the call: "Hey, I'm with a Chilean guy who wants to understand

Argentine football fandom, and I thought you could introduce him to Bebote." He sounded disappointed as he responded, "Oh, I see, he's laying low." He hung up and told me that Bebote was hiding in Brazil. *What the hell am I doing?* I wondered to myself—a question that loomed over my entire fieldwork.

Despite facing undeniable challenges, my initial months of fieldwork were also fruitful. Lucas significantly aided me in navigating the San Lorenzo fanbase. He and his father took me to games in the Nuevo Gasómetro, the San Lorenzo stadium, and provided extensive insights into the club's history and culture. While his father taught me about San Lorenzo's music history, Lucas educated me about current fan groups. I found Escuela de Tablones particularly fascinating—a collective of young hinchas known for uploading chants to social media that have gone viral not only in Argentina but also internationally. Later in 2016, Escuela de Tablones garnered significant attention, even being featured in major newspapers and sports magazines, providing valuable material for my later interviews. Until I met them, I assumed that Escuela de Tablones was the musical department of La Gloriosa Butteler (The Glorious Butteler), the barra that violently governs San Lorenzo's spaces and social relations—a group with which I found it difficult to engage. However, I soon discovered that Escuela de Tablones had no formal connection to La Gloriosa Butteler and, in fact, had a tense relationship with them. This tension largely stemmed from Escuela de Tablones's growing fame within the aguante world, which ultimately led to a rift between the two groups.

Thanks to the San Lorenzo hinchas I met and the experiences I gained in stadiums while following the team, I uncovered the connections between San Lorenzo and U. de Chile, the team I had supported throughout my entire life. While I had previously seen U. de Chile hinchas donning San Lorenzo jerseys in stadiums, I was surprised by the Argentine hinchas reciprocating this gesture in Buenos Aires. San Lorenzo hinchas pointed out the shared colors, the common experiences of football disappointment, and the sense of nomadic identity resulting from the absence of permanent home stadiums as resonances between the two clubs. These shared affinities not only facilitated my interactions with the San Lorenzo fanbase but also nurtured a growing sense of care and affinity for the club within me.

By the end of my second trip to Buenos Aires in 2017, I found myself significantly more at ease within the aguante world. I had attended numerous games independently and actively engaged with hinchas outside stadiums, participating in barbecues, parties, and other gatherings. The prominent presence of fan collectives, particularly Escuela de Tablones, on social media platforms facilitated the establishment of connections within the community. After months of immersive fieldwork, I felt I had gained a profound understanding of the interplay between aguante, creativity, mediation, and sense of place among San Lorenzo hinchas and, more broadly, within Argentine football fandom.

However, facing unexpected migratory issues while preparing for my yearlong fieldwork in 2018, I had to rethink my project. When I inquired with the IIE, my US visa sponsors on behalf of Fulbright, about the paperwork required for spending a year in Buenos Aires, I was informed that I could only stay in a foreign country if I took a leave of absence, resulting in the pausing of my migratory status in the United States during that period. Given that this option would also forfeit my Brown stipend, I asked for alternatives. The IIE explained that, during the academic year, I could only visit my home country, Chile. While initially enraged, I eventually viewed it as an opportunity to explore a series of questions that had intrigued me since I began my scholarly interest in football: Why do Chilean hinchadas sound like Argentine ones? Does this imply they have adopted aguante? Is this adoption purely stylistic or also ideological? And if so, what implications does this hold for aguante as a whole? Can it be understood as a transnational formation?

From May 2018 to December 2019, I conducted fieldwork in Santiago, my birth city and hometown, where I collaborated with hinchas of U. de Chile.[14] My connection with the club has been deeply significant since my father took me to a *Clásico Universitario* (University Derby) in 1993.[15] Naturally, as a lifelong fan, establishing networks happened rapidly, and within a week I found myself spending almost every day with hinchas from AHA, Las Bulla, and soon after, Los de Abajo. Throughout the week, I attended meetings, gatherings, and political activities among hinchas. While I traveled with them by bus, train, and foot to games during the weekend, every Saturday morning I participated in the alternative school that AHA and Los de Abajo established in Puente Alto, as depicted in the book's introductory vignette. Despite the inherent awkwardness of my researcher status, my personal bond with the club led U. de Chile hinchas to view me as a *camarada* (comrade), particularly since I demonstrated that the "recovery of the club" and the "reconstruction of its social fabric" were personally meaningful political endeavors that extended beyond my fieldwork. However, as I elaborate in the following section, the ease of networking and the almost immediate reciprocity, driven by our shared affection for U. de Chile, should not be conflated with moral commensurability. This is especially true with some of the leaders of Los de Abajo, such as the aforementioned Chalo, who always distrusted my presence.

Since I wanted to visit Uruguay in June 2019, intrigued by the adoption of aguante across the Rio de la Plata, I decided to postpone my plan to return to Argentina until the North American summer of 2020. However, the pandemic disrupted my travel plans, preventing me from returning to the Southern Cone until 2022. Although I had gathered enough material to write the dissertation that forms the basis of this book, I felt I had a gap in terms of interviews, especially with San Lorenzo and Uruguayan hinchas. Given the project's emphasis on digital mediation, conducting interviews remotely became a methodologically and analytically sound option. Many hinchas agreed, and we were able to converse liberally over Zoom and Skype. Upon my return to Chile in 2022, I continued conducting fieldwork on aguante while also dividing my ethnographic focus on a second project on sound, ecology, and violence among the Mapuche, the largest Indigenous nation in Chile.

ETHICS AND MORALS

Conducting ethnography on aguante raises several ethical and moral dilemmas. My discussions with outsiders about hinchadas swiftly become highly moralized, often condemning hinchas as immoral lumpenproletariat while questioning the ethics of my project. Simultaneously, outsiders frequently seem drawn to the aura of violence surrounding aguante, craving narratives about violence and criminality. While I acknowledge violence as a central aspect of the social life of hinchadas, my aim is to avoid sensationalism and provide a nuanced and ethically grounded ethnography of this world. In doing so, my goal is not to offer a solution to football violence but rather to comprehend it. By immersing myself in this ethically murky and morally volatile ethnographic sphere, I diverge from approaches that position the ethnographer as an advocate (Scheper-Hughes 1995; Hale 2006, 2008; Lipsitz 2008). Instead, I embrace a moral incommensurability between myself and my collaborators, acknowledging that, in ethnography, "equivocation always exists" (Viveiros de Castro 2004, 10).

Benjamin Teitelbaum (2017, 2019, 2022) has provocatively reignited reflections on the ethical and moral dimensions of ethnography. He posits that moral volatility is intrinsic to ethnographic research, suggesting that ethical concerns become particularly pronounced when the researcher's morality significantly diverges from the values learned in the field. Drawing on his experiences cultivating reciprocal and collaborative relationships with white nationalists in Nordic countries, he reflects on the ethical and moral implications of developing empathy and solidarity with groups that could perpetuate injustice. He contends that, when ethnography positions researchers in morally liminal spaces, "immorality imbues our enterprise" (Teitelbaum 2019, 415).

The moral misalignments outlined by Teitelbaum resonate deeply with my own ethnographic experiences. While I have been immersed in football fandom since childhood and have family members involved in barras, I am not an insider to aguante. Unlike hinchas, my upbringing in both Chile and Argentina was marked by economic stability. During my fieldwork, I initially received support from elite American institutions, which allowed me to bring US dollars into less affluent economies. Later, I was fortunate to receive funding from a generous grant from the Chilean government and had the opportunity to work in one of the most prestigious academic institutions in the country, if not all of Latin America. In essence, while I was born and raised in the Global South, my experiences in the field align closely with the privileges commonly associated with ethnographers originating from the Global North.

In fact, the sense of strangeness often observed by foreign ethnographers was heightened in my case, as fear and danger were palpable elements of my fieldwork experience. Violence was not merely a theoretical component but tangible reality, shaping the ethnographic landscape and creating moral tensions between my informants and myself. As noted by Walter Benjamin (2021), an act "becomes violence in the impressive sense of the word only when it intervenes in moral relations" (39). Violent acts were constant sources of moral discord between my informants—who often viewed them positively—and myself—who saw them as incompatible with the pursuit of just and egalitarian social projects. Although I did not always voice my disagreements for fear of violent reactions, I did express them on occasions with individuals I felt comfortable with. Unfortunately, these discussions often failed to find common ground, leading to awkward and unresolved situations.

Despite these tensions, reciprocity was also a fundamental aspect of my fieldwork. Although we disagreed over issues of violence, the vast majority of hinchas never treated me as a complete stranger, finding common ground with me through shared sports values and affiliations. Many hinchas welcomed me into their homes and neighborhoods, introducing me to their friends, partners, and families. As my fieldwork progressed, I gained a deeper understanding of the pervasive atmosphere of violence that permeated their daily lives. I began to question whether demanding someone inhabiting a necropolitical reality to fully disengage from violence was, in itself, an act of violence. The active and violent participation of hinchas in the social uprising that shook Chile in 2019 fractured my moral positionality even further, leading me to hear thanatopolitical overtones in liberal democracy. Ethnography unveiled the social and cultural productivity of violence while simultaneously urging me to see hinchas beyond mere villains.

Nonetheless, I never regarded them as heroes, struggling to fully advocate for their actions. Although I understood the circumstances that drove them to view violent acts as morally justified and witnessed several instances of political solidarity, I was troubled by their concurrent use of violence to maintain unjust power dynamics, impose social control, and partake in lethal conflicts. Throughout my fieldwork, which concluded in December 2023, I was consistently surrounded by danger and tension, frequently questioning my decision to undertake this project.

Understanding the ethnographic process as an intersubjective exchange that impacts both sides of the collaboration, my interactions with hinchas have also prompted reflection on my own political and subject position. In many respects, I have come to perceive myself as a contributor to the conditions that fostered the necropolitical formation depicted in this book. While I have personally benefited from the privileges afforded by the local and global inequalities that have radicalized aguante, my very project has also played a role in perpetuating its clandestine necropolitics. Respecting the principle that "los hinchas no sapean" (hinchas don't snitch), I have safeguarded the anonymity of all individuals involved in this ethnography, including those engaging in illicit activities. To preserve confidentiality, I have altered names and combined informants, while keeping the names of larger groups unchanged. I have withheld several instances of injustice and criminality I witnessed in the field, which has led me to question the social utility of this project. My ethnographic experience has ultimately placed me in a morally ambiguous position, "neither insider nor outsider, neither cheerleader nor opponent, and neither an accomplice nor an innocent" (Teitelbaum 2019, 421).

Has immorality thus imbued my ethnographic enterprise, to paraphrase Teitelbaum? While I understand his rhetorical augmentation, I find the proposal, along with the ensuing debate (Teitelbaum 2019), to be rooted in a dichotomy fraught with ethnographic and epistemological limitations. Arguing for ethnography to be labeled as either moral or immoral presupposes a world populated by heroes and villains, portraying certain subjects as morally upright and others as morally bankrupt. This debate promotes hegemonic positionalities as morally superior while stigmatizing any deviations as inherently immoral. Such a binary framework overlooks the inherent moral diversity of the human experience. Ultimately, reducing the discourse to a moral-immoral dichotomy fails to address the nuanced tensions inherent in ethnographic observation and interpretation.

In this sense, rather than viewing my ethnography as immoral, I prefer to interpret it as characterized by moral equivocation. Eduardo Viveiros de Castro (2004) argues that equivocation is inherent to ethnography, functioning as "a mode of communication par excellence between different perspectival positions—and therefore as both condition of possibility and limit of the anthropological enterprise" (3). While Viveiros de Castro links the equivocal process to the radical ontological alterity he associates with Amerindian perspectives, I perceive this incommensurability as a crucial aspect of ethnography itself, particularly in environments where vastly divergent moral frameworks intersect. An ethnographer immersed in violent atmospheres is consistently negotiating conflicting moral codes, often entirely incompatible and untranslatable. Rather than attempting to resolve these tensions, I have chosen to embrace my ethnography's moral ambiguity, inhabiting an uncertain terrain where disparate and conflicting moral systems converge. This means embracing a certain moral incommensurability with hinchas and speak from a liminal place of enunciation—an ambiguous and ever-evolving space characterized by both friction and reciprocity amid differing interpretations of violence. In this book, nothing exists in absolute binaries. There are no clear-cut heroes or villains, protagonists or antagonists. Everyone, including myself, is somehow entangled in this necropolitical landscape, emerging as ambiguous individuals navigating a violent reality. I argue that embracing this incommensurability, with all its ethical and moral tensions, is the most effective ethnographic approach to comprehending the contingent meanings, uses, and consequences of violence.

CHAPTERS OVERVIEW

Chapter 1 examines the crystallization and transnational developments of aguante, contending that the interplay of material, analog, and digital feedback has enacted (trans)local friction. These local and multisited encounters have culminated in the configuration of a simultaneously mediated and immediate public assembly, allowing hinchas to position themselves as the central component of football. Beginning with a stylistic overview of contemporary aguante, I then proceed to narrate the various processes that facilitated the emergence of chant creation and the introduction of murga porteña to stadiums during the first half of the twentieth century in Buenos Aires. These include the empowerment of the working class during populist governments and shifts in the production and circulation of popular and carnival culture. Subsequently, the chapter explains how social unrest and thanatopolitical dynamics led to the birth of aguante in the 1960s. The latter part of the chapter focuses on the transnationalization of aguante throughout the Southern Cone, examining the roles of migration, media, continental championships, specific border conditions, and the advent of digital technologies in its dissemination since the 1980s. This transmedia circulation has enabled hinchas to engage in reflexive discourse and construct alternative cosmopolitan imaginaries. Questioning the technological determinism present in recent scholarship on public formation, the chapter ultimately demonstrates how various modes of communication, whether digital, analog, or face-to-face, have decentered aguante from Argentine stadiums, allowing Southern Cone hinchas to participate in (trans)local encounters and disputes.

In the second chapter, I delve into creativity and attribution by focusing on the work of Escuela de Tablones. The chapter highlights that their creative work has allowed them to accrue honor and prestige within aguante. In contrast to the necrotic themes prevalent in most chants, their poetry primarily revolves around notions of place and belonging, establishing emotional connections between San Lorenzo, the Boedo neighborhood, and the stadium they lost there. While their lyrical approach significantly contributes to their reputation, their status is largely shaped by their auditory creativity—an interplay of various audile techniques that enables them to identify songs with the potential to serve as chants by imaginatively projecting the aguante style and stadium acoustics onto them. Their pursuit of aguante status through this form of creativity—which highlights everyday forms of aural ingenuity—has led to the separation of ownership from authorship. This division has given rise to a set of social norms governing attribution—an ideology of textuality that engages in both positive and negative feedback with copyright, thereby challenging both optimistic and pessimistic takes on intellectual property.

Chapter 3 shifts focus to Chile, examining issues of affect and labor among Los de Abajo. It narrates how, after decades of civic, democratic, and university-led administration, the club turned into a publicly traded sports company where participation became mediated by consumption and the stock market. In response, they have reframed the enactment of affective atmospheres not only as expressions of support but also as a means to cultivate stranger intimacy, shape match narratives, and denounce the club's exclusionary practices. In contrast to the profit-driven actions of club executives, U. de Chile hinchas exert their affective labor to generate interpersonal value and create a space for themselves in their clubs. Although Los de Abajo have developed a regime of value that differs from the profit-oriented approach of the company, the latter has effectively subsumed their labor into the club's production of economic value, ultimately denying their claims for rights and participation beyond consumption. Furthermore, Los de Abajo also deploy affect to engage in conflicts, create internal asymmetries, and exert social control—a valuation of violence over relationality that has eroded the club's social fabric, ultimately undermining their own community and political work. The chapter thus underscores the limits of affective labor to create alternatives in necropolitical and hyper-commodified contexts.

In the final chapter, I delve into hinchas' ideologies of voice vis-à-vis the social uprising that erupted in Chile in October 2019. It examines the underlying social, political, and economic dynamics that led to the social unrest—conditions that also influenced the adoption of aguante in the country. Alongside providing an overview of the social uprising, the chapter narrates the active participation of hinchas in the protests and how their involvement was perceived by public opinion. However, the chapter's primary focus is on exploring how hinchas perceive their sonic, material, and representational voices. It illustrates that hinchas interpret the destruction of their vocal organs as an assertion of agency and dignity, thus amplifying a necropolitics of the body wherein pain and physical damage are seen as embodiments of working-class morality. The chapter concludes by arguing that aguante's destructive vocality foreshadowed the use of violence as a necropolitical tool during the social unrest.

ONE

(Trans)local Feedbacks

Perched alongside Montevideo's *rambla*, an avenue that stretches along the coastline of the Rio de la Plata, I asked Cachila whether he concurred with my observation that aguante has facilitated transnational encounters in the Southern Cone. An hincha of Peñarol, Uruguay's most popular team, he paused while taking a sip of mate—a herbal beverage embraced throughout South America. He eventually answered:

> You aren't making it up at all. In fact, what you say can be extended to the larger Southern Cone, including Paraguay and Rio Grande do Sul. Today, in the case of hinchadas, you can see the Argentine phenomenon among Paraguayan hinchadas and even in the Grenal [between Grêmio and Internacional], which is the most important clásico in [southern] Brazil. In Rio Grande do Sul, they don't have torcidas; they have hinchadas. They have bombos con platillo, they have banners, and even the chants are the same as in Argentina.[1] Paraguayan hinchadas are like the Chilean ones, the Uruguayan ones, and the Argentine ones, with their umbrellas and banners. Here in Uruguay, it's the same. I tend to believe that we're more creative regarding chants—it's more creation than imitation. At least the Peñarol hinchada makes chants with Uruguayan popular music—either folklore, rock, or cumbia—instead of buying the melody or chant packaged from Argentina. We have both original and re-versioned chants. We make our own versions, like San Lorenzo in Argentina, which everyone ends up copying. Although they do that here too, the Peñarol hinchada, which I know the most, is famous for making their own chants. That's why they do it with local artists, for instance.

Cachila connects and mixes the entire Southern Cone when talking about aguante, using not only Argentine but also Chilean and Uruguayan hinchadas as models. His statement highlights the crystallization of a multisited forum where geographically distant groups come together to engage in discourse and practice. In-person, analog, and digital interactions have constituted a (trans) local formation that embodies a form of cosmopolitanism characterized by subaltern "practices, material technologies, and conceptual frameworks" (Turino 2000, 7). Aguante has evolved into the dominant imaginary of "how an hincha should be" (Alabarces 2014, 56) in Latin America, creating friction and feedback with local modes of cheering.

This introductory chapter traces the origins and (trans)local developments of aguante. My contention is that aguante, through its material, analog, and digital circulation, has sparked local and transnational dialogues, disputes, and conflicts. These encounters have led to the formation of a multisited public assembly that, while fragmented and disjunctively constituted, provides a material and mediated platform for geographically distant proletarians to converge and voice a shared belief in the centrality of hinchas in football's spectacle and social life.

The chapter commences with an introductory overview of the stylistic dimensions of contemporary aguante. It then delves into the emergence of chants in Argentina in the first half of the twentieth century vis-à-vis changes in the country's public sphere. From the early 1900s until the 1950s, Argentina emerged as South America's central hub for music, cinema, and radio production. This industrial growth coincided with the sonic integration of carnival and working-class culture into the public sphere. From the 1960s to the 1980s, the expansion of mass media coexisted with a series of social, political, and economic crises—turmoil that facilitated not only the crystallization but also the radicalization of aguante. The rest of the chapter discusses aguante's transnational circulation, emphasizing how various sounds, media, and individuals have contributed to the dissemination of a discourse and imaginary that has triggered tensions and conflicts among working-class hinchas in the Southern Cone. By connecting stadiums, people, and media, aguante's circulation has given rise to "feedback loops" (Novak 2015, 2020), generating "interconnection across difference" (Tsing 2005, 4).

Despite the significant role of new media in facilitating the (trans)local dissemination of aguante, this chapter challenges the technological determinism that underpins much of the scholarship on public formation. This body of literature suggests that networked technologies, with their affordances of persistence, replicability, scalability, and searchability, have fundamentally reshaped the reflexive circulation of discourse (Baym and boyd 2012; boyd 2011; Castells 2007; Crawford 2012; Gillespie 2010; Ito 2008; Sterne 2012; Papacharissi 2015). However, digital media's capacity to amplify, record, and share information has not altered but rather reinforced how hinchas engage with circulating practices and values. The transnational circulation of aguante and the (trans)local tensions it has generated should not be solely understood as a digital phenomenon. Instead, it is a feedback process that has been nurtured by the accumulation and overlap of face-to-face interactions, in-game experiences, analog forms of communication, and digital forms of dissemination. In essence, the core dynamics of aguante's circulation existed before the rise of social media and have continued to evolve alongside various communication methods.

THE SOUNDS OF AGUANTE

Sound holds a central position within aguante. Hinchas engage in a variety of sonic practices during football games, shouting, whistling, setting off pyrotechnics, playing drums and brass instruments, and singing contrafacta. These sounds significantly shape both in-person and mediated experiences. In this section, I provide a comprehensive description of the aguante style—a pedagogically necessary generalization that will be critically reexamined in the following chapters.

Hinchas never stop moving, accompanying their sonic practices with different body techniques. The most iconic movement of aguante is a rhythmic, back-and-forth motion of the arm in a semi-horizontal position, resembling an open-palm fist bump, with the full extension of the arm coinciding with the music's strong beat. They also accompany their vocalizations by jumping or shoving one another, among other body movements.

Balloons, umbrellas, and cloth banners serve to highlight the presence of hinchadas behind the goals. Typically, four to eight vertical banners stretch from the top of the terrace to the fence. Additionally, approximately three horizontal banners with the names of the barras cross the vertical ones. These banners usually display the teams' distinctive colors and drawings. While some instrumentalists and hinchas may have difficulty seeing the match due to the presence of these banners and flags, others become so immersed in their own performance that they do not see the game at all—or at least miss a significant part of it. Some hinchas intentionally disregard game events by standing with their backs to the field on para-avalanchas, encouraging other people to sing along.

Aguante's soundworld has noticeable connections with the *carnaval porteño*

FIGURE 1.1 Murga porteña.

(Buenos Aires carnival).[2] Along with a common interest in contrafacta, hinchadas have taken their drums and rhythms from these festivities. South American hinchas play murga porteña, a carnival genre complex that involves music, theater, song, and dance. Although both hinchas and carnival musicians use a wide variety of membranophones—including *surdos* (floor tom-like drums), *repiques* (tenor-like drums), and sometimes *redoblantes* (snare-like drums)—they regard the *bombo con platillo* (a double-headed bass drum with a mounted cymbal) as a synecdoche of murga porteña as a whole (O'Brien 2018). The *toques* (patterns) of murga porteña vary greatly, but they all tend to share a steady beat on the drum with a syncopated rhythm in its cymbal that emphasizes the duple meter's 3–3–2 division (O'Brien 2016). For example, figure 1.1 illustrates the traditional pattern known as *rumba* (video 1.1).

Some argue that hinchadas have merged murga porteña with the Brazilian genre samba reggae. Originating among Black communities in Salvador de Bahia, samba reggae was developed to establish transnational connections with Afro-diasporic formations elsewhere (Crook 1993). In addition to slowing down the basic samba beat to resemble reggae's loose shuffle feel, musicians divided "the low *surdos* into four or five distinct and interlocking parts while the high-pitched *repiques* and snare drums filled out the rhythm" (101). These patterns bear a striking resemblance to those played by the surdo and repiques in hinchadas, which could either confirm the incorporation of samba reggae, as some argue, or simply illustrate rhythmic resonances with murga porteña. Supporting the former viewpoint, Martin Liut suggests that Los Fabulosos Cadillacs' 1994 hit "Matador," which includes a batucada ensemble playing samba reggae, inspired hinchadas to fuse the Brazilian rhythm with murga porteña (personal communication; see also video 1.2). Although I have encountered mixed responses regarding this argument, these interconnections make sense within aguante's transnational feedback loops.

Hinchas vocalize an array of sounds, but football chants reign as the dominant component in their sonorous repertoire. These chants range from simple, rhythmic utterances with minimal variation in tone and pitch to more elaborate and conventional songs. The melodies of these songlike chants draw inspiration

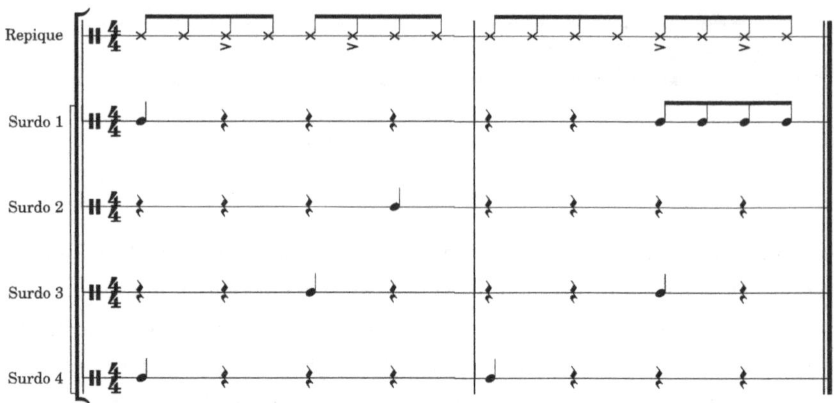

FIGURE 1.2 Samba reggae.

FIGURE 1.3 Hinchada percussion ensemble.

from diverse sources, including political marches, commercial jingles, and the latest hits promoted by the culture industries.

I define the act of (re)creating chants as *(re-)versioning*. This concept puts aguante's emic terminology in dialogue with Michael Veal's (2007) use of the term to discuss the ways in which dub challenges notions of musical uniqueness, originality, and authenticity:

> In Jamaican musical parlance the noun "version" was gradually transformed into a verb; that is, "to version." The dub plate can be considered the first step

in this process of "versioning," a method of serially recycling recorded material developed by producers desiring to ensure the longest commercial life for a given piece of recorded music despite economic constraints and a limited pool of musicians. The process of versioning was soon exploited to its fullest extent, as prerecorded backing tracks began to be used as a basis for a series of more distinct performances. (54–55)

Hinchas similarly employ *versión* to signify chant creation. *Versionar* (versioning) refers to the practice of finding melodies and altering their lyrics, while *re-versionar* (re-versioning) denotes the act of changing the texts of already existing chants.

The lyrical themes of aguante chants vary widely. Javier Bundio (2020) divides them into six different categories: self-praising, supporting, celebrating, insulting, teasing, and threatening. While most chants do not fit neatly into just one classification, this model proves useful in outlining the different topics present in the aguante songbook.

The self-praising and celebrating themes are closely connected. Glorifying belonging, dominance, and participation, these lyrics establish affective ties between hinchas, hinchadas, and clubs. See, for instance, the lyrics set by Racing Club's hinchada to the melody of "Esta noche me emborracho" (I Get Drunk Tonight) by fusion rock band La Mosca Tsé-Tsé (video 1.3):

Los momentos que viví	Everything that I've been through
Las cosas que yo dejé	The things I left behind
Por ser seguir a La Academia	To follow The Academy [Racing Club]
Nadie lo puede entender	Nobody can understand it
Yo no sé cómo explicar	I don't know how to explain
Que te llevo hasta en la piel	That I've got you under my skin
Sos la droga que en las venas me inyectaron al nacer	You're the drug that they injected when I was born
Se me para el corazón	My heart stops beating
Cada vez que vos perdés	Every time you lose
Me pongo de la cabeza	I get crazy
Y otra vez te vengo a ver	And come to see you again
Muchachos, traigan vino, juega La Acadé	Guys, bring wine, The Acade[my] is playing
Que esta banda está de fiesta	This band is turned up

Hoy no podemos perder	We can't lose
Muchachos, traigan vino, juega La Acadé	Guys, bring wine, The Acade[my] is playing
Me emborracho bien borracho	I get really drunk
Y El Rojo se va a la B	And The Red [Independiente] is relegated

The chant not only touches on conflict but also celebrates collective sociality through tropes of emotion, intensity, and rawness. It also gives voice to masculine modes of homosocial bonding and expression (Bundio 2020), a socioemotional release commonly found in different forms of masculinity (Gutmann 2006; Louie 2002, 2003). Many aguante chants narrate experiences of alcohol and drug consumption, emphasizing that hinchas often cheer for their teams in altered states of consciousness. Although aguante scholarship links substance abuse to the idea of forging masculine, resistant bodies through enduring damage (Alabarces and Garriga 2007, 2008; Garriga 2005), altered states of consciousness are also closely connected to the prioritization of affective states.

Related to these two categories is the supporting one. Often characterized by simplicity and brevity, these chants are aimed at encouraging players (video 1.4 🔊👁):

Oh, nosotros alentamos	Oh, we cheer
Oh, nosotros alentamos	Oh, we cheer
Pongan huevos	Grow some balls
Que ganamos	We're going to win

The expression "pongan huevos" (translated as "grow some balls") requires further discussion. In South American parlance, "huevos" (eggs) often symbolize testicles. The huevo trope is commonly used in chants and signifies concepts of male endurance, intensity, and bravado.

Examples of these self-praising, supporting, and celebrating chants can be more overtly hostile in nature, serving as illustrations of the necrotic themes dominating aguante chants. For example, River Plate's hinchada sings the following over the melody of "Imposible" (Impossible) by Argentine rock band Callejeros (video 1.5 🔊👁):

Todos los domingos a la tarde yo vengo a alentarte	Every Sunday afternoon I come to cheer for you
Venimos aguantando los trapos para verte a vos	We've been defending the banners to come to see you
Al fin va a decir la verdad el que escribe los diarios	The newspapers writers will finally tell the truth
Que River es el más grande todos y nunca abandonó	That River is biggest of all and never abandoned
Aunque ganes o aunque pierdas yo siempre te sigo	I always follow you even if you win or if you lose
Que me la chupen todas las hinchadas y el periodismo	All hinchadas and journalists can suck my dick
Yo no me voy antes de que termine el partido	I don't leave before the game is over
Banderas negras y parlantes no hay	There are neither black flags nor loudspeakers
Porque esta banda es puro carnaval	Because this band is pure carnival
La Boca y Avellaneda vamos a quemar	We'll burn La Boca and Avellaneda[3]
Y como siempre La 12 va a correr sin parar	And La 12 [Boca Juniors' barra] will run away nonstop as always

The chant emphasizes the loyalty, passion, and toughness of River Plate's hinchada. These expressions are interwoven with negative depictions of and violent threats toward rivals. In contrast to their own carnival, symbolizing an affective atmosphere, other teams require external technologies to support their sonic displays—black flags signify bitterness here, indicating a lack of aguante. In a rather dramatic turn, hinchas promise to burn rival neighborhoods, making violent threats that are fairly common in these chants. Another recurring theme is the desire to make other hinchadas, like La 12, Boca Juniors' barra, run away after confrontations. The chant also touches upon other common topics in aguante, including the defense of banners, critiques of journalism, and references to significant events in football history. Enduring police repression is present in several chants, although it is not explicitly mentioned in this particular one.

But while these first three themes aim to uplift and celebrate themselves, the insulting, teasing, and threatening categories serve to deride and belittle rival hinchadas. Bundio (2020) describes these dynamics as "radical othering," wherein alterity is constructed through the use of harmful sexist, homophobic, racist, xenophobic, and classist tropes. A chant by River Plate's hinchada serves as an illustration of this point (video 1.6):

Qué feo ser bostero y boliviano
En una villa tener que vivir
La hermana revolea la cartera
La vieja chupa pijas por ahí
Bostero, bostero, bostero,
Bostero, no lo pienses más
Andate a vivir a Bolivia
Toda tu familia está allá

How awful is to be a bostero [manure man, Boca Juniors hincha] and Bolivian
To have to live in a villa [impoverished neighborhood]
The sister sleeps with everyone
The old lady gives blowjobs somewhere
Bostero, bostero, bostero,
Bostero, don't think about it anymore
Move to Bolivia
Your entire family is there

In addition to the crude misogyny, the chant's radical othering also draws on pervasive assumptions about whiteness and poverty in Buenos Aires. While middle-class citizens are often portrayed as white, working-class communities are frequently stereotyped as immigrants of color. Despite the association of River Plate and Boca Juniors with the upper class and working class, respectively, the chant's classism is puzzling, as many of those who attend Argentine football matches, including River Plate hinchas, actually belong to the proletariat.

Many chants narrate stories of death and violence. See, for instance, this one by La Gloriosa Butteler, San Lorenzo's hinchada (video 1.7):

Saltando paredes
Yo no sé a quién vengas
Viniste al barrio
Te matamos a uno más
Y para el tercero
Te pido quemero
Que me vengas a buscar
Cumplieron cien años
Te volvimos a correr
Y ahora en La Boca
Nos volvemos a ver
Vos sos vigilante

Jumping walls
I don't know where you come from
You came to our neighborhood
We kill you another one
And for the third one
I ask you quemero [man-that-burn, Huracán hincha]
Come face me
You turned one hundred years old
We made you run away again
And now in La Boca
We'll face each other again
You are a snitch

Vos nunca la aguantaste	You never endured it
Con la Plaza Butteler	Against the Buttler Square[4]

The text not only celebrates but also immortalizes acts of deadly violence. The composition overtly glorifies the assassination of two Huracán hinchas, depicting death as a goal rather than an accident. Murder as a means of aguante domination is further emphasized by La Gloriosa Butteler's ominous vow to kill another rival hincha on the eve of a new encounter in La Boca.

GENEALOGIES OF AGUANTE

Although journalists have been describing Argentine stadiums as loud since at least the nineteenth century, the historical archive does not register melodic chants until the mid-twentieth century. According to Julio Frydenberg (2011), the emergence of "muchachadas" (bunches of boys) in the 1920s marked the first atomized association of fans. These young men would gather in spaces like bars and would demonstrate their maleness through drinking, posturing, and fighting. In the stands, however, these muchachadas rarely sang, simply vocalizing nonmelodic speech utterances such as "Bo-ca, Bo-ca" or the players' names (Bundio 2020). These chants would compete with various other sounds, as illustrated in this journalistic piece:

> From the top of the stands, the crowd seemed like a revolutionary rally: the voices, insults, swirls, stampedes, the back and forth of groups that momentarily break up and then signal to each other via shouting; the announcements of fruit, drinks, and magazine sellers; the rapid turmoil that causes a quarrel, quickly calmed by the neighbors, all this chaos of old and young, civilians and officers, people with shirts and pajamas rubbing shoulders with highly elegant spectators, produces a sensation of revolt, of a rally that is familiar to those who habitually attend the major sports events. (Quoted in Frydenberg 2011, 218)

In those same years, writer Roberto Artl defined the stadium's soundscape as cacophonous, modular, and material: "Not even a bunch of machine gunners could have made more noise than those eighty thousand hands that were applauding the Argentine success. So many people were clapping for the Argentine success. So many people were applauding behind my ears that the wind created by their hands buzzed by my cheeks. Then enthusiasm waned down, and I began to take notes" (2002, 263).

These accounts consistently lack references to contrafacta, but there is some evidence of the existence of melodic chants in the 1920s. For instance, Leandro, a San Lorenzo hincha, chant historian, and member of Escuela de Tablones, discovered a version of the tango "Buenos Aires" by Manuel Joves y Manuel Romero with lyrics about San Lorenzo:

San Lorenzo, campeón de primera	San Lorenzo, first-class champion
San Lorenzo, mi club más querido	San Lorenzo, my dearest club
Escuchá la canción que hoy te canto como un amigo	Listen to the song that I today sing to you as a friend
Yo te he visto luchar con bravura	I've seen you fighting bravely
Contra cuadros que fueron campeones	Against great champions
Sin que jamás la amargura manchara tus corazones	Without letting the bitterness stain your heart
Y en los partidos del campeonato	And in tournament games
Más de un mal rato por vos pasé	I had more than one sad moment
Días ingratos en que la suerte peor que la muerte yo vislumbré	Hard days when I faced a fate worse than death
Y al terminar la lucha ruda con mucha calma te vi triunfar	And when the hard fight was over I calmly saw you triumph
Porque si querés jugar	Because if you want to play
Lo que te sobra es el alma	The soul is enough
Y en la tarde linda de verano	And in a beautiful summer afternoon
Cuando vas a tu campo a entrenarte	When you go to your field to train
Al contemplar tanto afán	Contemplating so much effort
No me canso de admirarte	I can't get tired of admiring you

Tango's famous bitter, resigned fatalism acquires new meanings here. The lyrics present football as a space where the working class can find solace and compensation for the isolation caused by social inequality, romantic disappointments, and the disparities of modern life. Although the exact origins and circumstances of this piece remain uncertain, it serves as a precursor to the tradition of versioning.[5]

The first journalistic references to chants can be found in the 1940s (Bundio 2020). During this period, most of these compositions were rather concise and primarily focused on players, stating their names and short phrases related to their performance on the field:

Tenemos un arquero que es una maravilla
Ataja los penales sentados en una silla

We have a wonderful goalkeeper
He saves penalty kicks sitting on a chair

In these years, Argentina became the focal point of mass culture in South America, owing to the establishment of state-of-the-art radio, cinema, and music industries (Luker 2016; Karush 2007, 2010, 2012, 2017; Karush and Chamosa 2010; Nouzeilles and Montaldo 2002; Rios 2008, 2014). The expansion of cultural consumption during this era resulted in popular culture becoming accessible to wider segments of the population. While many of these cultural productions aimed to cater to consumers seeking cosmopolitan symbols, a significant portion also celebrated the dignity and solidarity of the proletariat, portraying them as morally superior to the elites, whom they depicted as selfish and immoral.

Unsurprisingly, cultural workers employed football as a means to exalt proletarian life. The film, radio, and music industries celebrated the practices surrounding football as the achievements of the working class, elevating hinchas as embodiments of proletarian dignity, solidarity, and passion (Karush 2010). These cultural productions reinforced the concept of the hincha as the moral protagonist of football (Alabarces 2007; Archetti 1999). One notable example is the movie *El Hincha* (1951), directed by Manuel Romero and featuring tango luminaire Enrique Santos Discépolo. The movie not only depicted hinchas as passionate and loyal supporters but also linked the hincha's role as the "twelfth player" to their vocal practices. Discépolo's character emphasized that hinchas should put all their effort into supporting their teams, singing "until hoarseness" and "breaking their lungs." The use of melodrama in *El Hincha* was a strategic approach to appeal to the non-elite audiences that frequented neighborhood movie theaters. By intertwining the essence of being an hincha with the values and struggles of the poor, the culture industries not only established strong connections between football and the proletariat but also effectively merged working-class culture with fan practice.

These developments in mass culture coincided with the rise of Colonel Juan Domingo Perón's populism. Perón, who had served as the country's Minister of Labor since 1930, introduced various programs of public assistance, earning him the support of labor unions and the working class (James 1988; Nouzeilles and Montaldo 2002). However, his populist policies also put him in conflict with conservative elites, leftist factions, and even some within the military. On October 9, 1945, Perón resigned from his position and was subsequently arrested. In response, hundreds of thousands of proletarians took to the Plaza de Mayo, the main city square, demanding his release and return to government. The military authorities ended up releasing him, allowing him to address the assembled crowd of workers. This momentous event not only calmed the protesters but also served as the launchpad for a political movement that would lead to Perón's victories in the presidential elections of 1946 and 1951.

Perón capitalized on the aforementioned narratives of the poor's moral superiority (Karush 2007, 2010, 2012). In addition to appealing to the proletariat through melodramatic tropes of dignity, he and his wife, Eva Duarte, negotiated salary increases and established systems of health, pension, and education that directly benefited the working class. The confluence of these policies and his populist rhetoric gave him the steadfast support and affection of the poor, which he motivated to take over the city's public spaces, first at rallies and later elsewhere. The physical colonization of Buenos Aires's landscape was accompanied by a sonic occupation of the city's soundscape through the bass drum, which became a symbol of Perón's supporters (Adamovsky and Buch 2016).

Starting in these years, the bass drum and later the bombo con platillo found their way into football stadiums, as evidenced by pictures from sports magazines of the time. The overlap between carnival and football has been a long-standing tradition in Buenos Aires's neighborhoods (Adamovsky and Buch 2016; Martín 1997; O'Brien 2018; Rossano 2009, 2012). As Coco Romero, an activist, composer, performer, and historian, elaborated during our conversation: "When you historicize football and when you historicize murga [porteña], both are parallel phenomena, that came [to the country] in the 1890s. So, in the first twenty years, you have a link between the kid that plays with the *pelota de trapo* [ball made of rags] and the carnival's [social] base. Since their emergence in this society, they've been close to each other. . . . Both cultural phenomena coexisted." At the turn of the twentieth century, murga porteña troupes established strong connections with football clubs, embracing their colors and emblems, and often sharing members and instruments. As stadium attendance surged in the 1950s, driven by the proletariat's increasing colonization of public spaces and active engagement in consumption (Alabarces 2007), the Peronist drum, and later murga porteña with the bombo con platillo, took center stage in stadiums.

In this context, hinchas versioned two chants that continue to resonate in stadiums to this day. The first one is the "Marcha Peronista" (Peronist March), the anthem of Perón's political movement. Originally recorded and performed by Hugo del Carril in 1949, this march quickly became an emblem of Peronist rallies, where thousands of hinchas collectively sang it to the rhythmic beat of drums (Adamovsky and Buch 2016).[6] A telling example of Peronist melodrama (Karush 2007, 2010, 2012), the chorus of "Marcha Peronista" carries the song's core message (video 1.8):

Perón, Perón, qué grande sos	Perón, Perón, you're the greatest
Mi general, cuánto valés	My general, you're priceless
Perón, Perón, gran conductor	Perón, Perón, great leader
Sos el primer trabajador	You're the number-one worker

The march began to dominate stadiums' soundscapes after the coup that ousted Perón in 1955. Amid a ban on pro-Peronist expressions, hinchas of different teams changed its chorus to "dale, campeón" (let's go, champion) or simply "dale, oh"(video 1.9). Boca Juniors hinchas are the authors of the second versioning still heard in stadiums (video 1.10):

Sí, sí, señores	Yes, yes, gentlemen
Yo soy de Boca	I'm a Boca fan
Sí, sí, señores	Yes, yes, gentlemen
De corazón	From the heart
Porque este año	Because this year
Desde La Boca	From La Boca
Desde La Boca	From La Boca
Saldrá el nuevo campeón	The new champion will come

The source is the popular song "Sinceramente" (Sincerely), a piece with touches of Brazilian *marcha* and composed by musician Santos Lipesker. Both examples not only marked the beginning of football chants but also laid the foundation for re-versioning, as they were readapted by other hinchadas.

During the 1960s, rapid changes in Argentina's mediascape accelerated these creative processes. This transformative decade witnessed the emergence of advertising as a pivotal mediator of consumption, an expansion of television channels and radio stations, a surge in the manufacturing and importing of electronic devices, and the establishment of offices by multinational recording companies in Buenos Aires, leading to an unprecedented production of LPs (Alabarces 2007). These developments flooded the country's public sphere with songs, jingles, and theme songs. Unsurprisingly, advertisement became the source of many chants. One such example is this versioning of a jingle for a sheet fabric:

Vaya, vaya con el campeón	Follow, follow the champion
A todas partes vaya con el campeón	Follow the champion everywhere
Si sos de Boca	If you're a Boca fan
Hacé el favor	Do us a favor
Andate a la puta que te parió	Go fuck yourself

This chant is also an early example of how attacks and profanities began to gradually dominate chants.

Coinciding with this rapid media and technological growth, Argentina also experienced three decades of constant social, political, and economic instability. The military junta that ousted Perón in 1955 made extensive efforts to dismantle his policies and tarnish his reputation, leading to severe persecution of his followers. Different de facto governments ruled the country until 1973, when an elderly Perón returned from exile and assumed office. Following Perón's death in 1974, his vice president and second wife, Isabel Perón, became president. Amid economic upheavals, left-wing insurgency, and reactionary activity from the far right, a US-backed military coup ended her presidency in 1976. An ensuing regime ruled the country from 1976 to 1983, using thanatopolitics to exert social and political control.

Through terror, the regime imposed neoliberalism as the new form of economic organization, consolidating power in the market and financial sectors. Foreign indebtedness sustained the Argentine model, making privatization, deregulation, and opening up to world markets prerequisites for obtaining loans from international organizations such as the International Monetary Fund (Teubal 2004). A stark departure from Argentina's tradition of state involvement in economic and social policies, this thanatopolitical restructuring of the country's foundations ultimately led to increased social exclusion, community fragmentation, and the erosion of classic forms of social integration (Grimson 2005).

The regime's thanatopolitics not only supported but were also shaped by neoliberalism. Within Argentina's "dirty war," violence operated within a private economy of terror. The regime established a clandestine market where entrepreneurs could collaborate with media corporations to spread disinformation, coordinate with companies to report opponents, and establish medical facilities to attend to the births of detained women, later selling their children to adoptive parents. In this death-market, a privileged role was played by task forces or *patotas*—independent groups formed by military, paramilitary, and security forces units dedicated to kidnapping, torturing, raping, murdering, and disappearing people. In addition to managing secret detention centers, these task forces profited by seizing victims' properties as war spoils. The regime ultimately subverted the state's monopoly on violence by privatizing it, allowing civilians to deploy violence for private goals that might not align with the regime's objectives.

Argentine scholars suggest that the regime's neoliberal thanatopolitics mediated the emergence of vicious lyrics, hostile sounds, organized combat, planned corruption, disregard for human life, and ultimately the necropolitics of aguante (Alabarces 2012; Garriga 2007, 2010). While violence has always been present in Argentine football, it began to be perceived as morally positive—a transactional form of capital that could be exchanged for social, political, and economic gains within larger networks of corruption. Through negotiations with various actors, including players, executives, and politicians, hinchas gained unprecedented power, reinvesting their capital in illegal forms of entrepreneurship, such as drug trafficking. As they competed over violent value production, clashes between hinchas naturally increased, leading to a corresponding rise in the number of deaths. Pablo Alabarces (2012) highlights that, amid the thanatopolitical liberalization of violence, barras adopted the model of task groups. Emerging within a death-market that displaced "life, death, and power from administration" (Emerson 2019, 3), aguante necropolitics crystallized as a subaltern appropriation of violence, becoming a material and symbolic resource amid state abandonment, social precarity, and irreconcilable conflicts.

Lyrics of the time illustrate the emergence of aguante proper. Chants became infused with stories of combat, death threats, insults to the police, and other violent utterances, highlighting the transformation of chants into symbols of radical defiance and deadly confrontation (video 1.11):

Yo te quiero, Millonario	I love you, Millionaire [River Plate]
Yo te quiero de verdad	I really love you
Quiero la Libertadores	I want to win the Libertadores
Y un bostero matar	And to kill a bostero

As necrotic themes began to dominate chants, the lyrics also started to portray hinchas as the protagonists of games, acknowledging the potential of sound to influence games and players (video 1.12):

Alentemos todos juntos	Let's cheer all together
Para que pongan huevos nuestros jugadores	So that our players grow some balls
Que los partidos se ganan dentro de la cancha	Because games are won on the field
Y acá en los tablones	And here in the stands
Que griten los cuervos	The cuervos [San Lorenzo hinchas] must sing
Si quieren salir campeones	If they want to win the championship

This chant illustrates the emergence of one of the fundamental principles in the aguante acoustemology: sound is a material force that can be deployed to affect, silence, and disorient minds and bodies. This affective and subjective weaponization of sound is in alignment with a broader shift toward necropolitics, underscoring an acoustemological transformation where practices of sounding, voicing, silencing, and musicking are now reframed in terms of conflict and violence.

The post-dictatorial governments continued the regime's economic policies, favoring large companies and economic groups. As Grimson (2005) writes, foreign debt, poverty, and the disruption of the productive system "reappeared in altered forms during the 1990s" (17). The Argentine neoliberal model faced a dramatic collapse during the 2001 crisis. Comparable to the Great Depression, the peso was devalued, wages plummeted, unemployment soared to 25 percent, and poverty escalated to 50 percent, leaving an indelible impact on Argentine society (Teubal 2004). After the crisis, as noted by football scholars, aguante necropolitics became the dominant mode of administering violence and death among hinchas (Alabarces 2012; Garriga 2007, 2010).

From this period to today, the core musical expressions of aguante have remained largely unchanged. However, there are a few notable exceptions. The incorporation of brass instruments has become prevalent, adding a new timbral and textural dimension to the collective vocalizations of hinchadas. This development coincided with the possible fusion of murga porteña and samba reggae. Additionally, there has been a noticeable shift in the sources for versioning, with popular music genres now being the primary influence. Leandro explains:

> Many chants of the '80s used the melody of "Sobreviviendo" [Surviving, by folk singer-songwriter Víctor Heredia] and the jingle "Bobby, mi buen amigo" [Bobby, My Good Friend]. This happened because there were fewer songs

available then. Now, we have a larger production of everything, especially in mass media. Until recently, when I was a kid, we only had five TV networks. Now, we live in a different world. My nephew, for example, who is six years old, is always on this [showing me his phone]. He spends his life on that thing. You have to consider that, especially in the '60s, '70s, and even the '80s, many chants came from jingles—they didn't come from authored songs. They were based on TV and radio ads. Over time, chants started to be taken from music bands because the advertising world changed. This shift illustrates the connection between football chants and everyday life. Advertisement changed, and now you barely have ads with jingles. What I mean is that the evolution of the world is always in feedback with football chant activity. Life itself and football chants feed off each other, both in terms of creativity and lyrics.

His statement resonates with Ochoa Gautier's (2006b) observations regarding contemporary shifts in the Latin American public sphere. She argues that the "intermediality of the sonic sphere—from face-to-face communication to radio, cinema and television, to the self-production of recordings to internet and cell phone communication—becomes an increasingly privileged site of constitution of a (contested) public sphere" (807). As a result of this increasing saturation and intermediation, the number of potential melodic sources for aguante chants has exponentially increased.

But the story told in this section remains partial. While aguante was gradually gaining prominence in Argentina during the 1980s, its circulation extended beyond the country's borders. In fact, Uruguayan and Chilean hinchas rapidly began to embrace, analyze, and debate the values and practices propagated through aguante chants, enacting resonances and frictions with local fan traditions. In stadiums and mediated spaces, hinchadas outside Argentina began to develop and publicly defend their fan worldview, all while examining themselves through a global lens.

THE FIRST STAGE OF (TRANS)LOCAL FRICTION

Due to border conditions, Uruguayan hinchas have been actively participating in aguante since the early 1980s. Instead of dividing Montevideo and Buenos Aires, the Rio de la Plata rather unites the two cities, forming a cohesive *rioplatense* region. Cachila explains: "It started in the '80s, and you have to consider that [aguante] arrived in Montevideo earlier than in Tucumán [a northern Argentine province], for example. It came earlier than in Córdoba [a city in central Argentina], which is like seven hours away from Buenos Aires. It's a movement where porteño culture is very present [in Montevideo]. The same in Asunción. I mean, [the television shows of Argentine anchors] Tinelli and Pergolini were aired live on TV at 10 [p.m.] on primetime. Here, you consume porteño culture. And sports too." Buenos Aires has strong and long-standing connections with Montevideo. Game footage from the 1980s reveals that the barras of Peñarol and Nacional (Uruguay's second most popular team) already exhibited similarities to Argentine hinchadas.

The specificities of South American football have significantly contributed to these exchanges. Peñarol and Nacional's active participation in Copa Libertadores since 1960 has led to repeated visits by Uruguayan hinchas to Argentine stadiums, and vice versa. Cachila states: "[The circulation of aguante] has always happened. For example, [Uruguayan and Argentine] teams have been protagonists of international competitions since the beginning of South American football. So, they have been traveling, border-crossing, playing finals. The Peñarol hinchada has gone twenty thousand more times than those of Colo-Colo and La U to Buenos Aires." As of 2019, Peñarol had achieved five Copa Libertadores titles and had been the runner-up in five occasions, while Nacional had won the tournament three times and reached the final in three tournaments.[7] Until recently, Argentina's big five used to play more games against these two Uruguayan squads than against teams outside Buenos Aires.

The use of murga porteña instead of murga uruguaya (Uruguayan murga) among Peñarol and Nacional hinchas exemplifies the (trans)local friction brought about by aguante circulation. While both genres incorporate borrowed melodies, they diverge in terms of rhythm and percussion. Played with cymbals, snare, and bass drums, murga uruguaya is characterized by two rhythms: a syncopated march-like beat known as *marcha camión* (truck march) and a pattern called *candombeado*, which imitates the Afro-Uruguayan drumming tradition known as *candombe* (Kirschstein 2007).[8] Apart from these musical distinctions, Uruguayans perceive the two genres as occupying distinct social spheres: murga uruguaya belongs to carnival, while murga porteña inhabits stadiums. As Cachila states, "murga uruguaya represents satire, socio-political critique, and, for Uruguayans, murga porteña represents football hinchadas. It's then a synonym of violence and aguante."

A revealing example of murga porteña's indexicality in Uruguay is the song "La violencia" (The Violence) by the renowned local ensemble Agarrate Catalina

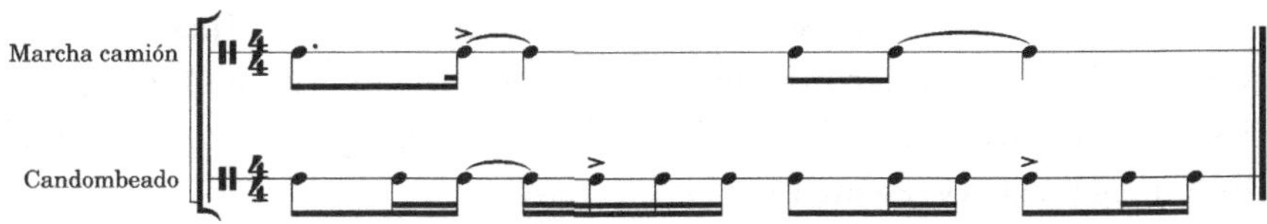

FIGURE 1.4 Murga uruguaya.

(video 1.13). Albeit a dystopian commentary on football, the song transcends mere condemnation of hinchas, making a broader critique of poverty and alienation within Uruguayan society. Instead of adhering to the traditional murga uruguaya rhythms found in all of their songs, Agarrate Catalina uses a bombo con platillo and adopts murga porteña in "La violencia." In doing so, it exemplifies the necropolitical connotations that a segment of Uruguayan society associates with the Argentine rhythm.[9]

The connections between poverty and aguante established in "La violencia" are common in Uruguay. Cachila, for example, posits that similar socio-urban conditions have made aguante appealing for working-class citizens throughout the Southern Cone: "The Southern Cone shares similar socioeconomic, penitentiary, and police state realities, resulting in similar impoverished contexts. The popular classes face the same issues and pressures, leading them to be attracted by the sonority and color of an hinchada." This aligns with what some scholars refer to as Latin American "structural poverty" (Grimson 2005, 82). Political economists have observed that South American countries share a "common peripheral condition," where economic growth primarily relies on "sectors with low levels of technological complexity (from natural resources extraction to labor-intensive assembly) and lacking an internal industrial core" (Ahumada 2019, 4). This type of peripheral growth has been linked to economic fluctuation and social inequality. Although Uruguay has made significant progress in reducing poverty over the past twenty years thanks to effective redistributive policies, urban marginalization and spatial segregation have remained prominent issues in the country (Serna and González 2017).

In Chile, conditions of precarity, repression, and marginalization compelled Garra Blanca and Los de Abajo—the barras of Colo-Colo and Universidad de Chile, respectively—to find aguante appealing during the 1980s. Although there has long been a tradition of violence (Elsey 2011), creativity (Grumann 2013), and loudness (Osorio 2023) in local stadiums, these barras have significantly transformed the style of these symbolic and material conflicts. These changes were especially noticeable in terms of sound practice. In fact, until the 1980s, these were limited to sporadic performances of liminal speech utterances and drumming practices resembling Brazilian samba.

Oral histories recount that Los de Abajo (The Underdogs, but literally "The Ones Below") emerged in the late 1980s—the waning yet most brutal years of General Augusto Pinochet's military regime (1973–1990). A group of teenagers sought to distinguish themselves from older supporters by critiquing their stylistic choices, connections with the club's administration, and endorsement of the military regime. Los de Abajo began occupying the bottom of the *Galería Sur* (South Stand), the National Stadium's most affordable section. While their name literally referred to the physical space they occupied in the stadium, it also symbolized their perceived social position: the underdogs of society. Armed with a small bass drum, these youngsters began imitating the singing voice and performing style of Argentine hinchadas.

The imitation of Argentine sonic practices was essential in establishing distinctions with older supporters. Rogelio, one of Los de Abajo's founders, states:

> We were part of the official barra. As such, we sang and followed the team. Obviously, because of age and friendship, a group of us became close and unbreakable. We started cheering for the team with more fervor . . . more or less fifty, sixty, seventy *bullangueros* [U. de Chile hinchas] who cheered differently began to gather here. Shirtless, naked torso, waving jerseys, close to the fence, sometimes on top of it . . . We were influenced by Argentine barras. At that time, we even sang with a "che" [a famous Argentine interjection] accent.

Deploying sonic intensity through aguante characterized the emergence of Los de Abajo. This desire to imitate Argentine hinchas was widespread among these teenagers, as Rogelio illustrates: "We were against [the older supporters]. First, we had a chant 'las cajas por la raja' [shove your snare drums up your asses]. We didn't want snare drums. We wanted the Argentine style—just a bass drum. The official barra had a Brazilian influence, with snare drums . . . Not like us. We wanted something slower where the voice was the protagonist and the bass drum set the pace." The centrality of the singing voice became a core value among Los de Abajo—an axiom that persisted even with the shift from the bass drum to the bombo con platillo in the 2010s. In the 1980s and 1990s, these adolescents were not yet aware of the murga porteña style that Argentine hinchas were actually playing, primarily because the drum's sounds were not adequately amplified by the technologies mediating their listening practices. Rogelio continues:

> We had an Argentine influence. In that time, Argentine football was broadcast by [sports commentator] Tito Awad. That's when we started to see the Argentine barras. The chants, the atmosphere, started to capture our attention. We put our ears close to the TV [speakers] but we couldn't hear much. To understand the lyrics, the chants. Tito Awad only said stupid shit, and we wanted to listen to the barras—not the commentaries. And that's where we took our first chants. And Pablito Boca or Pablito Anormal [Abnormal] was also among Los de Abajo's founders, who came from Argentina, from Harvard, from studies in La 12.[10]

In addition to highlighting the role of immigration in the (trans)local feedback of aguante, Rogelio emphasizes the aural friction enacted by the precarious mediation of television. Veal (2007) has demonstrated that fragilities, limitations, and low-quality technologies can give rise to contingent musicalities. This resonates with the adoption of aguante in Chile, where the limited sonorous quality of football broadcasts led Los de Abajo to perceive only the lower sounds of bombos con platillos, shaping their initial interpretation and performance of aguante.

Los de Abajo crystallized not only amid technological but also sociopolitical precarity. In the 1980s, facing mounting local and international pressure, the Pinochet regime became even more brutal and further restricted civil liberties. U. de Chile games became one of the pioneering spaces for public protest against the dictatorship (Matamala 2015; Nadel 2014). As Rogelio explains: "The typical [chant] was 'y va caer' [and he's going to fall]. That shit was unstoppable. Usually, not always, it started where we were. A lot of us were coming from high school with that burden. And also, many college students gathered there. Guys who came from college, who were studying, sang with us, who were younger. A really important social movement against the power of the Pinochet regime started there." Sonic aguante also allowed Los de Abajo to redress the erosion of the U. de Chile fanbase due to poor sports campaigns. Rogelio continues:

> Los de Abajo is an ideal . . . we were all one. We didn't have a boss, we didn't have a leader, everything was democratic. If something was decided and you were in the minority, you ended up supporting and rowing in the same direction, even if the decision wasn't what you wanted. That's helped us grow. That ethos, that brotherhood . . . Los de Abajo's first dream wasn't about winning a

championship: It was to see the entire South Stand singing and cheering for La U. Because at clásicos, the Colo-Colo hinchada started at [gate] 16: from the scoreboard, at 16, to Andes [an expensive section of the stadium]—the entire stadium. And La U [people] was the stadium's twentieth, thirtieth percent. Just one sector . . . La U people were quieter and didn't go [to the stadium]. When we moved to gate 14 of the South Stand and took over the area, we began to change that.

As historians Gabriel Salazar and Julio Pinto (1999) point out, hinchadas became spaces where working-class adolescents responded to their sociopolitical exclusion by creating their own modes of expression, forms of sociality, and articulation of democratic ideals.

But the adoption of aguante was also informed by violence. Los de Abajo's crystallization occurred in one of the most violent periods in the country's history. Rogelio explains: "Politically, socially, we were coming out of something that was very heavy, which was the dictatorship. The Pinochet period was coming to an end. People really began to open up. In '87, when we started getting together, to know each other, we all came from school, from different places that repressed us. The dictatorship was really tough on us. We're the sons of the dictatorship. We were educated by Pinochet." Hegemonic thanatopolitics helped enact alternative necropolitics. The emergence of Los de Abajo was marked by brawls with the embryonic Garra Blanca. During the late 1980s, Colo-Colo hinchas began attacking U. de Chile supporters, stealing their flags and banners. Attending games as a group became essential for U. de Chile people to safely leave neighborhoods dominated by the Colo-Colo fanbase. This need for self-defense further exacerbated Los de Abajo's tensions with older supporters. As Rogelio remembers: "When there was conflict, we went directly to the clash. And [the older fans] said, 'No, don't mess with them.' Why wouldn't we go if they were attacking the blue family?! We were a little bit more extreme. It was diametrically different from what was happening before. If we saw that our people were being attacked, we would defend them. We were not going to be passive agents—we were going to be active agents." However, these teenagers quickly moved beyond mere self-defense and began actively engaging in banner warfare, viewing violence as valuable capital. The stories of combat, stolen banners, and intensified conflicts present in aguante chants resonated with local rivalries and prevailing conditions of alienation and repression. While these practices empowered hinchas, they also fueled a necropolitical feedback loop between aguante and local dynamics of violence.

THE SECOND STAGE OF (TRANS)LOCAL FRICTION

Changes in the Southern Cone's mediascape amplified the reflexive circulation of aguante in the 1990s and early 2000s. A significant development was the emergence of cable television. Although TyC Sports, ESPN Latin America, and Fox Sports Latin America headquarters were in Buenos Aires, they functioned as transnational networks, broadcasting the same content to Chile and Uruguay.[11] As a result, viewers in the Southern Cone got access to high-quality broadcasts of Argentine games on a weekly basis. Moreover, the shows produced by these channels began to dedicate a significant portion of their airtime to hinchas, extensively depicting their rituals and values (Salerno 2006). This (trans)local feedback helped cement a multisited assembly that perceived itself as an essential, if not the most crucial, component of the football spectacle (Alabarces and Rodríguez 1996).

TyC Sports' *El Aguante* significantly mediated the transnational circulation of aguante for more than a decade. Its founders, Martín Souto, Pablo González, and Mariano López, originally wanted to create a show that discussed the relationship between football and popular music. However, since a similar program already existed, they decided to focus on the sounds of aguante. From 1997 to 2008, "the hinchas' show," as the anchors called it, conducted interviews with Argentine and South American fans and broadcasted their practices to the entire Southern Cone. Through rankings, showdowns, and other music-centered segments, the hosts celebrated the aesthetics of musical aguante, pitting hinchas against each other in terms of musicality. Media scholar Daniel Salerno (2006) points out that, by centering the football spectacle around hinchadas, the show amplified the aguante aesthetic, presenting it as the ideal model of fandom in the region.

In addition to underscoring chains of contrafacta, *El Aguante* dedicated significant airtime to highlighting connections between chants and their musical sources. Every chant they broadcasted was treated like a popular music song. Similar to music television networks, each video was accompanied by captions in the left corner, including the name of the respective hinchada, the title of the chant, the name of the song, and the musicians who originally composed it. The show also invited the musicians who created the melodies for interviews and to play arrangements of the contrafacta made by hinchadas. Musicians consistently expressed excitement at the possibility of hearing their melodies sung by thousands of people. For example, a member of rock band Katanga once stated: "When we started our career, when an hinchada sang one of our songs, you don't understand how important that is . . . When hinchadas sing songs by [musical] bands, it surpasses [the realm of] popular music. You make a song, and it's insane that someone hears it and creates new lyrics for it" (quoted in Salerno 2006, 144). *El Aguante* validated (re-)versioning practices, making hinchas aware that composers and musicians wanted their songs to be arranged and collectively sung in stadiums.

The section "El Aguante Internacional" (International Aguante) specifically aired Chilean and Uruguayan practices. Focusing on rivalries like Colo-Colo versus U. de Chile and Peñarol versus Nacional, the hosts interviewed local hinchas about aguante, enabling them to engage in transnational public discourse. Other episodes featured continental games between Argentine and other South American teams, highlighting sonic clashes between hinchadas. These (trans) local comparisons allowed hinchas in Chile and Uruguay to participate and perceive themselves as insiders within the fandom, opening the door for feedback processes that would stylistically and ideologically diversify aguante.

As Argentine public opinion began to discuss the role of aguante lyrics and their circulation in inciting violence, *El Aguante* faced increasing pressure. Sports commentators, politicians, and football authorities posited that the show was dangerously amplifying the aguante discourse, radicalizing hostile relations among hinchadas. TyC Sports eventually decided to cancel the show in 2008.

Meanwhile, CONMEBOL (the South American football Confederation) expanded the number of continental championships in the 1990s. Although the Copa Libertadores remained the most prestigious tournament, the addition of competitions such as the Supercopa Sudamericana (1988–1997), the Copa CONMEBOL (1989–1997), the Copa Mercosur (1998–2001), the Recopa Sudamericana (1989–1998, 2003–present), and the Copa Sudamericana (2002–present) significantly increased the number of continental matchups. This expansion allowed more teams to compete with the Argentine, Uruguayan, and Chilean barras that had already engaged in aguante.

During this period, these barras began to purposefully and effectively disseminate their sonic practices of fandom in their own countries. Hinchas of other teams not only heard them vocalizing chants in stadiums but also had the opportunity to listen to them through media technologies, as they started recording their contrafacta on cassettes and later compact discs. The first analog recordings were produced in Chile, including Los de Abajo's *Dale León* (Let's Go Lion) from 1992 and Garra Blanca's *Se Viene el Albo Campeón* (The White Champion Is Coming) from 1998 (video 1.14). Produced by record label Alerce and sold in shops like Feria del Disco, the circulation of these recordings was massive, not only among the respective fanbases but also among hinchas of other teams, who used them as models when (re-)versioning aguante. In fact, a significant portion of the contrafacta sung in Chilean stadiums in the 1990s and early 2000s came from these recordings. It is also noteworthy that Chilean, not Argentine, recordings were the first to be publicly released, highlighting the early transnationalization of aguante.

The circulation of aguante did not result in the passive adoption of Argentine necropolitics across the region. Transnationalization did not lead to a one-way invasion where Argentine sounds contaminated and transformed peaceful groups into violent ones. Instead, these (trans)local encounters functioned as feedback processes, creating friction between local and transnational forms of fandom. A brief detour to Brazil, one of South America's football hotspots, supports this point.

During the 1960s, as barras began to crystallize in Argentina, a parallel process unfolded in Brazil, giving rise to torcidas organizadas (hereafter, torcidas) (Lopes 2013; Lopes and Reis 2017; Reis and Lopes 2016; Teixeira 2016). These organizations comprised *torcedores* (fans or supporters) who introduced typical carnival music, particularly samba and its percussion ensemble known as *bateria*, into stadiums (Marra 2009, 2014, 2017, 2018, 2021; Marra and Trotta 2019). Since their inception, torcidas have been officially registered with clubs, recognized as formal, nonprofit associations with structured positions such as president, director, and deliberative body. Despite their official status, these groups have engaged in conflict with fellow supporters, club management, football authorities, and broader state authorities, employing violence both as insurrectional action and as a means of establishing hierarchical relations within their fanbases.

Although the necropolitics of torcidas resembles that of hinchadas, the predominant circulation of aguante in the 1990s and early 2000s created unexpected processes of feedback in Brazil. Over the years, dissident groups within torcidas have sought to defy the hierarchies and asymmetries imposed by dominant collectives (Costa and Toledo 2022; Santos 2016; Vimieiro 2015). Since the 2000s, these groups have appropriated aguante as a sanitized, nonviolent form of fandom, deploying it to challenge the norms and politics enforced by those who govern torcidas. They have advocated for a festive, family-oriented fan culture, adopting the performative style of hinchadas as a way to collectively embrace the supporting experience without the dangers and risks associated with violence. While embracing aguante practices, these groups have simultaneously reframed and dislocated them, incorporating elements from the torcida soundworld. This merging of influences has given rise to an original formation that has created both ideological and aesthetic friction with both hinchadas and torcidas.

THE THIRD STAGE OF (TRANS)LOCAL FRICTION

The digitalization of aguante began in the late 2000s, when videos of hinchadas started to saturate social media. As Cachila puts it, "the dispute is now on the YouTube comments." Nevertheless, this period's media and technological developments were not entirely novel. Instead, they expanded and reinforced the feedback loops already established through in-person and analog interactions.

Escuela de Tablones, a collective comprising approximately a dozen San Lorenzo hinchas, has risen as influential trendsetters in the aguante world through their media work. Their commitment to creating chants has not only expanded traditional chant pedagogy but has also fostered intertextuality, transforming digital media into the primary platform for aguante creativity. This shift has allowed hinchas from outside Argentina to participate more actively in collective deliberations, effectively turning aguante into a fully transnational forum.

The emergence of Escuela de Tablones has been linked to the rise of social media. Orti, one of the members of Escuela de Tablones, elaborates:

> We met creating new songs during previas, an hour before games, early [gatherings under the stands where hinchas sing chants until games start]. And we were always the same, and we started to meet each other, and we created a group just for [creating chants]. Escuela de Tablones emerged in 2014, 2015. We realized that with social media it was easier to disseminate [the chants] than in previas. Because [in previas] people didn't know [the chants]. Before, you had to use your lungs and little flyers. Social media helped a lot. Now you circulate a chant, and everyone comes to the previa knowing it already. Before, you used to come to the previas an hour before under the stands with the drums and it was difficult to learn the long chants we created.

Digital technologies have allowed Escuela de Tablones to streamline a chant's insertion into the aguante canon. The already quoted Leandro states:

> The process is: we create it, record it, and then always sing it during what we call the previa, under the stands, where many people attend with cellphones to record and sing. That's Escuela de Tablones's signature. Otherwise, it doesn't reach the stands, which is the next step. You also have to consider that getting those in the center to sing it is one thing. Then, it has to go viral and spread to the sides. Finally, it has to reach the *plateistas* [fans in the most expensive section of the stadium]. The hardest part is making people like the chant so that they appropriate it and it ascends into the stands.

In the past, technologies with limited circulatory affordances such as flyers and photocopies mediated these pedagogies. Leandro continues: "in the stands you found photocopies with the chant on the floor, or they handed them to you. And then we sang them. It was something more on the field, in situ . . . you learned them there." In addition to employing the creative possibilities of the messaging app WhatsApp (Achondo 2022), Escuela de Tablones further enhanced their pedagogical approach by utilizing platforms such as Facebook, Twitter, Instagram, and YouTube to upload digital recordings. Leandro adds:

> Unlike before, what we do with the guys of Escuela de Tablones is to record them ourselves. It's a professional recording but homemade—nothing like a producer for a super band in the US. But we disseminate it that way. So, when people arrive at the stadium for what we call the previa, which takes place under the stands—if you go to YouTube, you'll find thousands of videos of us there—they already know the chant. Unlike in the past, when you learned it on the spot, now you have to adapt to the times and the speed with which information circulates. Everything is online now, so we use the tools of social media.

Escuela de Tablones not only saturates social media with recordings but also with live streams of their previas.[12] This allows Escuela de Tablones to amplify this pedagogical space, enabling the participation of fans who are physically absent. Media scholar Zizi Papacharissi (2015) argues that social media allows users to "*feel* their own place in current events, developing news stories, and various forms of civic mobilization," encouraging users to "tune into events they are physically removed from by imagining what these might feel like for people directly experiencing them" (4; emphasis in the original). Indeed, chant pedagogy is now immediately and mediately read, heard, observed, and imagined.

By saturating various platforms, Escuela de Tablones ensures the continuous circulation and accumulation of viral capital for their videos. They simultaneously benefit from the participatory aspect of aguante, as other hinchas contribute by sharing their videos online. For example, when YouTube took down their version of "Despacito," it continued to circulate on other social networking sites, and other users reuploaded it to the video-sharing platform. Especially relevant in this context is the media influence of Musicuervo, a YouTube channel dedicated to sharing videos of San Lorenzo's hinchada. With millions of views and likes from fans worldwide, Musicuervo has played a pivotal role in disseminating the creative expressions of San Lorenzo fans on a global scale. As Leandro affirms, "Musicuervo helped a lot. But I insist, it also has to do with internet waves, mass media, and virality."

Escuela de Tablones's utilization of social media has broadened the creative influence of the San Lorenzo fanbase from the local to the global. Their presence on social media platforms highlights that their chants are embraced not only by Argentine fans but also by enthusiasts from around the world. Videos showcasing Latin American, European, and Asian supporters performing Escuela de Tablones's chants saturate YouTube, Facebook, Instagram, and Twitter. Orti reflects: "The uptake is surprising, even for us. Every time we upload a new video, we have more reproductions. More and more. International news shows make segments about us." Views, likes, shares, and comments on their videos have evolved into the primary indicators of Escuela de Tablones's prominence within aguante. Lucas, a San Lorenzo hincha, notes: "Hinchas of other teams greet the San Lorenzo hinchada with comments like, 'respect from the hinchada of [Brazil's] Corinthians,' or 'respect from the hinchada of Colombia's Atlético Nacional.' These comments reflect the popularity of these groups due to social media circulation and demonstrate how other teams recognize the inventiveness and creativity of San Lorenzo's hinchada. You can visit the videos, and the comments illustrate this process clearly."

Escuela de Tablones now mediates aguante both locally and globally. Lucas continues:

> San Lorenzo is recognized as the most creative hinchada in Argentina, known for creating music, lyrics, and chants. A song like "Despacito," for example, becomes popular, and then the lyrics are changed and adapted by other teams. San Lorenzo's hinchada is praised for its imaginative and creative capacity by other teams, despite football rivalries, problems, and teases. As long as I can remember, San Lorenzo has a strong tradition of football chant creation, as well as in terms of circulation. Initially, this creativity mostly circulated among Ar-

gentine hinchadas. Now, with globalization, everything crosses borders faster, so you can find chants versioned by San Lorenzo's hinchada in other countries.

The frequently reiterated phrase "the hinchada that other hinchadas listen to" has expanded to encompass a global scope. And Escuela de Tablones is acutely aware of this transnational phenomenon. Phrases like "this is the one that the entire world listens to" have now become a common presence in their lyrics and declarations.

By inspiring other hinchadas to emulate their media work, Escuela de Tablones has contributed to the decentering of aguante from Argentine stadiums. In an era where social media serves as one of the primary evaluators of creativity, hinchas outside Argentina can actively engage and assert their dominance in this competition. The feedback processes of (re-)versioning have intensified aguante's chant ecology, which now operates digitally and transnationally. This has nurtured practices of remediation that, in turn, have amplified the (trans) local publicness of aguante.

The website *Barra Brava* (barrabrava.net) has assumed a pivotal role in fostering (trans)local competition among fanbases. The platform centers around a transnational ranking system where each hinchada is assigned "respect" points based on user votes. While the website continues to maintain an important level of activity, social media has emerged as a crucial arena for user engagement. On platforms such as Facebook, Twitter, and Instagram, *Barra Brava* administrators share videos featuring various South American hinchadas, encouraging users to determine winners through likes, shares, comments, and polls.

The digitalization of aguante has had repercussions on drumming practices outside the Rio de la Plata. While media technologies initially captured only the deep sounds of bombos con platillos, YouTube has heightened the prominence of cymbals, consequently emphasizing the previously unheard murga porteña rhythm. In Chile, Los de Abajo emerged as one of the early barras to incorporate the drum and embrace the murga porteña style. Scooby, the founder of their ensemble La Banda de la Chile, explains:

> [I created the ensemble] to make the people sing. Because in the 1990s, the style was with a bass drum, shirtless, everyone singing. It was beautiful, it was spectacular. But singing stopped for a while. So, what was murga porteña trying to do? To put the fiesta [party, which signifies a carnivalesque performance] together. Nothing more than putting the fiesta together. And we threw the

fiesta. Yes, we did it with murga porteña. Singing murga porteña to pep people up. It didn't have any other purpose but to liven up. We also added some brass instruments. Just trumpets. The trumpets' function was to play the same melody that the hincha is singing. To give the pitch to the people. So, murga porteña was a carnivalesque accompaniment so that people would sing.

Throughout the years, U. de Chile hinchas have steadily viewed musical performance as a means to elicit collective singing. During both the bass drum and the murga porteña periods, Los de Abajo have understood instruments as supplementary to vocal practice.

All in all, social media has helped redirect aguante away from Argentine stadiums. It has enabled hinchas from different regions to partake in (trans)local feedback loops, creating friction with local modes of fandom. These encounters have given rise to new styles that have either bypassed or directly influenced Argentine barras. Uruguayan and Chilean hinchas now see themselves as cosmopolitan insiders to aguante, adapting its practices and values while simultaneously contesting the dominance of Argentine barras. As Cachila states:

> Aguante has taken root in hinchadas. For instance, the hinchadas of Peñarol and Nacional boast larger crowds and have more aguante than many prominent hinchadas in Argentina. They perceive themselves as greater than many Argentinian hinchadas. When competing with other hinchadas, they stand out exceptionally. We all believe that we're the spectacle, not those twenty-two fuckers on the field. Here, we embrace the concept that "we're the owners of the fiesta, of the carnival." I remember when Peñarol was trailing 4–0 against [Colombia's] Atlético Nacional de Medellín at [Montevideo's] Centenario Stadium during the Copa Libertadores group stage, and the stadium was electric. Every time [Atlético Nacional] scored, we sang louder. We couldn't afford to lose both battles [i.e., on the field and in the stands]. It's about the idea of being the protagonist.

Aguante has thus become a multisited public assembly. Hinchas have engaged in a public discourse that circulates not only in national public spheres but also in transnational circuits. This process has provided marginalized groups dispersed across geographic boundaries with cosmopolitan yet alternative "ways of imagining stranger-sociability and its reflexivity" (Warner 2002, 88). Aguante circulation has offered hinchas a (trans)local platform to assert their significance within the realm of football while concurrently accentuating the decline of working-class livelihoods within the region.

Despite the influence that digital remediation has had on aguante's (trans)local publicness, it is important not to attribute its transnationality solely to digitality. Although social media has allowed hinchas "to self-actualize online and offline as they develop their own voice(s) and connect to diasporic publics around the globe" (Papacharissi 2015, 110), it has not fundamentally altered the reflexivity and performativity of the aguante discourse. Rather, its digital circulation has grown out and reinforced existing modes of feedback. In this sense, it is more productive to think of contemporary aguante as a bundle of face-to-face, in-game, analog, and digital forms of public relationality and (trans)local engagement.

CONCLUSION

This chapter has mapped the local genealogies and (trans)local flows that have turned aguante into a transnational public assembly. It all began in Buenos Aires during the initial decades of the twentieth century, where the intersection of football and carnival converged with broader sociopolitical transformations, especially the proletarian reclamation of public spaces, a phenomenon amplified by the emergence of Peronism and the escalating saturation of Buenos Aires's mediascape. A series of thanatopolitical crises contributed to the necropolitical radicalization of aguante, redefining violence as a positive type of transactional capital.

The transnational circulation of aguante has been propelled by various factors, including border conditions, advancements in media technologies, the heightened circulation of media, and the expansion of continental championships. Social media has further amplified aguante's (trans)local feedback loops. Platforms such as YouTube, Facebook, Instagram, and Twitter have enabled hinchas outside Argentina to publicly participate in the fandom's competition, asserting their identity as part of a multisited public assembly that perceives itself as the primary component of the football spectacle. While aguante has provided an avenue for working-class subjects to construct alternative imaginaries and amplify their marginalized social circumstances, it has also intersected with local thanatopolitical and necropolitical dynamics. The death threats, stories of combat, glorification of criminality, and discriminatory slurs filling the chants and informing the circulation of aguante have resonated with local conditions of violence and precarity, contributing to the radicalization of crowds and subjectivities throughout the entire Southern Cone. Yet aguante's transnational feedback has not led to uniformity and homogenization. Rather, it has generated friction and miscommunication. The subsequent chapters delve into the contingent meanings, uses, and effects of the sounds of aguante. The exploration begins by analyzing issues related to creativity and attribution among Escuela de Tablones.

TWO
Attribution and Creativity

On February 16, 2017, after reaching one million views in ten days, YouTube took down the video "'Despacito' – Escuela De Tablones" due to copyright violations. The video was an audio recording of a dozen male hinchas singing their own lyrics over the melody of "Despacito" (Gently) by Puerto Rican musicians Luis Fonsi and Daddy Yankee. Although the reggaeton track had been circulating in Argentina's public sphere for over a month, it had yet to achieve its viral, record-breaking status.

With a static red-and-blue flag in the background, the video starts with a trumpet playing the melody. A syncopated murga porteña pattern played by a bombo con platillo accompanies the brass instrument—sounds harmonized by claps, whistles, and shouts. Once the trumpet finishes the first melodic phrase, the hinchas begin to sing while the lyrics roll down. Prioritizing intensity over pitch precision, the men sing in a loop for over four minutes (video 2.1):

Ciclón, vos sos mi locura, no puedo parar
Y cada domingo me enamoro más
Por estos colores doy la vida entera
Oh, vamos, San Lorenzo, vamos a ganar
Este año la vuelta queremos dar
Para que Boedo vuelva a estar de fiesta

Cyclone, you are my madness, I can't stop
And every Sunday I fall in love even more
I give my life for these colors
Oh, let's go, San Lorenzo, let's win
We want to win the championship this year
So that Boedo can celebrate once again

San Lorenzo, es inexplicable todo lo que siento	San Lorenzo, I can't explain everything I feel
Estaré contigo en todo momento	I'll always be there with you
Porque la azulgrana yo la llevo adentro	Because I carry the blue-and-red inside of me
Pongan huevo y vayan al frente para ser primero	Let's grow some balls and fight to be the number one
Esta es la gloriosa banda de Boedo	This is the glorious band of Boedo
Es la que escuchan en el mundo entero	The one that the entire world listens to
Yo llevo una vida a tu lado siguiéndote	I've been following you all my life
Desde que nací junto al Ciclón	Since I was born, I was with the Cyclone
Sé que no hay distancia que nos pueda separar	I know that no distance can separate us
Vayas donde vayas voy con vos	I go wherever you go

These locally rooted yet transnationally directed lyrics belong to Escuela de Tablones, a group of hinchas who create chants to cheer for the Argentine football team San Lorenzo, also nicknamed Ciclón (Cyclone) and Cuervo (Crow). Their lyrics blend tropes of aguante with nostalgic expressions about Boedo, a neighborhood they cherish as their home, despite losing their stadium there during the last military regime (1976–1983). Hinchas in Argentina and beyond widely recognize the San Lorenzo hinchada as the most innovative and creative on the continent, rejoicing in their ability to draw inspiration from unexpected melodic sources.

Despite the video's short life, it sparked substantial debate. The day after Escuela de Tablones uploaded the chant to YouTube, Luis Fonsi praised it on Twitter: "This is incredible! I want to witness this in person." The chant also caught the interest of fans from Latin America, Europe, and Asia, whose comments flooded Escuela de Tablones's social media platforms. The day after YouTube took down the video, Escuela de Tablones posted the following statement: "Yesterday, YouTube decided to remove the video due to copyright, which got more than one million views and made the San Lorenzo hinchada travel around the world through its creativity. Outraged by the situation, but stronger than ever, because 'they could never stop this hinchada,' we'll keep uploading videos and making chants, despite the censorship, as we've been doing for the past ten years." In the following weeks, "Despacito" would match the chant's viral success while hinchadas in Argentina and abroad would start modifying Escuela de Tablones's contrafactum to cheer for their own teams.

Participatory understandings of auditory culture inform the perceived censorship. Aguante chants constitute a shared repertoire, accessible to all hinchas regardless of nationality or club affiliation. The very existence of this corpus relies on the idea that the sounds circulating in the aural sphere belong to the public at large. But the statement's defiant tone also foregrounds that conflict also shapes the authorial, proprietorial, and creative values surrounding this collectively owned and collaboratively composed songbook—dynamics of attribution that are both in tension and harmony with neoliberal approaches to intellectual property (IP).

This chapter discusses notions of attribution and creativity among hinchadas, arguing that they understand them as granting status within the aguante conflict. Fanbases compete with each other in order to be known as the most creative in Argentina and abroad. In this context, creativity extends beyond creating original lyrics and includes the imaginative ability to discover unexpected melodic sources for chants. This auditory imagination involves deploying a series of interrelated listening techniques to diagnose which melodies could be adapted into chants by imaginatively projecting the aguante style and stadium acoustics onto them. While these chants are embedded in relations of competitive authorship, they are also seen as part of a public ecology, accessible to both local and foreign hinchas. The fact that they promote the socialization and adaptation of their own chants to accrue authorial and creative reputation complicates straightforward assumptions about attribution and creativity. Indeed, this participatory yet competitive ethos illustrates the existence of an alternative, contingent set of social norms to regulate attribution—conceptualizations of ownership and authorship that both align with and deviate from IP principles.

CREATIVITY, OWNERSHIP, AND AUTHORSHIP

Serving as a sphere where to claim and exert dominance, aguante creativity goes beyond merely creating innovative lyrics but rather centers on a series of interrelated *audile techniques* (Sterne 2003). Music scholars have explored various auditory forms of creativity, illustrating how audiophiles engage with the sonic qualities of music (Perlman 2004), how composers audibly evaluate their materials during the creative process (Cook 2018), how producers and engineers reimagine the sounds crafted by musicians (Meintjes 2003; Porcello 2004), and how music fans turn listening into an expressive act of consumption (McDaniel 2024). The aural creativity of hinchas involves applying acoustemological knowledge related to stadium acoustics, chant musicality, and socio-sonic relations among hinchadas to discover unexpected melodic sources that could resonate within stadiums and go viral on social media. This auditory framework is equally applied to private modes of music listening and attentive soundwalking in public spaces, fostering an imaginative and generative approach to diverse musical styles as potential aural representations of aguante. Unlike the myth surrounding canonical composers, which suggests that the work of art exists as a nonsonic auditory image in the minds of creators (Cook 2018), this creative process occurs while actively listening to existing, sounding melodies. Enacted through, not despite, sound, this auditory creativity brings attention to the significance of everyday acts of listening and moves away from notions of musical creativity linked solely to performance, composition, and production.

Aguante's creative prestige relies on highlighting attribution. Chants constitute a public aural ecology that is open to all hinchadas. The intersection of this collective ownership and the fact that creators have remained largely anonymous has led commentators to mistakenly assume that authorship is incidental in this culture of fandom (see Alabarces 2015; Bundio 2020; Parrish and Nauright 2013). However, authorial recognition plays a crucial role in establishing hierarchies both within and between hinchadas. To underscore their auditory creativity, hinchas not only highlight melodic sources but also actively circulate their chants for peers to learn and rival hinchadas to re-version them. The process of (re-) versioning allows hinchas to gain creative status within their own hinchada and the aguante world. Nonetheless, these dynamics of attribution have also contributed to intra-group hostility, as demonstrated by the tensions between Escuela de Tablones and La Gloriosa Butteler (the San Lorenzo barra).

Aguante's ideology of attribution provides insight into the contingency of intellectual property. (Ethno)musicologists have criticized copyright as ethnocentric and incompatible with communities where musical creation arises from dynamic, collective, and sometimes anonymous creative practices (Cook 2018; Fossum 2025; Manuel 2006, 2010; Manuel and Marshall 2006; McCann 2001). Critics argue that IP maximalism, which treats creativity as a means of capital production, can be detrimental to groups that have developed their own social norms for governing attribution—communities that operate outside and sometimes contrary to copyright law (Bollier 2008; Dent 2020; Katzenbach 2018).

Examples from various professions, such as chefs, tattooers, graffiti writers, hip-hop producers, and the creative commons movement, challenge IP assumptions "that creativity cannot thrive without legal rights of exclusion, that widespread copying is inevitable without legal intervention, and that law dictates the way the public interacts with creative works" (Darling and Perzanowski 2017, 10). However, despite the tension created with intellectual property due to the massive circulation of contrafacta, aguante creativity continues to flourish even in the face of strict copyright enforcement. Aguante's emphasis on competitive authorship, and its resonance with the creative competition favored by neoliberal approaches to intellectual property, has unexpectedly benefited both hinchadas and corporate owners. This questions contentions on both sides of the debate over copyright: that the law is necessary to sustain creative relations, on the one hand, and that legal regulation endangers noncommercial economies of musical creativity, on the other hand.

THE BIGGEST NEIGHBORHOOD CLUB IN THE WORLD

San Lorenzo's history is indissolubly tied to Boedo, a neighborhood in the heart of Buenos Aires. The team was founded in 1908 when Father Lorenzo Massa offered the teenage squad Los Forzosos de Almagro (The Forceful Ones of Almagro) blue-and-red jerseys and a field in Almagro, a bordering neighborhood of Boedo. The team was later renamed San Lorenzo de Almagro in honor of the Battle of San Lorenzo in the Argentine War of Independence. In 1916, San Lorenzo built a stadium, the Gasómetro, on Boedo's 1700 La Plata Avenue. Since then, as Matthew Hawkins (2017) writes, the neighborhood has become "synonymous with San Lorenzo" (121).

Boedo is a quintessential "barrio porteño," mostly settled by Italian and Spanish immigrants during the city's urban expansion in the early twentieth century. Over time, Boedo evolved into a hub of carnival, tango, literature, and Buenos Aires's distinctive café culture. The presence of San Lorenzo played a crucial role in setting Boedo apart from other porteño neighborhoods, fostering an ethos that intertwined sociality, physical surroundings, popular culture, and football fandom.

The landscape of Boedo is now filled with iconography that seamlessly combines the club and the neighborhood. Numerous bars, cafés, libraries, and cultural centers bear the name of the team, and colorful murals depicting musicians, writers, and artists sporting San Lorenzo jerseys adorn the area. Notable erudite

FIGURE 2.1 San Lorenzo's headquarters in Boedo.

yet fervent fans include Pope Francis, Vicentico from Los Fabulosos Cadillacs, Viggo Mortensen (who spent his childhood in Buenos Aires), and writer Fabián Casas, who has extensively explored the relationship between the club and the neighborhood in his writings. The barra's name, La Gloriosa Butteler, further emphasizes this socio-spatial connection as "Butteler" refers to a square in Boedo where San Lorenzo hinchas gather and socialize.

Figure 2.2 showcases the fusion of proletarian football and erudite art. Created by the Grupo Artístico Boedo (Boedo Art Group), the mural features the neighborhood alongside an angelic depiction of the writer Osvaldo Soriano, accompanied by the quote "One is always looking for origins. Our identity!" Although the quote originated from an interview where Soriano was reflecting on writing and national identity, San Lorenzo hinchas have linked it to his well-known passion for the club. Soriano's works frequently explored football as a central theme (Kunz 2001), but his writings about San Lorenzo were limited to a short story in which he fictionalized the later years of one of the club's founders:

> Among the San Lorenzo hinchas who ecstatically celebrated the 1972 championships, walked a seventy-nine-year-old man, his face weathered like a nut-

> shell, with faded eyes that only permitted a faraway gaze. He didn't feel the usual pain in his liver or nose, broken by a ball seventy years ago. In his back pocket, he carried a worn-out leather wallet, housing two hundred pesos, a San Lorenzo lifetime membership, and a gold medal. Despite his presence, no one recognized him, nor did anyone offer gratitude. Upon returning to his rooming house at 3700 Monte Street, he locked himself in his cramped three-by-three room. There, he extinguished his kerosene lamp, peeled three potatoes, and boiled them. Seated in the solitary chair, he turned on the radio, listening to how a group of men, comfortably living off football, experienced glory. (Soriano 1996, 115–16)

The sense of loss and melancholy evident throughout the text reflects essential aspects of the San Lorenzo identity.

While San Lorenzo has become one of the most successful and popular teams in the country, its surrounding imaginary has been shaped by traumatic events

FIGURE 2.2 Mural of Osvaldo Soriano in Boedo.

that occurred during the last military regime. In 1976, the de facto government of Buenos Aires closed down the Gasómetro due to safety concerns. Four years later, amid economic difficulties, the San Lorenzo administration reached an agreement with the authorities to grant the city part of their land on La Plata Avenue. In return, San Lorenzo received recognition of their ownership over a lot in Bajo Flores—a neighborhood close to Boedo where they wanted to build a massive sports complex. In 1981, San Lorenzo was the first of the big five to be relegated to the second division. Although it came back to the first division the following year, San Lorenzo did not win a tournament for twenty-five years. The courts later ordered San Lorenzo to sell a second portion of the Boedo terrain to cover unpaid debts in 1982. That same year, the club sold most of the remaining land to a corporation based in Uruguay, which later sold it to the French supermarket Carrefour. Today, San Lorenzo hinchas overwhelmingly blame the loss of the stadium on the regime, claiming that the military controlled the Uruguayan-based company.

Although San Lorenzo inaugurated the Nuevo Gasómetro in the 1990s—a new stadium situated in the notoriously dangerous and conspicuously inhospitable Bajo Flores—Boedo and the old stadium continue to haunt the imagination of San Lorenzo hinchas. This phenomenon persists even among those who were born after the stadium was lost, as this statement by Lucas illustrates:

> One aspect that sets San Lorenzo apart from other teams is its ability to connect two almost antagonistic characteristics of so-called big and small teams. It shares the history, tradition, people, and strong culture of the big teams, along with their sports success. However, it also carries a strong association with suffering, more commonly found among small teams. This suffering is not only related to sports issues but is also tied to a specific period, starting in the late 1970s and culminating in the loss of the stadium and relegation in 1981. This placed San Lorenzo in a new and challenging position, unlike anything experienced by the club or any other big team before. This adversity led to a football revolution, with fans rallying around San Lorenzo to relaunch the club. Additionally, closely connected to this narrative is the phrase "San Lorenzo is the biggest neighborhood club in the world," which underscores the team's unique identity and deep connection to its place of origin.

Listening to the memories of those who actually socialized in the old Gasómetro inspired young hinchas with the concept of *La Vuelta a Boedo* (The Return to

Boedo): a fan-funded initiative aimed at repurchasing the land from Carrefour and reconstructing a stadium on the site. Lucas elaborates:

> I didn't grow up in that cultural and football environment, and I still haven't experienced it firsthand because the stadium is no longer there. For me, it's more about a narrative passed down from my dad. I'm a San Lorenzo hincha because of my father. It's about envisioning what he did as a child with my grandfather. My family's connection with San Lorenzo begins with that grandfather. The stories my dad shares with me—taking the train, bringing food, watching minor league games until they finally got to see a first division game—connect me to the area, to Boedo. Although I haven't lived there personally, I still feel a sense of belonging to that space.

Shared past experiences of and in the stadium "produced a narrative from the club's past, using and transforming the memories of older *cuervos*, that in turn influences how *hinchas* of San Lorenzo understand their relationship with their club" (Hawkins 2017, 327). The Return to Boedo has become an affective longing for a place of socialization, cultural activity, and political engagement. Lucas continues: "[The Return to Boedo] is not just about building a stadium where we can play every fifteen days, but rather about recovering those dynamics, those social bonds that were at some point stolen. The loss of the stadium, which was caused by the military regime. It's a defense of that cultural tradition." The idea that reclaiming a physical location and rebuilding a material structure would inherently revive the past social and cultural atmosphere of Boedo has been notably mediated by Escuela de Tablones's lyrics. They have intertwined this longing for a sense of place with tropes of aguante.

TROPES OF PLACE AND AGUANTE

While Escuela de Tablones use their lyrics to mock rivals, their compositions differ from typical aguante chants as they tend to avoid necrotic stories. Orti, one of its members, states: "Within so much dirtiness, we try to inject some color and carnival spirit. I remember when I was a kid, my old man used to bring me along, and it was a big deal for fathers to teach the chants to their kids. We want the whole family, the kids, everyone, to learn the lyrics. That's why we're very careful with the words we use, to not focus too much on violence, even though such topics are part of the stadium culture." While Escuela de Tablones does not glorify aguante warfare, they do view conflict as the overarching, structural concept of fandom.

Their first chant to reach the stands was a contrafactum of "Se me ha perdido el corazón" (I've Lost My Heart) by Argentine cumbia singer Gilda (video 2.2):

Y dale, dale, Matador
A todas partes voy con vos
Hasta que me muera
Yo siempre te voy a seguir
Dejando el alma en el tablón
Ganes o pierdas
Volver a Boedo
Esa es mi ilusión
Quiero la vuelta
Quiero verte campeón
El sentimiento que hay en mí
No te lo puedo explicar
Es algo que se lleva adentro
Volver a Boedo
Esa es mi ilusión
Quiero la vuelta
Quiero verte campeón
A donde vayas, Matador
Contigo siempre voy a estar
Por los colores de este amor
Vamos, Ciclón
Vamos a ganar
Y La Gloriosa va a festejar
Por la Azulgrana voy a morir
Sin el Ciclón
No sé vivir

Let's go, Matador [San Lorenzo]
I go everywhere with you
Until death
I'll always follow you
Leaving the soul in the stands
Win or lose
To return to Boedo
That's my dream
I want to come back
I want to see you winning the championship
The feeling inside me
I can't explain it to you
It's something you carry inside
To return to Boedo
That's my dream
I want to come back
I want to see you winning the championship
Wherever you go, Matador
I'll always be with you
For the love for these colors
Let's go, Ciclón
Let's win
And La Gloriosa will celebrate
I'll die for the Azulgrana
Without the Ciclón
I don't know how to live

This chant distinguishes itself from those of other hinchadas in two distinct ways. First, its lyrics are extensive, incorporating choruses and multiple verses, which diverges from the short and repetitive nature of traditional chants. Second, the chant elaborates not only on aguante themes but also on the merging of sociality, materiality, and locality embodied by Boedo. It also became one of the earliest instances where the desire for the Return to Boedo became audible in stadiums. This fusion of aguante's physical resilience with San Lorenzo's emotional reservoir—characterized by steadfast melancholy and nostalgia for an idealized past—has significantly shaped how hinchas perceive and feel about the Return to Boedo.

The lost stadium and its location often work as synecdoches of the neighborhood in their lyrics. See, for instance, their version of "I'm Yours" by Jason Mraz (video 2.3):

Avenida La Plata 1700	1700 La Plata Avenue
Ahí nació este amor	This love was born there
Ahí nació San Lorenzo	San Lorenzo was born there
Ahí vamos a volver	We'll come back there
A levantar la cancha otra vez	To lift the stadium again
Las casas, Muñiz, Inclán, José Mármol, Salcedo	The houses, Muñiz, Inclán, José Mármol, Salcedo
Encierran este sueño del Gasómetro nuevo	Enclose this dream of a new Gasómetro
Tus calles mis venas son	Your streets are my veins
El barrio mi corazón	The neighborhood my heart
Boedo es un festival	Boedo is a festival
Todo el año es carnaval	It's carnival all year long
Toda mi vida te di	I gave you all my life
Por vos yo voy a morir	I'll die for you

Merging tropes of spatiality and viscerality, the lyrics vividly portray the neighborhood's distinct geography, forging tangible connections between the team, the hinchada, and Boedo. This creation of a material continuum weaves a narrative that seamlessly intertwines the past, present, and future of the club, the fanbase, and the neighborhood. This conflation of bodies, landscapes, and the lost stadium sets their poetry apart from that of other hinchadas. Leandro, another member of Escuela de Tablones, elaborates: "Other teams have pretty chants . . . but they're limited to singing to their team, or to do some sort of revisionism with the team's achievements, or the love for the colors. We have a history of creativity that has pushed us to create lyrics not only about winning a championship—which we have—not only about winning the clásico—which we have . . . San Lorenzo sings about exile, return, comeback, loyalty."

Many chants similarly intertwine the lost stadium's location and materiality, serving as a justification for the revival of a once-communal relationality through the construction of a new material structure in the very same space. One example is their contrafactum of "Y dale alegría a mi corazón" (And Give Happiness to My Heart) by Argentine rock star Fito Páez (video 2.4):

Y dale alegría a mi corazón	And give happiness to my heart
La Vuelta para Boedo es mi obsesión	The Return to Boedo is my obsession
Tener una cancha como la de tablón	To have a stadium like the wooden one
Y en Avenida La Plata salir campeón	And to be champions on La Plata Avenue
Vamos a volver	We'll come back
Al barrio que a San Lorenzo lo vio nacer	To the neighborhood where San Lorenzo was born

The use of wood as a metaphor is common in their chants. Although *tablón* (wooden stand) generally means "stand" in the Southern Cone, in the case of San Lorenzo, it also alludes to the old Gasómetro's rustic materiality.[1]

Despite their strong emphasis on locality, sociality, and identity, conflict is present in some of Escuela de Tablones's chants. Leandro admits: "We try to tell San Lorenzo what happens to us with San Lorenzo—that we love it. Now, obviously, there're songs [like] 'Huracán, you'll be relegated,' 'Racing you sold your sentiment,' 'you're our son.' Aggressions in lyrics or ironies, jokes, or black humor, which is part of football fandom and will always be present." See, for instance, their arrangement of "Una guitarra y una muchacha" (A Guitar and a Girl) by Argentine balada singer Sandro (video 2.5):

Si pasa el tiempo y no te veo	If time goes by and I don't see you
Yo pierdo la razón	I lose my mind
Y no me digan de ir un loquero	And don't tell me that I should see a shrink
Soy hincha del Ciclón	I'm a Ciclón hincha
Te conocí un domingo a la tarde	I met you on a Sunday afternoon
Y de vos me enamoré	And I fell in love with you
Pasan los años, pasa la vida,	Years pass by, life goes by

Y siempre te vengo a ver
Yo llevo tus colores desde Boedo a la eternidad
Para que lloren todos los de la Boca y de Huracán
Y los de Avellaneda son amargos de verdad
De River mejor no hablemos, prendieron fuego el Monumental

And I always come to see you
I carry your colors from Boedo to eternity
So that those of Boca and Huracán cry
And those of Avellaneda are really bitter
Let's not talk about River, they set the Monumental on fire

Leandro explains: "That chant is mine and I like it. In fact, people are starting to sing it. People like it because you tease everyone. And it has the right phrase: 'let's not talk about River, they set the Monumental on fire.'[2] That's it. You can't come back after that." Although Escuela de Tablones engages in the aguante conflict, they generally avoid resorting to expressions of violence toward rivals. As they state in a newspaper interview: "We never insult, we try to put some creativity to the typical 'we'll kill you'" (quoted in Gavira 2016). As implied in the quote, however, Escuela de Tablones does perceive chants as means to participate in symbolic disputes with rival teams, encompassing a spectrum from ingenious jokes to more direct insults.

A more hostile example is their contrafactum of "Algo en tu cara me fascina" (Something in Your Face Fascinates Me) by salsa singer Elvis Crespo (video 2.6):

Hay una banda de putos
En el barrio de La Quema
Son poquitos y boludos
Nunca la tribuna llena
Globo no hagas reír
Te lo pido por favor
Yo sé que te gusta mucho
La poronga del Ciclón
A los quemeros les fascina
A los quemeros les fascina
Chuparme la pija
Chuparme la pija

There's a band of putos [homophobic slur][3]
In La Quema neighborhood
They're not many and they're dumbasses
They never fill the stands
Globo, don't make me laugh
Please, I beg you
I know that you really like
The Ciclón's cock
The quemeros love
The quemeros love
To suck my dick
To suck my dick

Hay una cosa en tu escudo	There's something in your badge
No me para de asombrar	It never stops surprising me
Cada boludés que pasa	Every dumb thing that happens
Vos te ponés a bordar	You start embroidering
Globo, no me hagas reír	Balloon [Huracán], don't make me laugh
Te lo pido por favor	Please, I beg you
Nunca vas a ser un grande	You'll never be a big team
La puta que te parió	Son of a bitch
Algo en tu escudo me da risa	Something in your badge makes me laugh
Algo en tu escudo me da risa	Something in your badge makes me laugh
Son las estrellitas	It's the little stars
Son las estrellitas	It's the little stars

In addition to provoking Huracán hinchas in terms of manliness, Escuela de Tablones taunts their archrivals for sewing a star on their jersey to celebrate a minor local cup—a practice usually reserved for major international championships. Leandro explains the use of such violent tropes as follows:

> Some sing that "they'll kill them four," that "they'll set fire to La Bombonera [Stadium]," that "they'll kill them all." But be cautious, I always say that, in the stadium, in the chant culture, everything is valid. When the game is over, as you can imagine, I come back to my house. I wouldn't even think about fighting someone or saying something. Actually, that's kind of fascist. To tell someone with La U jersey "hey, we'll kill you" is stupid. I don't like what happens when barras fight. In fact, I get very scared when barras fight. I can't see them . . . But I find it funny when you sing "we'll kill you" to another team.

Like Leandro, many hinchas claim that these kinds of utterances are harmless components of football fandom. They contend that they do not uphold discriminatory views, stating that listening to misogynistic, homophobic, racist, xenophobic, and classist expressions does not truly affect them or bystanders.

Yet the sonorous expression of violent utterances has immersive and omnidirectional effects (Daughtry 2015). Beyond victimizing discriminated minorities and normalizing differences as undesirable deviances, the act of vocally performing threats, necrotic stories, dehumanizing expressions, and discriminatory slurs can also impact the singers themselves. Herrera (2018) points out that collective vocalization can lead to states of "deindividuation," where hinchas momentarily engage in and normalize behaviors that deviate from societal norms. However, as discussed in the forthcoming chapter, the vocalization of violent utterances can also have more lasting and profound effects, contributing to the radicalization of subjectivities, intensification conflicts, and incitation of further violence.

Nevertheless, the dehumanization of rivals is infrequent in the chants of Escuela de Tablones. In fact, the nature of their lyrics has been shifting, becoming less inclined to mention rivals. Leandro connects this shift to the fact that hinchas of rival teams are unable to attend away games in Argentine football:

> In Argentina, [football fandom] has changed a lot with the issue that rival hinchas can't come. A lot was lost there. That's key for me . . . When I was a kid, in the '80s and '90s, when we had rival hinchas, a really fun competition occurred. Really fun, and that doesn't happen anymore. Because when we play against Huracán and Boca, the clásicos, none of them are there. I'm a fervent advocate for [having rival hinchas]. I want them to come, and I want to go to La Boca and Parque Patricios. If I lose, I lose. If I win, I win. That's the fandom: the laugh, the jokes. That doesn't exist anymore . . . The football chants have changed a bit. In fact, I rarely make chants to make fun of a rival team. Because, why? If they don't come, whom do we sing against?[4]

As a result, lyrics are turning increasingly inward in nature, primarily addressing their own histories, identities, and clubs. While some journalists and scholars argue that the prohibition has only intensified internal conflicts, it can also be argued that it has contributed to a shift away from expressions of violence in the lyrics. However, this does not imply that the aguante conflict no longer influences music-making, as the competition has now shifted from the lyrics to the act of versioning itself.

AGUANTE CREATIVITY

Aguante creativity is now less about teasing rivals through lyrics and more about standing out as resourceful in finding and versioning unexpected musical sources. While poetry remains essential, the aural ability to discover songs that could potentially work as chants has become crucial. This auditory imagination involves the capacity to listen to and envision the sounds circulating in private and public spaces as future chants.

San Lorenzo hinchas constantly seek to assert their creative domination over rival hinchadas. For example, Leandro states:

> When you talk to an hincha about football chants in Argentina, you talk about San Lorenzo. The thing is that in recent years journalism is creating the notion that in Argentina only two clubs exist. We don't have a big five anymore. It's Boca, River, and the rest. In that terrible pedagogy that they're making with football, they're trying to suppress, censure, and close down everything that's not about Boca and River. But when you talk to an hincha, he's going to tell you that when you're talking about football chants you're talking about San Lorenzo.

The historical dominance of the San Lorenzo fanbase is a point they stress systematically. Leandro continues: "The truth is that, humbly, we're the avant-garde of Argentine football chants—and worldwide because many copy us. And among all of those [San Lorenzo] schools [of versioning], I generally like the chants of the '70s a lot. They're not sung anymore, but, for example, I sing them when I'm the shower. I don't care. Or sang them to my friends. At the end of the '80s, a group called Los Pibes de Devoto [Devoto's Kids] appeared. They invented a lot of songs that I love." By anchoring their originality in San Lorenzo's history and social fabric, they establish connections between their creative practices and Boedo. Leandro adds:

> There's a rich history. [Versioning] was born in the Boedo neighborhood, which is a very special neighborhood. [Our creativity] has [also] to do with the Boedo neighborhood. A neighborhood of tango, on the one hand, of poetry, on the other, of tradition, of carnival, of murga porteña. Boedo has always been a tango neighborhood. You have what's called the Boedo Generation in literature. It has always been a neighborhood of protest. Historically, San Lorenzo has been an avant-garde team against the powerful. That's in the essence of the Boedo neighborhood. A neighborhood of murga porteña—there're many chants that come from murga porteña songs. I don't think that [our creativity] is just sharpness and rapid creativity. It seems to me that there's a history behind it that's related to the neighborhood, which boosts that creativity. Even in exile.
>
> Matías Lammens, the former president of the club, thinks similarly:
>
> It's rooted in San Lorenzo's history. San Lorenzo has always been the club that created the most creative chants. There's a rich history here. And seeing kids

> involved in creating chants shows that this tradition has been passed down from generation to generation. It's also tied to the neighborhood. San Lorenzo is not just a national club with four million hinchas, but it's also a neighborhood club. That's why we say we're the biggest neighborhood club in the world: because it belongs to Boedo . . . This neighborhood, with a strong emphasis on public education, which produced poets and writers who have contributed significantly to Argentine culture. San Lorenzo stands out because of this: it embodies the *porteñidad* [the essence of Buenos Aires]. (Quoted in Gallo 2017)

As discussed previously, San Lorenzo hinchas view Boedo as a vortex of porteño popular culture. Although most of the hinchada no longer socializes in the neighborhood, Escuela de Tablones believes that the creative traditions have persisted within San Lorenzo hinchas themselves, passed down from generation to generation. The neighborhood, the club, and the fanbase form a social circuit that distributes creativity transhistorically. This allows them to assert that creativity is an inherent quality among them. "It comes out naturally," Leandro concludes, stating that making songs is part of the San Lorenzo "idiosyncrasy—it's activated naturally."

These associations with porteño popular culture are partly strategic. Morgan Luker (2016) explains that tango functions as a strategic signifier in Buenos Aires, elevating "certain figures, instances, or subjectivities while silencing others" (38). By interweaving tango's discursive power with references to the neighborhood's carnival and literary traditions, San Lorenzo hinchas position themselves within broader economies of musical and poetic creativity in Argentine culture and society. In so doing, they manage to differentiate themselves from rival hinchadas through practices and traditions imbued with power and cultural capital in Argentina.[5]

But these statements also highlight the musicality of their creativity. One of the most celebrated characteristics of Escuela de Tablones is their aptitude for discovering unexpected melodies that, once versioned, quickly become popular among Argentine and foreign hinchas. For instance, take note of this journalist's emphasis on musicality when discussing their contrafactum of Creedence Clearwater Revival's "Bad Moon Rising":

> Creedence Clearwater Revival's members likely never imagined that one of their songs from the 60s and 70s would become a hit in the stands, let alone that this melody, adapted for the occasion, would travel the world thanks to

> Argentines who turned it into an anthem during Brazil's 2014 World Cup, forty years after the band's breakup. Similarly, Enrique Iglesias, accustomed to breaking chart records, probably didn't anticipate that part of his playlist would proliferate throughout the world as a football chant. These are the peculiar achievements of San Lorenzo hinchas . . . Yes, the Cyclone, through its people, creates tradition. Escuela de Tablones, in this case. Because a group of ordinary neighborhood kids, who study and work, dedicates their free time to keeping the football world's largest Spotify always updated. The hinchada that other hinchadas listen to . . . Their latest creation, Enrique Iglesias's "Duele el Corazón," crossed all borders: it was featured in sports newspapers like Spain's Marca and As, and Greece's Web Sports 24. In South America, their verses were played on every website or sports channel, while hinchas across the country, regardless of the club they support, found themselves humming the catchy San Lorenzo chant. (Paulich 2016)

The focus on sources is not accidental as Escuela de Tablones explicitly emphasizes the significance of melodies when crafting chants. Leandro elucidates: "When you're creating a football chant, seventy percent of the work is done with the melody. I think that there are two keys to football chants. Not only the ingenuity and creativity when writing lyrics but also knowing what melody would hit and what melody people would like." The ability to imagine whether a melody has the potential to become a chant intertwines previously acquired audile techniques.

Immersion in the soundworld of hinchadas has cultivated a unique acoustic attunement to melodic elements, influencing the creative process of song selection. Hinchas explain that not every melody can seamlessly transition into a chant; they must conform to specific contours, range, rhythm, and phrasing. Songs that have evolved into aguante anthems typically exhibit reduced melodic movement, a limited range, and nonmelismatic endings—characteristics closely linked to stadium acoustics, as discussed in the following paragraph. Pitch and tonality take a backseat in importance, as hinchas unconsciously adjust them to fit the customary baritone range. While tempo is also of lesser concern due to their tendency to accelerate chants, a melody's agogic quality remains essential, creating rhythmic dynamism by establishing interlocking connections with murga porteña. Understanding this style, I have been told, can only be achieved by immersing oneself in aguante chants in stadiums, previas, and online platforms.

This stylistic knowledge is interconnected with an acoustemological understanding of the stadium's "aural architecture" (Blesser and Salter 2006, 2). Listening to how sound reverberates within the stadium plays a pivotal role in determining the musical suitability of a chant. Specifically, the resounding and amplifying characteristics of stadium acoustics favor the execution of chants with limited melodic variation, a restricted vocal range, and nonmelismatic endings. While the stadium enhances phrases ending with long, sustained notes, it can also pose challenges when vocalizing melodies with excessive movement and an abundance of melisma as these tend to become sonically blurred due to reverberation. Practicing and listening to melodic drafts, both in advance and within the stadium, enable them to understand how collectively sung melodies sound in this aural space.

In the quest for potential chants, these listening techniques are intentionally employed during private modes of music exploration. Although Escuela de Tablones members evaluate songs they enjoy, their critical listening approach remains unbound by genre or personal taste. Whether it is reggaeton, folk, or balada, genre and personal connections take a back seat to a source's potential. Leandro elaborates:

> The songs I choose are those that I think might work for a San Lorenzo chant. It could even be a song by [Uruguayan pop singer] Natalia Oreiro. With this, I'm not making a homage to the history of music. It's not that I'm saying "OK, I like [Led] Zeppelin, so I use a song by Zeppelin because it's an amazing band." No, I like Zeppelin, and if someday I find a song by Zeppelin that could work as a football chant, I'd start writing. I have lyrics with songs by the Beatles [and] Natalia Oreiro—whose music sucks. I don't have prejudices. If I feel that a melody sounds well and could become popular [I use it].

Escuela de Tablones neither seeks to engage in musical criticism nor aims to disseminate their most cherished songs through versioning. Instead, their selection of a melody is primarily based on its potential for chanting. As Joshua Tucker (2013) points out, changing conditions in the Latin American public sphere complicate attempts to "align one system of symbols and meanings with a single class, culture, and nation," underscoring that consumers can be "promiscuous and fickle, using different media forms for different purposes at different moments" (9). Escuela de Tablones's use of the diverse sounds that populate the public sphere exemplifies these complexities. While power dynamics undoubtedly shape soundscapes and music circulation, individuals do possess a certain degree of agency within this sonic and media saturation. However, as demonstrated by Escuela de Tablones, users not only appropriate symbols based on identitarian or emotional impulses but also harness them to generate alternative forms of value.

Indeed, San Lorenzo hinchas' practices demonstrate a keen understanding of popular music consumption and circulation. Their versioning of "Despacito" serves as an illustration of their awareness of the viral potential of popular music. Orti further explains: "We're always talking about new songs, what's trending everywhere, and 'Despacito' was the hit of the year, so we said that we must make a song with it. We're all attentive to new songs, of the phrases you can use, of how new songs are made." Escuela de Tablones uploaded their chant online almost a month after "Despacito" was released. The fact that the creative process takes several weeks indicates that they recognized the hit's potential immediately after its release. In other words, even before the song saturated social media, Escuela de Tablones had already identified its viral potential. This suggests an awareness of popular music's patterns of consumption and circulation—a knowledge they strategically deploy to accrue creative status.

These private forms of aural analysis extend beyond popular music and encompass other media forms. For instance, Escuela de Tablones has identified potential chants while watching television or movies. As they state in an interview with journalist Diego Paulich, "We have one that never got popular with the opening of Mirtha Legrand's show ('Mirtha is here, she's here again'), [and] another one with [the main theme of] the movie *The Godfather*" (quoted in Paulich 2016). The utilization of acoustemological knowledge for the identification of potential chants is not limited to private settings; it also extends to public spaces. This auditory creativity involves an active and generative auditory disposition to the sounds populating the public sphere as potential chants—an ongoing and engaged reflection through and in sound of musical potentialities. Escuela de Tablones walks through Buenos Aires while listening attentively to promising melodies. "You must be attentive," they state in the already quoted newspaper interview, "you could run into a hit at any time" (quoted in Paulich 2016). In fact, they have found potential contrafacta in the most unexpected places, such as grocery stores: "The one by Enrique Iglesias ('Duele el Corazón') came up in a Chinese Supermarket. They put it on the speakers, and I proposed an initial idea to the group, everyone liked it, and we began composing. Now it's sung every weekend" (quotes in Gavira 2016). Or the public transportation system: "I was on the 126 [bus]. A musician got onto [the bus] and began to sing 'Mi Historia Entre Tus Dedos' by [Italian balada singer] Gianluca Grignani with a ukulele, and I thought that it would be a great football chant. During the trip, which lasted half an hour, I came up with two stanzas. Once at my place, and during three weeks, I finished it and sent it to the WhatsApp group, where we all fixed it" (quoted in Gavira 2016).

Escuela de Tablones's aural imaginativeness is, in many ways, a form of soundwalking—a "process of moving through urban space while actively listening" (Galloway 2015, 134). Escuela de Tablones's attunement to the sounds populating the public sphere illustrates that modes of analytical listening can also occur in mundane social spaces. Through their aural reflections, songs actualize as new virtual creations and novel meanings emerge, showcasing the creativity inherent in everyday acts of listening.

ATTRIBUTION AND COPYRIGHT

Attribution is neither transparent nor straightforward in aguante. While competition informs their understandings of authorship and creativity, hinchas also conceive of chants as publicly owned. "They aren't San Lorenzo's property," Leandro explains, "the chants belong to everyone." Escuela de Tablones understands chants as part of a public ecology that rival and foreign hinchas can freely re-version and remediate.

Aguante's simultaneously conflictive and participatory nature accounts for the apparent tension between competitive authorship and public ownership. Here, gaining recognition for creativity means being acknowledged as the authors, not the owners, of chants. More than ownership, hinchas strive to be recognized as the creators of viral and influential chants. Once they are versioned, they become part of a public auditory culture, and rivals are free to re-version and remediate them. As Escuela de Tablones emphasizes in the interview repeatedly: "We're proud. With so many chants out there, they take the ones we created, that is, they liked them so much that they have to replicate them. We have a motto every time we create a new chant: Keep copying us" (quoted in Gavira 2016). It is attribution that ultimately imbues hinchadas with creative status and reputation, which challenges the common-held assumption that (re-)versioning is all about anonymity (Alabarces 2015).

The presumption that anonymity and lack of authorship characterize aguante aligns with what Marc Perlman (2019) terms "peripheralized authorship": a meta-ideology of textuality asserting that a community places minimal significance on "authorial individuality, originality, or ownership" (266). However, the downplaying of authorial reputation by aguante scholars constitutes a nonfactual assertion that aims to reduce working-class culture to orality and anonymity, ultimately disconnecting proletarian expressions from creativity and musicality.

As mentioned earlier, attribution links in aguante have often been broken. Social networking sites have helped change these dynamics. Lucas explains:

> Many times, the boundaries of the original version [are blurry]. One could think that each chant has three stages. The first would be the original song, not associated with football and sung by musicians—either popular, independent, consecrated, or musicians who don't sing it anymore. That would be the original version. Then, you have the first time an hinchada took the song and versioned it. And then you have the re-versionings of the football chants. I think that the boundaries and authorships are always blurry there. What often ends up happening and makes San Lorenzo's hinchada different is that San Lorenzo hinchas created the chant. And you also have the role of social media. Because these groups many times upload the versioned football chants with lyrics before singing them in the stadium. There's a capacity to unite the creator with the chant that didn't exist before.

A digital archive, social media highlights authors and indexes dates. Mentions of original sources and the use of hashtags for pedagogical purposes has helped reinforce attribution links. However, the fact that social media has underscored intertextuality does not mean that this is a new concern among hinchas. Hinchadas have long sought to credit sources and include attribution links. See figure 2.3, for example, which includes the title of the original song. Furthermore, intertextuality has always been a part of (re-)versioning as chants have often contained phrases from original sources and versions. In this sense, social media has realigned issues that were already present in previous modes of media work.

Aguante (re-)versioning and (re)mediation align with theories emphasizing the transmediality of popular music circulation (Goldschmitt 2011; Novak 2010, 2013). Music media, massively interconnected, operates within disjunctive yet overlapping loops, enabling songs to reach unexpected spaces and platforms. Notably, aguante contrafacta have propelled locally known melodies onto the transnational stage, creating modes of virality unforeseen by the music industry. The fact that fans of Liverpool and AC Milan are singing melodies by Argentine musicians such as Fito Páez or La Mosca Tsé-Tsé underscores the role of football networks in fostering new modes of consumption and remediation of popular music.

Cuando empenzo el campeonato
Estaba vacío el gallinero,
Vos siempre haces lo mismo
llevas la gente si vas primero,
gallina hija de puta
te digo algo de frente mar,
Esta tarde te cogemos
y damos la vuelta junto a central.
La vuelta junto a central,
Junto a central, junto a central

Música (autenticos decadentes: tuta tuta)
Los pibes de AGRELO.

FIGURE 2.3 Flyer with a chant's lyrics, authors (Los Pibes de Agrelo), and source ("Tuta Tuta" by Los Auténticos Decadentes). Photo courtesy of Leandro.

The global circulation of aguante has created tensions with copyright, which I exemplify with the controversies surrounding "Vengo del barrio de Boedo"—Escuela de Tablones's contrafactum of "Bad Moon Rising." In addition to stressing their loyalty, the chant highlights the significance of the neighborhood and its meaningful forms of socialization:

Vengo del barrio de Boedo	I come from the Boedo neighborhood
Barrio de murga y carnaval	A neighborhood of murga and carnival
Te juro que en los malos momentos	I swear to you that in the bad moments
Siempre te voy a acompañar	I'll always be there for you
Dale, dale, Matador	Let's go, Matador
Dale, dale, Matador	Let's go, Matador
Dale, dale, dale, dale	Let's go, let's go, let's go, let's go
Matador	Matador

Escuela de Tablones often mentions this pithy chant as their favorite one. Personal connections to "Bad Moon Rising" do not inform this predilection as they were not even familiar with the song before creating the chant. According to one member of the group: "A friend of mine gave me the Creedence audio. He told me that I should put lyrics to it, and then I started creating. Once I finished it, it took years to be sung in the stands" (quoted in Gavira 2016). Three factors contribute to making this chant their most cherished one. First, it simply yet compellingly reiterates the ties between Boedo and San Lorenzo. Second, it carries a romantic nostalgia for the specific moment when it first reached the stands: the 2011–2012 season when San Lorenzo was on the verge of being relegated to the second division—a testament to their unwavering loyalty. Finally, the chant's subsequent (re-)versionings and remediations by other hinchadas serve as evidence of Escuela de Tablones's trendsetting powers and their uncontested creative status within the aguante world.

During the 2014 World Cup, a video of hundreds of Argentines collectively singing in Rio de Janeiro's Atlântica Avenue went viral. They were outside the hotel of the Argentine national team, which was debuting the following day. Their hopes for this tournament's edition were particularly high—especially due to Lionel Messi's record-breaking performances in the years leading to the event. The chant voiced this optimism:

Brasil, decime qué siente
Tener en casa a tu papá
Te juro que, aunque pasen los años,
Nunca nos vamos a olvidar
Que el Diego los gambeteó
Y el Cani los vacunó
Están llorando desde Italia hasta hoy
A Messi los van a ver
La copa se va a traer
Maradona es más grande que Pelé

Brazil, tell me how it feels
Having your daddy here at home
I swear that all these years later
We're never going to forget
That Diego [Maradona] dribbled you
And [Claudio] Cani[ggia] banged it home
You've been crying since the Italy [World Cup]
You're going to see Messi
He's going to bring the cup home
Maradona is greater than Pelé

The piece is based on an adaptation that Boca Juniors hinchas made of "Vengo del barrio de Boedo." The Boca Juniors version mocks River Plate's historical relegation to the second division:

River, decime qué se siente
Haber jugado el nacional
Te juro que, aunque pasen los años,
Nunca lo vamos a olvidar
Que te fuiste a la B

River, tell me how it feels
To have played in the second division
I swear that all these years later
We're never going to forget
That you were relegated

Quemaste el Monumental	You set fire to the Monumental
Esa mancha no se borra nunca más	That stain will never be erased
Che, gallina, sos cagón	Hey, chicken [River Plate], you're a coward
Le pegaste a un jugador	You hit a player
Qué cobardes Los Borrachos del Tablón	Los Borrachos del Tablón are so cowardly

"Brasil, decime qué se siente" defiantly narrates a hypothetical scenario in which Argentina occupies Brazilian territory and wins the tournament, humiliating the host. The chant strategically picks a previous game to exemplify a supposed sports dominance of Argentina over Brazil. In the round of sixteen of the 1990 World Cup held in Italy, the Argentine national team defeated the Brazilian squad with a late goal by striker Claudio Caniggia and an outstanding performance by national hero Diego Maradona—who also allegedly gave Brazilian left-back Branco a bottle of water spiked with sedatives. The chant conveniently forgets recent victories of the Brazilian national team over the Argentine squad—including two Copa América finals in the 2000s. The lyrics reinforce this dubious dominance by restating the Argentine argument over who is the greatest football player of all time, either Maradona or Brazilian icon Pelé.

The chant quickly turned into Argentina's second national anthem during the tournament. Videos of the Argentine players singing it began to circulate on social media, fueling excitement across the nation. As the national team progressed through the stages, reaching the tournament's final against Germany, the chant took on a prophetic character: Lionel Messi would finally follow in Maradona's footsteps and lead Argentina to its third World Cup victory. Unfortunately, the Argentine aspirations were painfully crushed when German midfielder Mario Götze scored an extra-time goal, securing Germany's victory in the final.

"Brasil, decime qué se siente" fulfilled a long desire among Argentines: a chant to cheer for the national team. Until the 2014 World Cup, Argentines complained about the lack of singing during Argentina games, signaling the lack of creative chants as the core of the problem. "Brasil decime qué se siente" finally brought local fandom's creativity to games of the national team. Commentators contend that the chant presents common themes and tropes of aguante, showcasing narcissistic men asserting their presence and dominance over rivals in a somewhat homoerotic manner (Alabarces 2015).

However, "Brasil, decime qué se siente" was actually re-versioned by outsiders to aguante. Two upper-middle-class publicists, Ignacio Harraca and Patricio Scordo, came up with the chant on the eve of the 2014 World Cup. They had the financial means and freedom to spend thirty-five days in Brazil, where they printed four hundred copies of the lyrics and distributed them among fellow Argentines in Rio de Janeiro. The chant's popularity led Harraca and Scordo to explore the potential for profit using Argentina's IP law. Upon returning from Brazil, they swiftly registered the chant with the National Office of Copyright. This strategic move turned out to be highly successful, both in terms of economic gains and media attention. As a result, the two fans became regular guests on sports and morning shows, generating income each time the chant was reproduced on air. The media predominantly focused on the legal tactics employed by Harraca and Scordo, commending their entrepreneurial skills rather than highlighting the creativity behind the chant itself.[6]

These events stirred ambivalent feelings among Escuela de Tablones. "What happened with the Creedence one made us mad at first, but then you feel some sort of pride," they explain in an already quoted newspaper interview, "the reality is that if San Lorenzo hadn't sung it first, it wouldn't had been sung in Brazil." Leandro explains further:

> What happened was that it was a spectacular chant—which, as I told you, took years to become popular. People started to sing it. I remember, maybe I'm confused, that teams in Brazil, like Grêmio, began to sing it before Argentines. It was a total success. Then, Boca sang it. They made a catchy chant about River's relegation, and it became a Boca anthem. And, from Boca's chant—which had some of San Lorenzo's chant, some of San Lorenzo's lyrics—a group of Argentines made a song for the World Cup, maintaining some of San Lorenzo's chant and some of Boca's chant, but more associated with Boca's than San Lorenzo's lyrics. A chant that deserves only one star. But you can imagine that people sang it. And also, during the World Cup, as always, with the World Cup fever, it was sung by TV anchors who never attend games, models who never attend games. They made sketches with the chant. They created an entire circus, and "Brasil, Decime Qué Se Siente" got popular.

In contrast to how Escuela de Tablones reacted to other hinchadas copying their chants, their response to Harraca and Scordo's actions was more ambiguous and convoluted. On the one hand, they expressed resentment at Harraca and Scordo's lack of attribution for their original source. They criticized "Brasil, decime qué se siente" by characterizing it as a product of fetishism and unoriginality, linking it to market and copyright dynamics that deviate from the norms guiding (re-)versioning. On the other hand, Escuela de Tablones recognized the virality of "Brasil, decime qué se siente" as a means of reaffirming their own creative reputation. Since social media had already documented their initial versioning, the media attention garnered by the chant eventually provided Escuela de Tablones with an opportunity to gain exposure in mainstream media. In fact, the newspaper interviews mentioned in this chapter took place when journalists realized that Escuela de Tablones was the original group behind the versioning of "Bad Moon Rising."

The dominance of intellectual property (IP) in neoliberal contexts serves as the backdrop for these debates over attribution. Alexander Dent (2020) argues that neoliberalism has fostered the notion that creators must either profit from their creative works or refrain from expressing their creativity altogether. He contends that copyright laws have instilled an "ethics of accumulation" (Dent 2012, 31), establishing a moral framework wherein individuals who adhere to and compete within the social, legal, and economic norms of intellectual property can optimize their creative and financial endeavors. Dent concludes that the neoliberal logic underpinning copyright maximalism has led many "consumers and producers of texts such as movies and music [to] experience the intellectual property (IP) system as profoundly broken" (Dent 2020, 3).

Indeed, it might be tempting to use the controversies surrounding their contrafacta of "Despacito" and "Bad Moon Rising" to support the argument that "contrary to the neoliberal ideologies that have driven the exploitation of copyright as an instrument of privatization, there are contexts in which a culture of ownership is no culture at all" (Cook 2018, 187). Alabarces (2015) echoes these sentiments when discussing Harraca and Scordo's legal actions, suggesting that the processes of commodification facilitated by IP have directly undermined aguante creativity: "it seems that, once again, the populist temptation to celebrate the anonymous, collective, and popular authorship of mass phenomena must recede to the capitalist, spectacular, and industrialized organization of mass culture" (8).

However, while aguante presents social norms that are in conflict with IP's conceptualizations of attribution, such assertions do not fully capture the complexities and tensions surrounding creative practices that exist both in harmony and discord with larger patterns of musical consumption. Although hinchadas assume that chants are publicly owned, their creative practices are nonetheless rooted in authorial competitive logics that align with neoliberal understandings of authorship as a platform for competition. Far from disrupting chains of contrafacta, the controversies surrounding their versions of "Despacito" and "Bad Moon Rising" actually encouraged re-versioning processes. This, in turn, allowed Escuela de Tablones to gain creative prestige within the aguante world and beyond. While Harraca, Scordo, and Universal Music Latin (the owners of "Despacito") profited economically from these events, Escuela de Tablones accumulated creative capital, enabling them to claim victory in aguante's noncommercial contest of musical creativity. Arguments that hyperbolically posit copyright as either the savior or the nemesis of creativity fall short in analyzing spaces like aguante.

CREATIVITY, ATTRIBUTION, AND NECROPOLITICS

Although many San Lorenzo hinchas take pride of Escuela de Tablones's reputation, their creative status has also stirred necropolitical tensions within the fanbase. Readers may have noted that Escuela de Tablones frequently references La Gloriosa Butteler in their lyrics, despite not being part of the barra or participating in aguante warfare. The relationship with La Gloriosa Butteler is an elusive topic, but my hypothesis is that, since the barra holds the authority to decide which chants are sung during games, Escuela de Tablones strategically mentions them to ensure the performance of their chants. Unfortunately, as Escuela de Tablones's fame grew, La Gloriosa Butteler began to perceive them as a threat, leading to a rupture in their social relations.

For years, Escuela de Tablones actively participated in previas, disseminating their chants intertwining Boedo, the lost stadium, and San Lorenzo. During games, the barra sang their contrafacta, allowing Escuela de Tablones's repertoire to dominate the soundscape of the Nuevo Gasómetro. Their prominence within the San Lorenzo community was so conspicuous that they even had a massive banner at the center of the stands, positioned above the two banners displayed by La Gloriosa Butteler (see figure 2.4). The lyrical references to La Gloriosa Butteler, as well as Escuela de Tablones's frequent presence in shared spaces of socialization, led many to assume that they served as the barra's official musical department. This perception contributed to the belief that La Gloriosa Butteler was responsible for composing the chants that were being re-versioned and remediated by numerous South American hinchadas, thus solidifying their status as the primary creative force behind aguante.

Tensions erupted around 2018, however, when journalists and hinchadas

FIGURE 2.4 La Gloriosa Butteler.

began attributing San Lorenzo's chants to Escuela de Tablones rather than La Gloriosa Butteler. Escuela de Tablones's banner vanished from the stands, and La Gloriosa Butteler stopped singing their compositions. During previas, the barra asserted its authority by imposing its own chants whenever hinchas attempted to sing those created by Escuela de Tablones. Tellingly, La Gloriosa Butteler often sang this contrafactum—a re-versioning of a chant by Los de Abajo—when outshouting the San Lorenzo peers who wanted to sing Escuela de Tablones's compositions:

Vamos, San Lorenzo	Come on, San Lorenzo
Siguiendo a Boedo	Following Boedo
No importa si es lejos	Doesn't matter if it's far away
No importa si es lejos	Doesn't matter if it's far away
Te vengo a alentar	I come here to cheer for you
La banda de Boedo	Boedo's band
Zarpada de gira	High on tour
Quiere cocaína	Wants cocaine
No puede parar	It can't stop

Que todo está bien	Everything is all right
Es la Plaza Butteler	It's the Butteler Square
Es tu hinchada la más fiel	It's your most loyal hinchada
La que te sigue	The one that follows you
A donde jugués	Everywhere you play
La banda más loca	The craziest band
Para en Cobo y Viel	Hangs out at Cobo and Viel[7]

The chant's focus on cocaine-infused states and expressions of spatial dominance contrasts sharply with Escuela de Tablones's place-centered approach to aguante themes and tropes.

Due to their aural exclusion, San Lorenzo hinchas began to perceive that Escuela de Tablones no longer attends games, calling for their return on social media, where the collective kept uploading chants. Lucas explains the socio-sonic dynamic within the fanbase as follows: "The barra is censoring us. They don't let us sing the songs we like. They have to cut it off with the coke [chant]. Everyone knows and has heard that every time we want to sing a new chant [by Escuela de Tablones] they outshout us, the same with the trumpet players, singing another song on top, cheering for coke. It's clear that they do not want new songs by Escuela de Tablones. [At some point] their cocaine song was outshouted by the people with a 'Sanloré, Sanloré' [chant]." These tensions exemplify the impact of necropolitics on aguante's creativity and attribution. As Escuela de Tablones's fame began to overshadow La Gloriosa Butteler, internal conflicts erupted within the fanbase. The barra members perceived their dominance and hierarchies were under threat, prompting them to silence Escuela de Tablones and other peer collectives. Despite attempts from other San Lorenzo fans to sonically defy this silencing, La Gloriosa Butteler succeeded in asserting their authority in these sonic and creative conflicts. Ultimately, this reaffirmed the barra's position as the primary social entity within the hinchada while eroding social bonds within the San Lorenzo fanbase.

CONCLUSION

On July 27, 2019, I was invited by Peter, an U. de Chile hincha, to his house to discuss his musical project Trovazules (see Achondo 2022). U. de Chile was playing at noon, so we met early in the morning. It was my first time visiting his parents' house in La Granja, a working-class neighborhood in southern

Santiago. To avoid territories dominated by U. Católica and Colo-Colo hinchas, Peter provided me with a map that indicated areas controlled by rival factions.

The morning was chilly, and his room, a homemade second floor, felt freezing. Although my initial intention was to ask him about remediation and (re-)versioning, we ended up spending almost an hour watching videos of Escuela de Tablones. As he told me: "They feed all the barras in the world. We [also] want other teams to imitate us. Every hincha wants its hinchada to be known as the most creative one. [Also] there's a resonance between the Return to Boedo and our recuperation of the club." Peter underscored the significance of creativity and attribution in the aguante conflict, emphasizing Escuela de Tablones's unparalleled dominance. His statement also highlighted that Escuela de Tablones has not only mediated the emotional significance of the Return of Boedo but also facilitated its transnationalization, forging resonances and establishing social connections with politicized hinchadas elsewhere.

This chapter has contributed to theories of creativity and attribution in music studies. In addition to pushing (ethno)musicology to think of musical creativity as enacting and contributing to conflict, I have promoted a novel understanding of auditory ingenuity. Hinchas' active, generative, and reflective interlocking of various listening techniques enables the creation of new compositions by imaginatively projecting the aguante style and stadium acoustics onto sounding melodies. This highlights creative forms of listening beyond traditional musical agents and spaces. I have also demonstrated that the relationship between authorship and ownership is not always straightforward, thereby illustrating the contingency of (meta)ideologies of textuality. In the aguante world, hinchas seek recognition and prestige by being known as the enactors, not the owners, of chains of contrafacta. In using social media to highlight attribution links, their media and creative work have forged new transnational paths for music circulation and (re)mediation, creating both tensions and resonances with intellectual property. Copyright law, while sometimes silencing hinchas temporarily, has not truly threatened Escuela de Tablones's production and accumulation of creative value, underscoring the need for more nuanced humanistic approaches to intellectual property.

The (trans)local circulation of these chants has also contributed to the spread of aguante's necropolitics. As the following chapter shows, while these practices of fandom have affectively empowered proletarian Chileans, they have also intersected with contingent conditions of alienation and precarity, overloading subjectivities, radicalizing local hostilities, and leading hinchas to visceral forms of violence and criminality.

THREE

Affect and Labor

Dozens of red flares lit up the Ester Roa Stadium of Concepción in March 2019. The hundreds of fireworks and firecrackers launched by Los de Abajo forced the referee to stop the match between their team and Universidad de Concepción. The stadium's architecture amplified the collective voice of the hinchada, who sang loudly and intensely over the explosions (video 3.1):

Que se vaya Carlos Heller	Carlos Heller must leave
Que se muera Azul Azul	Blue Blue must die
Que se vayan esos buitres	Those vultures must leave
Que no aman a La U	They don't love La U

The cacophony of voices and pyrotechnics saturated the stadium's soundscape, silencing the local team's petite barra. Los de Abajo also put up two blue-and-red banners: "Leave Carlos Heller, Leave Azul Azul" and "Azul Azul, Passion for Money." The match broadcast reported that Carlos Heller, the largest stockholder of Azul Azul, left his box and ran away to the dressing rooms. When the pyrotechnics were over, the referee recorded the event, waited for the smoke to fade away, and resumed the match. U. de Concepción ended up winning the game, a defeat that kept U. de Chile in the relegation zone.

Heller resigned the board's presidency once the game was over, stating: "Delinquency has won again in this country—fan delinquency. I have death threats on my phone. A long time ago, I received death threats. Graffiti in my workplaces. You watched the poor spectacle done by the corrupted hinchas. . . . The delinquents have won again." U. de Chile's recently hired coach, Uruguayan Alfredo

Arias, sympathized with Heller and asked: "He's a good guy. . . . It's OK if he has to go because the fans are hurt because the team is losing. But, beyond cheering, what else have they done [for the club]?"

U. de Chile hinchas celebrated Heller's resignation, signaling it as a small victory toward the "recovery of the club." After the game, Los de Abajo posted the following statement on social media:

> [This was] the day when our voices were heard stronger than ever. Thousands of hinchas demonstrating their love for their colors. But also, thousands of hinchas demonstrating their discontent with the Azul Azul administration. Discontent with the country's hegemonic powers, which have done whatever they want for years with only one goal: profit. . . . That's real delinquency. But since they own every business in the country (football channels, retail stores, football security, other football teams, among others) they have the voice of power, and they can confuse people with their media. But listen, gentlemen, this is La U, and La U people have a huge heart. You, not even with all your power, will be able to silence us. And this is not delinquency. . . . We're showing our discontent with the [club's] current administration. We have knowledge, identity, principles, and values. We're not delinquents. But also remember that we're hinchas, and to be an hincha means fighting for the colors we love and respect until the end.

The text then blasted the coach's rhetorical question:

> Arias asked what we do besides cheering. Maybe this is his first time in a big team. . . . Here we give up our lives for La U, and we're there when we're needed the most. Ask your players. . . . We don't want to start our relationship badly. We forgive you this time, but we also remind you what a coach that was very successful in Chile once said: "the hinchas are the only irreplaceable ones in football." You'll leave eventually—we'll be here forever.

Safe Stadium Plan, the state policy on football violence, punished Los de Abajo for their "bad behavior" and "grave incidents," prohibiting them from bringing their musical instruments to stadiums for the next six months.

U. de Chile hinchas have historically seen themselves as the club's essential constituency, proclaiming that "La U is big because of its people" and "La U is its people." Miguel, an hincha leading a campaign against Azul Azul, elaborates:

"If La U wouldn't have such a level of fandom, passion, organization, and everything, it practically wouldn't exist. That's why CDF [football channel] pays what it pays. That's why international stars want to play in La U. It's not because La U has won a lot of titles. We must realize that we [the hinchas] are La U's true owners. We're La U's essence, we're the original popular power that makes it what it is." In the mid-2000s, controversial events challenged this sense of ownership. A new law that forced clubs to become public limited sports companies coincided with U. de Chile's bankruptcy due to a polemical reinterpretation of the tax code regarding player bonuses. In 2007, the consortium Azul Azul took over the club's management, ending decades of democratic administration. The company reframed U. de Chile hinchas as consumers, excluding them from the club's spaces and decision-making processes.

This chapter argues that Los de Abajo conceptualize sound practice as a form of affective labor. By producing and manipulating affect, they not only express their support for the team but also cultivate stranger intimacy, shape matches narratives, and carve out space for themselves in the club's current neoliberally organized, sports advertisement structure. In so doing, they present themselves as indispensable members of the institution, an idea significantly shaped by decades of representative club democracy. However, the club's board has effectively subsumed their affective labor into their production of economic value, disregarding their demands for participation beyond mere consumption. Furthermore, operating within a regime of value where violence holds significant sway, Los de Abajo's affective production also serves to assert social control, establish hierarchies, and engage in radical conflicts, both internally and externally. The prioritization of violent over relational value has led to antisocial dynamics that have ultimately undermined their own community efforts. In illustrating the commodification and weaponization of affect in perpetuating internal asymmetries, this chapter underscores the limitations of affective labor in challenging neoliberal structures.

AFFECT, LABOR, VALUE

Defining affect as the capacity to affect and be affected, fundamentalists frame it as an unqualified intensity that, functioning at the level of the visceral, intertwines different sensory domains (Goodman 2010; Gregg and Seigworth 2010; Massumi 2002). These theorists differentiate affect from emotion by stressing the unmediated character of the former: affect is presubjective, precognitive, prelinguistic, and precultural. The inherent immanence and immateriality of affect, they add, have the potential to liberate the political body from the constraints imposed by socially constructed and power-mediated ways of knowing and being. Problematically, this "romantic (and complicit) attachment to a fantasy of immediacy" (Mazzarella 2009, 294) ends up divorcing the material and immaterial realms (Leys 2011; Lutz 2017; Navaro-Yashin 2009). When understanding that "mediation is the social condition of the fantasy of immediation" (Mazzarella 2009, 303), affect emerges as a rich analytical category as it illustrates that mass publicness is "always moving between immanence and qualification" (304).

Ethnomusicology has underscored the inevitability of affective mediation and signification (Garcia 2020), emphasizing sound's role in creating and sustaining affective publics (Figueroa 2022; Garcia 2015; Gill 2017; Gray 2013). Affective sonorities can nurture "stranger-intimacy—that is, the gestures of social warmth, sharing, and vulnerability between strangers" (Garcia 2023, 2). These intimate connections, forged through sound practice, have also become critical sites for "the construction, implementation and animation of political projects and ideologies" (Desai-Stephens and Reisnour 2020, 104). Amid neoliberal decay and neglect, sonic affect has enabled communities to navigate and articulate their precarious realities (Hofman 2020a, 2020b; Tatro 2022). The creation of affective atmospheres has empowered marginalized groups to forge radical social movements, providing a platform to publicly voice dissent against neoliberal inequalities (Jack 2021a, 2021b, 2022, 2024).

These insights resonate with the affective politics of Los de Abajo. They conceptualize affect through tropes of the carnivalesque, using the terms *fiestas* (parties) and *carnavales* (carnivals) to describe their performances. Involving sonic intensity and kinesthetic participation, these atmospheres saturate the senses and create affective ties between the peers and strangers populating the stadium. Hinchas use the term *descontrol* (out of control) to signify the ideal state for experiencing fiestas. While descontrol can refer to altered states of consciousness brought about by alcohol and drugs, it also underscores an overload of the sensorium. Through their affective performances, they seek to foster stranger intimacy, influence game events, express dissent, and carve out space for themselves in the club's hyper-commodified structures.

Since U. de Chile hinchas conceptualize the production of carnivalesque atmospheres as labor, I propose to understand it as affective labor—that is, the "creation and manipulation of affect" (Hardt and Negri 2000, 293). Scholarship on musical labor treats affect as an object for commodity exchange (Garland 2020, 2024; Gill 2017; MacMillen 2019; Miller 2017), illustrating how affective production is materially arranged within different regimes of value (Appadurai 2013; Graeber 2001, 2005). Embedded within institutional and relational structures (Tochka 2017), affective labor can enable marginalized communities to "explore alternative relationships to work and notions of value, using the hard work of their bodies to ground their imaginings of alternative ways to make meaningful social contributions, beyond earning a wage" (Tatro 2022, 130). However, affect can sometimes be socially and politically constrained (Tausig 2019), especially in "contexts where life is caught in complex and ambiguous structures of political, social and economic power" (Hofman 2020b, 313). Indeed, affective production can reinforce "inequities and structures of power just as much as it might subvert them" (Desai-Stephens and Reisnour 2020, 105). Understanding the types of value generated by affective labor and their intersections within overlapping regimes of value is crucial for comprehending the social and political impacts of sonic affect.

This chapter foregrounds the material constraints that arise when affective labor operates within necropolitical and hyper-commodified regimes of value. Through their sonic exertions, Los de Abajo strive to cultivate social relations for their own sake, akin to what Julia Elyachar (2010) describes as phatic channels and infrastructures. Within the hyper-commodified realm of football, however, affective labor generates not only relational but also economic value, positively affecting the club's production of capital. In fact, Azul Azul has easily appropriated and transformed Los de Abajo's noncommercial, interpersonal forms of value into profit, perpetuating the socioeconomic conditions that marginalize and reduce them to mere consumers. Simultaneously operating within aguante's regime of value, where violence is regarded as the primary symbolic and material resource, Los de Abajo's atmospheres frequently escalate into violence. While they deploy sonic affect to materially rebel against neoliberal asymmetries, it also serves as a means to exert social control, create asymmetries, and navigate radicalized conflicts that can only be resolved through force. In illustrating that value production ends up favoring profit and enmity over relationality, this chapter ultimately underscores the limits of affective labor to produce social alternatives amid social formations mediated by necropolitics and neoliberalism.

THE BIGGEST UNIVERSITY CLUB IN THE WORLD

The club's history is tied to the Universidad de Chile, the country's most influential public institution. Although historians disagree on the team's exact founding date, there is consensus that it emerged in the early twentieth century due to the student body's desire to engage in competitive football. Emerging as a sports embodiment of the university, the club has long been shaped by principles of direct democracy. Until 2006, U. de Chile functioned as a democratic, nonprofit organization, when it was compelled to undergo a significant transformation toward a corporate and for-profit model of administration.

Following its transition to a professional team in the late 1930s, U. de Chile quickly garnered a strong following among non-college-educated citizens (Matamala 2015). The team's popularity experienced a significant surge in the 1960s, particularly during the era of the *Ballet Azul* (Blue Ballet), when the team dominated local football. However, the 1970s marked a period of sports, financial, and administrative turmoil. To address the team's financial needs, the university established a nonprofit organization called Corfuch to oversee the management of the club. In addition to continuing to prioritize noncommercial values, the organization expanded U. de Chile's direct democracy. Although non-college-educated fans had been supporting the club for decades, its management had predominantly been in the hands of university alumni and authorities. With the establishment of Corfuch and its separation from the university, proletarian hinchas were finally granted full participation in the club's everyday and political life. In fact, more than thirty thousand hinchas became club members, granting them access to spaces, the ability to participate in assemblies and democratic elections, and opportunities to engage with players, coaches, and authorities (Ruete et al., 2021). According to Miguel, Corfuch transformed the club into a genuinely inclusive institution: "after Corfuch, La U was no longer linked only to the university. Before becoming popular in impoverished neighborhoods in the '80s, it was an elitist football club. With Corfuch, U. de Chile finally became a popular force."

However, Corfuch's administrative inefficiency also worsened U. de Chile's financial and sporting challenges. The team went twenty-five years without winning a league title and was eventually relegated to the second division in 1989. During this period, the nonprofit also lost its property in Parque Araucano, where they had planned to construct a stadium. Today, U. de Chile continues to play at the state-owned National Stadium. Despite the ongoing crisis, the club continued to attract new members and maintain popular support, particularly among young proletarians. It was during the late 1980s that these hinchas founded Los de Abajo.

The return to democracy coincided with U. de Chile's revival. Under the administration of René Orozco, a professor of medicine, improvements were made to the club's finances, competitive players were signed, and the team ended the twenty-five-year championship drought. Although Orozco's plan aimed to further commercialize the club through sponsorship deals, he was also committed to preserving Corfuch's noncommercial values. He ensured that any profits generated would be reinvested into the team and fan programs, prioritizing sports and communal relations over economic value. As part of his socially minded project, Orozco embraced and adopted Los de Abajo. In a 2019 newspaper interview, he explained:

> Do you know what they used to tell me about "the bandits," as they define Los de Abajo? . . . The cops told me: "doctor, your kids are behaving well." That's what we achieved: we stopped the drug consumption, we built a school, fifteen kids who were living on the streets studied and got college degrees. . . . Those things happened in La U. We built it again. We gave it new values. Some didn't like that we treated the barra as people. . . . Los de Abajo made La U. They helped make it. They were able to end their drug addictions, study, and leave the streets. (Quoted in Fernández 2019)

Orozco posited that the club, as an extension of the university, should embrace and support working-class youths. In keeping with Corfuch's democratic principles, he provided Los de Abajo with access to the club's headquarters and assisted them in setting up an alternative school to complete their high school education. Unsurprisingly, Orozco garnered substantial grassroots support and consistently won club elections by significant margins.

Orozco's socio-sports project began to unravel at the turn of the century, leading to the emergence of Azul Azul. The crisis was aggravated by a controversial reinterpretation of the tax code, which mandated clubs to retroactively pay taxes on player bonuses. Similar to Colo-Colo in 2002, a judge compelled Corfuch to declare bankruptcy in 2005. Simultaneously, during the mid-1990s, Los de Abajo solidified a hierarchical and transactional organization mediated by violence. The barra's leaders not only gained notoriety for their violent clashes with the police and rival groups but also exploited Corfuch's facilities for storing weapons and engaging in illegal activities such as drug trafficking. Both the corruption within fan groups and administrative instability affecting Colo-Colo and U. de Chile provided justification for the approval of Law 20019 in 2005, which mandated that clubs transform into publicly traded sports companies. Azul Azul acquired the club's license, rights, and administration in 2007, and subsequently went public in 2008, allowing right-wing businessmen, who had been vying for control of the club for many years, to assume management. U. de Chile hinchas claim that the collapse of Corfuch and the subsequent rise of Azul Azul were part of a conspiracy orchestrated by the country's business and political elites.[1]

The implementation of Law 20019 coincided with the enactment of Law 20620. This legislation served a dual purpose: delineating the responsibilities and obligations of public limited sports companies to ensure safe conditions and providing a legal framework for the police to maintain public order. This law led to the creation of Safe Stadium Plan, designed to facilitate efficient resource allocation and collaboration with local authorities for the collection and provision of attendee data. Law 20620 placed public security at the forefront of football's norms and policies, creating a social environment where the police could freely target hinchas, irrespective of their actual involvement in violence. By establishing a disciplinary framework for social control, this violent encroachment of the law (Benjamin 2021) ultimately sought to protect Law 20019 and, by extension, the corporate football model.

Amid this drastic and coerced privatization of football, some U. de Chile hinchas began to voice the idea that Azul Azul wanted to impose "corporate football" and reframe hinchas as consumers instead of club constituency. As Miguel explains:

> Participation in sports is not understood as a social right. Right now, for legal purposes, we're consuming Azul Azul's tickets. That's the only relationship [between us and the club]. Azul Azul is an event producer. Azul Azul produces events. The events are called "La U games." And the rules are set by the producer, like with any producer that brings a music band. And Azul Azul owns the spectacle. It has all the rights. Because those who participate aren't understood as having the right to participate in what's happening. That's something that in the '60s to '70s the state not only supported but also encouraged.

Recognizing the tradition of civic and democratic engagement associated with football clubs (Elsey 2011), Miguel and other U. de Chile supporters have launched a campaign to "recover the club" from Azul Azul and reinstate democratic forms of participation. They have taken legal action to challenge Corfuch's bankruptcy status, engaged in lobbying efforts with politicians and university officials to reform the stock-market model, and united the hinchada around democratic, community-oriented, and anti-corporate values.

Nevertheless, influential factions within the barra continue to engage in criminal and violent activity, considering violence as aguante's most precious asset.

Violent action still mediates conflicts with rivals and shapes internal relations. Tuto, a frontline member, explains: "singing, traveling, aguante, and kicking the asses of the Indians [Colo-Colo hinchas]. That's it. That's what makes you a La U hincha and gain prestige within a barra." Since authorities have only sought to prevent football violence inside and nearby stadiums, aguante necropolitics has silently expanded and radicalized in impoverished neighborhoods. Gunfire, kidnapping, torture, and murder have become ubiquitous, instilling fear and terror in local communities. Criminal syndicates have noted the sense of alienation, dispossession, and marginalization generated by the public limited sports companies, exploiting and expanding their existing networks to recruit hinchas as sentinels. Some members of Los de Abajo have now become involved in narco warfare, further escalating hostilities with the drug dealers who also hold sway over the U. Católica and Colo-Colo barras.

The necropolitical radicalization of aguante has led to the fragmentation of the hinchada's social fabric. Miguel explains: "To wear La U jersey is no longer enough to have camaraderie with another hincha. Factions have atomized and started to have problems with each other." He and others argue that the violent radicalization of Los de Abajo is tied to the feelings of alienation stemming from the club's exclusionary practices. Many U. de Chile hinchas believe that the concentration of power and wealth in the hands of a few tycoons has eroded the club's sense of community, leaving enmity as the only remaining social bond within the hinchada. It is at the intersection of necropolitics and privatization that the social world of U. de Chile has become structurally asymmetrical, leading to the valorization of violence as the most prized resource.

AFFECT AND FIESTAS

In October 2018, I attended the Clásico Universitario between U. de Chile and U. Católica at the National Stadium. Hinchas filled the area and street vendors loudly promoted their products for sale. The air was filled with the strong smell of *choripanes* (chorizo sandwiches) and *sandwiches de potito* (cow rectum sandwiches). Hundreds of people came out from the new subway station—located right next to the human rights nonprofit that supervised the monument memorializing the stadium's past as a torture center during the Pinochet regime.

Graffiti stating "Los de Abajo Anti Azul Azul," "We'll Come Back," and "No to Corporate Football" adorned the walls of the dusty southern entrance. About two hundred feet away from the stadium, I could already hear the sounds coming from the space underneath the stands where Los de Abajo usually gather before games. After two guards aggressively searched me, I showed my ID to a female guard who inserted it into a machine. As I ascended the concrete stairs, the cacophony of voices and instruments resonated intensely.

The Police Special Forces observed the performance with defiance. Red and blue fabric separated the barra's frontline from the other hinchas. La Banda de la Chile positioned themselves on each side of the rectangle, with brass instruments, bombos con platillos, repiques, surdos, and redoblantes. The musicians sported shirts with the ensemble's motto, "Cantar para Ganar" (Sing to Win). In the center, two teenagers held a large bass drum, while two hinchas wearing work gloves played a steady tempo with two mallets each. The drummers raised their hands as high as possible before striking the instrument with force, causing their arms to elevate instantly. While their faces conveyed strength and effort, they also radiated enjoyment and camaraderie as they made friendly eye contact with other hinchas. Meanwhile, the frontline jumped, sang, and hugged, all while documenting the performance with cameras and recorders. They also aggressively demanded even greater intensity from those outside the rectangle, who sang, jumped, and recorded with their phones. The concrete space magnified the volume. Closer to the game, the crowd created a passage for the ensemble to access the stands. Thousands of hinchas had already filled the area, but I managed to find a spot to the right of La Banda de la Chile.

Los de Abajo had raised more than four million pesos (approximately, four thousand dollars) and had worked for weeks on the *recibimiento* (reception or pre-game fiesta). Hundreds of flags filled the already packed stands. At the bottom, Los de Abajo's official banner covered the wall separating the field from the stands. Eight yellow elevator trucks, guarded by a dozen hinchas, were positioned on the track field. Several television cameras were pointed at stands, where a hundred-foot-long, folded piece of fabric rested on the ground. Meanwhile, the stadium chanted "Oh, sale León" (Oh, come out, Lion) over the chorus of "Estrechez de corazón" (Narrow Heart) by local rock stars Los Prisioneros.

The stadium reverberated with Los de Abajo's collective voice as the players entered the field. Flares were ignited, fireworks were launched, and shredded newspaper filled the air as the elevators raised the long fabric resting on the track field. After a few seconds, a magnificent thirty-foot-tall piece of art was visible. On it, six all-time U. de Chile idols stood in iconic moments from the club's history. The three versions of the club's badge were displayed in the center of the piece. The stadium sang even louder when La Banda de la Chile raised their

FIGURE 3.1 Clásico Universitario's fiesta. Screenshot taken from U. de Chile's YouTube channel.

drums, each bearing a letter forming the sentence "play like them." I recalled what Tuto had mentioned a few days earlier: "Young hinchas must learn about our history." Giant banners began to cover other sections of the stadium. The guards began to expel the hinchas who had supervised the installation on the field. While most left the track field jumping and celebrating, one mimicked firing an imaginary shotgun at one of the guards. Meanwhile, a clearly emotional stranger hugged me while singing. I felt a lump in my throat as we vocalized together. The players approached the stands and applauded the hinchas, who clapped back at them. U. de Chile went on to win the Clásico Universitario 2–0 (video 3.2).

After the match, current and former U. de Chile players congratulated Los de Abajo on social media. Although some journalists questioned that "some delinquents were on the track field," most commentators defined the performance as "outstanding," "spectacular," and "touching." An hincha who had gained prestige for writing short stories about Los de Abajo on Facebook, and who had been critical of the recent influence of Escuela de Tablones on the hinchada, posted: "I was moved to tears. It was truly beautiful. I thank all of those who were behind this enormous effort wholeheartedly. A [Facebook] page that is made for emotion can only stand up and applaud." The manager of *Barra Brava Foto*

Chile, the unofficial arbiter of local aguante on social media, commented on Los de Abajo's photos on Instagram: "The number one—that's it. Light years ahead from everybody else."

As depicted in this vignette, Los de Abajo place great value on affective sensation, believing that their atmospheres have a material impact on football spaces and structures. Apart from reveling in altered states of consciousness, U. de Chile hinchas enjoy singing in locations that offer resonant, immersive, and overwhelming acoustics. One example is the area beneath the stadium stands, where hinchas spend hours appreciating how the enclosed, concrete architecture amplifies and enhances sound. They also prefer stadiums with features that facilitate resonance, such as roofs and stands in proximity to the field. This emphasis on resonant acoustics extends beyond stadiums to spaces like buses. While traveling to stadiums, U. de Chile hinchas sing continuously, but their vocalizations become even louder in underground passages. Similarly, as they walk toward stadiums, they often pause at tunnels, using them as spaces for singing. These places serve as impromptu performance venues, where hinchas sing inside or even alongside them.

Hinchas intertwine visceral sensation with the club's emotional repository. Linking fiestas to the communal principles that have historically characterized the fanbase, U. de Chile hinchas value them as phatic expressions of stranger intimacy. Evaluations of the Clásico Universitario's fiesta exemplify these beliefs. Tuto, one of the performance's organizers, states:

> We want to have the fiesta everywhere. What we did against Católica was to show historical moments against Católica. We tried to capture and express those three historical heroic deeds. I remember when I was with my dad in the stadium [in the 1994 Clásico Universitario], I was eleven, and the stadium fell apart after [Marcelo] Salas's goal. Everybody cried, you must remember it. It was insane, nobody could believe it, everybody cried. And that's what we tried to do: to make La U people shiver, to shake them up with emotion. We want to show pure history. We want to teach La U history because Azul Azul doesn't do social work. As I told you before, we gather the largest social force of La U hinchas, that's why we believe that we have a social role. Alongside the fiesta and everything, we must teach history.

Although Tuto emphasizes mediation and qualification when talking about the emotional specificity of these performances, he also stresses their viscerality:

> La U—and that's what we wanted to do with the fiesta—excites you, man, it's visceral shit, it's feeling. This is not a trend that comes and goes. It's for your entire life, it encompasses all society, beyond education, everything. There're La U hinchas everywhere. We know that Colo-Colo has more fans, but we are more loyal. That's why we bring more people to the stadiums than them, even though they have more fans. Those who support La U are die-hard hinchas. We want the center of the barra, [Gates] 14 and 15, to be out of control. That shit has to be insane. Why? Because we have to inject everyone else in the stadium. It must be out of control. That's why a lot of people who were going to the *codos* [the sides of the South Stand] are coming back. They have come back to [Gate] 14. Emblematic singers, people we've seen exciting others for years and making that space a space of craziness, carnival, chaos.

These tropes of disorder and contagion underscore the carnivalesque sociality of visceral sensation. In conflating affective experience with the social, communal, and personal meanings that he attaches to the club and hinchada, Tuto coincides with Sara Ahmed (2014) when she states that "impressions" emerge in the encounter "between bodily sensation, emotion and thought" (6). Precisely, sonic stimuli do not affect all bodies similarly as contingent meanings, relations, and emotions mediate perception and thought. For example, the lump I felt in my throat during the Clásico Universitario was directly tied to the fact that I am a lifelong hincha of the club—an ethnographer less invested in the club's history, sociality, and emotionality would have probably reacted differently to the fiesta's sensorial chaos and the hug from the hincha.

Interweaving personal experience, club principles, communal relationality, and visceral sensation, hinchas value fiestas' capacity to foster stranger intimacy. The hug that the hincha gave me during the Clásico Universitario is common during U. de Chile games. During fiestas, sound creates emotional and affective connections among strangers, transforming the hinchada into a cohesive community of peers. While some hinchas and cliques may be acquainted with one another, the fanbase as a whole is ultimately a community of strangers bound together by a shared loyalty. It is during games that the hinchada emerges as a tangible, material, embodied social entity.

In addition to fostering stranger intimacy, Los de Abajo seek to affect games through their sonic practices. Their musical ensemble's motto "Sing to Win" demonstrates that they believe that they can affect players through their sonic affect. Tuto explains:

> We started the game ahead on the score with that fiesta, for sure. I saw the Católica players with their pants crapped. The U. Católica goalie, he committed a beginner's mistake against [U. de Chile's Francisco] Arancibia. At minute one. So, yes, they crapped their pants. We've scored with La U. The barra has won games when it roars in its best singing, in its splendor. With the drum heartbeat, with the people singing and jumping, La U has come back in games, it has won games with its hinchada. I remember a unique moment—with the fervor of lions and the hinchada out of control in a way that other hinchadas in Chile and South America don't get out of control. It was when we lost the first final against U. Católica 2–0 [in 2011]. I can tell you that we [Los de Abajo] won that final. Fifteen minutes and [the hinchada] was out of control. It was chaos.

Functioning as potent manifestations of collective unity, U. de Chile hinchas portray fiestas' climactic moments in weaponized terms, employing words such as "explosion" and "burst" to capture the heightened intensity and chaotic energy they embody. In these moments, the stadium, the hinchas, and the players all resonate together, forging a forceful presence that collectively asserts dominance over rivals.

However, the stadium's soundscape extends beyond collective singing, as various other sounds complement aguante chants. Hinchas shout "¡ole!" when a player successfully evades an opponent, "¡eh!" in response to a foul, and "¡uh!" when the ball comes close to the net. They also use clapping to show approval for a particular play, scream insults at rivals and referees, and unleash an endless, thunderous "¡gol!" chant when a goal is scored. Whistling is another common sound employed by hinchas. It serves multiple purposes, including mocking a player who misses a goal, expressing disdain toward the police, criticizing referees, and creating rhythmic fills during musical interludes. These sounds overlap and interact with one another, causing the volume and intensity of the stadium's soundscape to constantly shift and evolve. While the majority of Los de Abajo engage in singing and music-playing throughout the entire game, others contribute additional sounds on top of the songs, resulting in layered sonic clusters. The diverse forms and levels of participation generate sonic waves that are in a constant state of flux, exerting a continuous influence on the narrative and emotional dynamics of the matches.

Moments of high involvement and energy do not necessarily occur when the team is performing well—the relationship between games and fan behavior is more intricate. Instances of extreme loudness and high participation can occur after a wide range of situations: a goal, a good play, a fault, a fight, or even a bad performance. In this sense, the game and the stadium's soundscape constitute a symbiotic relationship: While the game influences people's participation and intensity, hinchas also try to affect the match through their behavior.

Los de Abajo employ fiestas as a means to assert control over the modular flexibility of the stadium's soundscape. Through their voices, fireworks, drums, and brass instruments, Los de Abajo create carnivalesque atmospheres in which they override the sounds produced by other fans. Julian Henriques (2011) introduces the concept of "sonic dominance" (xv) to describe environments where sound overwhelms the senses and immerses individuals in a heightened state of vibrational intensity. Similarly, fiestas enable Los de Abajo to exert dominance over the stadium's auditory space and influence others through intense vibrations.

Beyond their impact on match dynamics and narratives, many hinchas perceive fiestas as acts of dissent that exceed the realm of athletic competition. In the face of club censorship and exclusion, sound practice allows them to make their voices audible, offering a platform to criticize Azul Azul and the hypercommercialization of football. Tuto explains: "We want the people to be listened to, that the hincha is listened to, and that our voice, our opinion matters within the club. We want to provide our point of view, our opinion, and be listened to. We don't use the law to demand [rights], we don't use that medium. The only place where we can defend ourselves, where we can protest is the stadium." The statement also highlights their recognition of the stadium as a technology of amplification. Miguel similarly emphasizes the political potential that arises from the convergence of stadiums and sound practice:

> Today, football goes beyond the field and has become a mirror of the country's social and political reality. They have made silence the norm by repressing organized hinchas. The typical elements that give life to the hinchada have been forbidden. Entering a stadium seems like entering a prison [and] police abuse is common every Sunday. Also, since the arrival of the sports limited public companies in 2005, hinchas have fewer spaces. These administrations have sought to make the hincha invisible, framing it as a simple consumer of a product, establishing a market relationship. The only space where we, the hinchas, can make ourselves audible is in the stands. We have brought different banners against Azul Azul, against the model of administration, against the current moment, for months, even years. But those banners have never

> achieved anything. They have never gotten a page in any newspapers, in any tabloid, [not] a minute in news programs, they have never gotten a minute in any radio show covering football, etc. So, when we have demonstrated peacefully, demonstrations in which, in quotations, we don't harm anyone, the people haven't paid attention. We were never heard, and now that we make ourselves audible through pyrotechnics the people condemn us.

Hinchas perceive fiestas and stadiums as tools to amplify their critiques of the neoliberal dynamics that have reduced them to mere consumers.

Many also perceive the National Stadium as a repository of affect. During the Pinochet regime, the military infamously employed the stadium as a detention center. The post-dictatorial state designated the structure as a cultural heritage site, constructed a memorial that resembled the wooden stands of the 1970s, and established a nonprofit organization to oversee guided tours. As U. de Chile is currently the only club that uses the stadium, its hinchas have reclaimed the space and its history. Many U. de Chile hinchas believe that the prisoners' affective residue has become embedded within the materiality of the stadium. Andrea, a female hincha, explains: "As La U hinchas, we know the place's history. The emotional, symbolic, historical, violent burden of a place that was a torture center. It's different being in a place literally than making an empathic exercise, like 'Oh, that was terrible.' You can empathize rationally. But it's different to feel those people's heartbeat in your heartbeat. If you create that communion, it's powerful. Every time you enter the stadium you remember that." U. de Chile hinchas engage in a form of "spatial melancholia" (Navaro-Yashin 2009, 16), in which they strive to "re-signify" these tortured affects through their carnivalesque fiestas. They regard this affective process as a form of labor.

THE SUBSUMPTION OF AFFECTIVE LABOR

Los de Abajo talk about the production and enactment of fiestas in terms of labor. Tuto explains:

> Personal profit doesn't exist here. We want this barra to keep growing both in the stadium's fiesta and the social part. Los de Abajo work for making La U bigger. When I was a kid, La U wasn't big for winning championships. We fell in love with those people's aguante. Those who started this [barra]. We don't

> want the younger generations to lose this essence. The essence of this is singing, aguante, love for the colors. It's the people who make this work. It's everyone's work, [players should] play like hinchas.

Much like Tuto, who supplements his income from a copy center with activities penalized by the law, many members of Los de Abajo are either unemployed or engaged in informal, illegal, or labor-intensive jobs that fail to provide them with complete satisfaction. The prevalence of promarket ideologies in the labor code, limitations on unionization, and the dominance of informal and low-skilled work have resulted in a state of job precarity for the Chilean proletariat (Ahumada 2019). Unsurprisingly, Los de Abajo perceive their support for U. de Chile as their primary occupation—a way of life that intertwines leisure and labor. They assert that their affective work is dedicated to the betterment of the team and fanbase, placing greater importance on fostering social connections, expressing themselves, and achieving success in the realm of sports, rather than prioritizing economic productivity. Although aguante's necropolitics complicates this idealized understanding, Tuto's speech illustrates that Los de Abajo's regime of value departs from neoliberal logics.

Despite this emphasis on interpersonal relations, their affective labor does have economic implications. Julia Elyachar (2010) explains that the channels created by social relations can create phatic infrastructures upon which economic value can be generated. Precisely, in fostering stranger intimacy and affecting the outcomes of games, Los de Abajo's affective labor has helped cement an economy that has directly affected the club's finances. Nevertheless, while they know that their fiestas have profitable implications, they see economic value as not only secondary but also subordinate to relational value.

Tuto's aforementioned statement also underscores that segments of Los de Abajo have sought to distance themselves from traditional forms of aguante transactionality. This moral distancing is indissolubly tied to the revalorization of the hinchada as the core constituency of the club. The necessity to carve out space for themselves within the club has radicalized this proposition, leading them to sever transactional connections with club workers and celebrate non-commercial forms of value. U. de Chile hinchas have come to value the sociality of their affective labor, arguing that the club's social, sporting, and administrative life have been mainly shaped by relational, rather than economic, value.

This emphasis on the historical dominance of relationality over capital deserves serious consideration. The fact that the hyper-commodification of football has reframed every expression and relation in capitalistic terms does not mean that the sport is inherently a commercial enterprise. Indeed, Arjun Appadurai underlines the temporality of commodification processes, arguing that commodities are "things that, at a certain *phase* in their careers and in a particular *context*, meet the requirements of commodity candidacy" (2013, 16; emphasis in the original). The prioritization of market relations and the concentration of power among the elites are a relatively recent developments in the history of U. de Chile. For decades, relationships driven by nonprofit motives were the norm. As Miguel aptly expresses, unlike Corfuch, "Azul Azul is an institution whose work is to loot the blue sentiment."

Azul Azul is deeply aware of the economic implications of Los de Abajo's affective labor. See, for instance, the following statement by Azul Azul's sports director Rodrigo Goldberg: "We're competing with clubs with budgets that triple, quadruple our budget. But this club has something else. It has something that makes you fall in love, that seduces you, and that's why so many players want to come back afterward. That's something we take into consideration because there are players that have realized what U. de Chile means and have changed their minds. From not showing any interest at first to saying, 'Wow, it's La U, it's something important.'" In a documentary, Goldberg more explicitly links value production to Los de Abajo: "When they tell us, 'You didn't win a championship in twenty-five years,' [I respond,] 'Yes, and I'm proud of it. Because in those twenty-five years the most important hinchada in the country was born.'" A former U. de Chile player appointed by Heller when he resigned from the board, Goldberg highlights the importance of the phatic channels created by Los de Abajo. He recognizes that U. de Chile's sports and economic dominance is rooted in and dependent on the stranger intimacy and in-game relations enacted by sound practice. In essence, Goldberg suggests that without the affective support of Los de Abajo, U. de Chile would not have achieved its current status.

However, a fundamental disagreement exists between Azul Azul and Los de Abajo concerning the exchange subordination of the various forms of value associated with the club, with the company prioritizing profit over fan relationality. As Timothy Taylor (2016) observes, capitalism possesses an inexhaustible ability to co-opt and assimilate alternative value systems and modes of production in its pursuit of capital accumulation. Similar to other football contexts (Jack 2024), Azul Azul has effectively reversed the relationship between relational and economic value within the club, subsuming Los de Abajo's affective labor while denying them any rights beyond consumption.

The subsumption of Los de Abajo's affective labor by Azul Azul has also led to the appropriation of fan practices themselves. A striking example was the *banderazo* (roughly, "big flagging") on the eve of the Superclásico against Colo-Colo in October 2019. Typically, a banderazo involves a fiesta during the team's final practice before a major game—a final display of affection toward the players. These events usually draw tens of thousands of hinchas and are held at the National Stadium. However, on this occasion, Azul Azul took control, implementing stringent ID checks, limiting access for fans with criminal records, and banning the use of pyrotechnics and musical instruments.

These measures sparked widespread outrage, prompting fan organizations to urge U. de Chile hinchas not to attend. As a result, Azul Azul's banderazo was attended by only a few hundred people, mainly consisting of players' families. In response, Los de Abajo organized their own banderazo outside the hotel where the players were staying the night before the game. They shared the following message on social media:

> The love we have for this jersey is immense and we've never turned our backs to our players. We believe in supporting the team on the eve of the game in a more direct way, without fences and restrictions. [That's] the true support our players and coaching staff need. That's why we call the entire hinchada to a traditional *hotelazo* [banderazo outside the team's hotel] where we'll give all our aguante to the team we love. . . . Los de Abajo never abandon, because when the vultures are no longer present, we'll keep singing loudly! . . . We just want to sing to our team in these difficult times . . . we want our players to feel the love we have for these colors.

Once at the hotel, Los de Abajo sought to sonically amplify this message, voicing their dissatisfaction with the club's current state (video 3.3):

Han pasado muchos años	Many years have passed by
Muchos jugadores	Many players
Muchos dirigentes	Many directors
Se llenaron los bolsillos	They lined their pockets
Lo único que queda es la gloriosa gente	All that remains is the glorious people
Esta hinchada se lo dice	This hinchada says it
Para que lo sepan esos jugadores	So that the players know it

Aunque no salgan campeones	Even if you don't win the championship
Hay que poner más huevos por estos colores	You must grow some balls for these colors
Y vamos, leones	Let's go, lions
Mojen esa camiseta	Work up a sweat
Y vamos, leones	Let's go, lions
Que queremos dar la vuelta	We want the championship

Despite their plea for inclusion, the hotelazo was met with harsh police repression. Law enforcement responded with tear gas and water cannons, forcibly dispersing men, women, and children who were expressing their affective support for the club.

Azul Azul has managed to absorb and exploit the affective labor of Los de Abajo while simultaneously excluding them from the club. This corporate subsumption highlights the limitations of affective labor within consumer communities as they remain vulnerable to commodification and fetishization. Despite the efforts of U. de Chile fans to disrupt the neoliberal takeover of their club, their affective actions have inadvertently reinforced the very structures that have marginalized and silenced them.

The politics of affective aguante resonate with social struggles in football scenes elsewhere. Max Jack (2024) demonstrates that European *ultras* use "atmosphere as a medium of public and political expression that [works] in place of democratic representation in the context of football fandom" (131). However, akin to Los de Abajo's affective labor, "ultras' subversive rhetoric and collective action are ripe for appropriation by the clubs and governing bodies that use culture and affect to market the sporting event, in effect making it available for consumption" (52). Moreover, political aspirations within hyper-commodified sports environments become increasingly restricted when become tainted by violence, rendering affect highly unpredictable. Amid necropolitics and neoliberal precarity, Los de Abajo emerge as a "utopian-dystopian figure" (Mazzarella 2009, 304). In this context, affect not only disrupts unequal power dynamics but also serves as a tool for social control, participation in radical conflicts, and establishment of hierarchical asymmetries within the hinchada itself. Los de Abajo's prioritization of violent over relational value has ultimately undermined their efforts to foster community amid the hyper-commodification of U. de Chile.

NECROPOLITICAL CONFLICTS

The fiesta I observed during the game between U. de Chile and Palestino at the National Stadium in May 2018 exemplifies the ambiguous potential of affective labor. A few minutes into the second half, Los de Abajo turned on countless red flares and launched hundreds of fireworks while singing loudly and intensely. The stadium's architecture amplified the cacophony of voices, pyrotechnics, and brass and percussion instruments. The conspicuous marijuana smell merged with the gunpowder odor coming from the flares and fireworks. Los de Abajo became an intense, colossal whole moving and singing along (video 3.4):

Bulla de mi vida	Noise of my life
Bulla de mi amor	Noise of my love
Puro sentimiento	Pure sentiment
Más que una pasión	More than a passion
Para donde vayas	Anywhere you go
Siempre te acompaño	I'll always be there
Y por esta hinchada	And this hinchada
Vamos a ser campeón	Will make us champion

In the second part of the chant, the percussionists began to play half instead of quarter notes, creating a slower, more dramatic mood. The hinchas accompanied the drums by raising their hands and clapping above their heads. The lyrics not only rejected hegemonic norms, controls, and mediations but also underscored the disruptive potential of the hinchada:

Todos saben de un gran amor	Everybody knows about the great love
De un bullanguero que no se vendió	Of a bullanguero [U. de Chile hincha] who didn't sell out
Ni a los pacos ni a la represión	Neither to the cops nor the repression
Ni a las mentiras de la televisión	Nor the television's lies
La más fiel de la capital	The city's most loyal one
La más gloriosa a nivel mundial	The world's most glorious one
A esta hinchada no la callarán	This hinchada won't be silenced
No la callarán	Won't be silenced

When the chant looped back to the dynamically faster section, Los de Abajo chaotically exploded alongside the fireworks. As soon as the referee stopped the game due to the smoke and fireworks, the hinchas unveiled numerous banners.

While some expressed solidarity with the Palestinian cause for self-determination (see Achondo 2021), a group of female hinchas criticized the ineffective investigation into a recent gang-rape committed by U. de Chile hinchas. "In Chile," their banner read, "it's easier to find an hincha than five rapists!" The sign conflated the sexual abuse with Los de Abajo's main cause for protesting: the sanction against an hincha who made fun of Raimundo Tupper, a beloved U. Católica player who committed suicide in 1995 by jumping off a building. The offender wore a Superman costume and a mask with Tupper's face during the Clásico Universitario played a few weeks before, suggesting that the player had tried to fly like the superhero. U. Católica hinchas denounced the incident on social media, and the authorities banned the U. de Chile hincha from stadiums for one year.

Many banners displayed offensive and insulting messages toward Los Cruzados, the U. Católica barra, labeling them as *sapos* ("toads," slang for "snitches"). Others insulted and mocked the deceased player. One banner featured the phrase "I rub Tupper on my dick," while another displayed an upside-down headshot of the player with tears streaming down his face, accompanied by the message "Your idol abandoned you." Los de Abajo perceived the sanction imposed on the hincha as an overreaction to what they considered a creative expression of aguante—hence their disruptive behavior.

Amid the overwhelming cacophony of voices, instruments, and fireworks, a shirtless hincha engaged in aggressive behavior toward a teenager trying to climb the metal bar where he was standing. Despite his efforts to deter him, the young fan managed to climb and began singing from the structure. The older hincha, still singing loudly, asserted his dominance through spitting, slapping his shaved head, and aggressive arm movements. Their proximity and exaggerated movements resulted in the older hincha's arms going beyond the teenager's body. But the young hincha did not seem intimidated and kept singing on the metal structure. The sonorous dispute eventually escalated into an outright fistfight. The fiesta not only accompanied but also intensified the conflict, drawing in the friends of the brawlers. Once the fireworks concluded and the banners insulting Tupper were put away, frontline members of Los de Abajo intervened, using posturing and threats of retaliation to halt the fight. Nevertheless, the hostilities between the two groups persisted beyond that day, spilling over into subsequent games and events.

This ethnographic scene underscores the ambiguous productivity of affective labor. On the one hand, it proves how sound can gather strangers around shared meanings and intensities. On the other hand, it makes audible the antisociality of aguante. In a context of radicalized conflict, some hinchas have dangerously hyperbolized the competitive nature of fiestas—carnivalesque events that have concurrently overloaded hostilities and subjectivities with disruptive meanings and sensations. The necropolitical overwhelming of the aguante conflict has turned these performances into events capable of both fostering stranger intimacy and fueling enmity between and within hinchadas.

During this particular fiesta, Los de Abajo invoked a traumatic event from U. Católica's history to assert their communal dominance over their rivals. While some hinchas used sound practice to express solidarity with the Palestinian cause and to address issues of gendered violence, the majority of Los de Abajo employed it to rally around a fellow hincha who had been punished. In doing so, they not only endorsed but also amplified their peer's behavior, exacerbating the initial prank. This performance further escalated existing hostilities with Los Cruzados, reaching a peak a few weeks later when U. Católica hinchas ambushed a bus carrying U. de Chile people, resulting in a series of stabbings.

This fiesta ignited conflicts not only with Los Cruzados but also within the U. de Chile hinchada itself. The chaotic environment stirred the sonic, kinesthetic, and ultimately fistfight combat between the two hinchas and their respective factions. Many internal antagonisms have started following clashes resembling the one depicted in the ethnographic vignette. Fiestas, with their carnivalesque intensities, create immersive environments in which radicalized sounds and movements can enact internal hostilities and asymmetries that would not manifest otherwise. During these moments, hinchas weaponize sound to assert dominance and establish hierarchies with their own peers. Radicalized individuals and factions employ sound as a means to challenge fellow hinchas, thereby turning fiestas into unpredictably aggressive events that, affecting all entities populating the stands, create asymmetries within hinchadas. Chaotic intensity, overloaded subjectivities, and radicalized aguante relations have turned fiestas into immersive, omnidirectional, and disruptive events. In solidifying the dominance of certain groups, affective labor has simultaneously strained communal bonds within hinchadas, imposing enmity and force as the sole modes of relationality.

Affective labor creates immersive atmospheres in which violent tropes and aggressive behaviors become pervasive, impacting subject positions. Michel Wieviorka (2009) argues that the superabundance and omnipresence of meaning can affect the frames of reference that previously defined the social, political, or cultural dimensions of reality. Amid club exclusion, fan hostility, and narco warfare, the aggressive vocalization and intense listening to threats of rape, torture, and murder violently overload hinchas' ethical and moral frameworks. Ultimately, fiestas forge necropolitical subjectivities that extend beyond states of deindividuation (Herrera 2018; Marra 2021).

The use of sound to exert social control transcends the realm of game sociality, having a material impact on everyday relations. In numerous cases, it has even resulted in the complete disintegration of social groups. The subsequent section delves into the socially degenerative effects of affective labor by exploring the brief yet intense existence of Las Bulla.

AGUANTE, FEMINISM, AND MISOGYNY

Asserting that the club's recovery should embrace feminist principles, a collective of female hinchas established Las Bulla in 2017. Although some women had previously participated in Los de Abajo, their contributions were often confined to invisible labor, as male hinchas excluded them from the decision-making process. Nonetheless, some of these pioneering female hinchas managed to navigate these hypermasculine networks. Emma, one of these women, articulates her experience:

> Even if you're a woman, you're inserting yourself into a world of men. So, you have to act like them more than expressing what's being a woman or feminist. Because everyone will always judge you. If a man fools around with ten different girls, no one will say anything. But you'll always be a whore. You have to be careful about not being like that so that they consider and respect you. That's why a La U woman who wants to be considered has to start acting like a man. But in the good stuff: supporting, cheering, being there, fighting.

While these women had to adhere to sexist standards, Las Bulla aimed to empower female hinchas by giving them visibility and challenging misogynistic dynamics within the hinchada. Although they understood aguante as a sphere where they were subjected to gendered violence, they also believed it could provide tools to counteract sexism. Precisely, their *feminismo bullanguero* intertwined feminism, aguante, and the values surrounding the club.

Las Bulla sought to performatively carve out space for themselves in the stadium's politics and sociality through their affective labor. They employed various strategies to achieve this, including modifying the gendered aspects of the lyrics by incorporating female pronouns, adjectives, and nouns while eliminating homophobic and sexist expressions.[2] These changes contributed to their visibility, audibility, and ultimately empowerment. Andrea, a former member of Las Bulla, explains:

> By changing the lyrics to feminine, first, I'm more identified with what I'm singing. So, I can sing stronger. Because if I say "soy bullanguero de pendejo" [I'm a bullanguero since I was a little boy] sounds ridiculous. But if I say "bullanguera"—it comes from inside. That's power. It's about realizing that you're not singing about someone else but about yourself. And that changes your relationship with La U. [It makes you realize] that my relationship with the club is not so much about how I've been told, or how I always thought that it should be—a traditional, masculinized relationship. I'm a La U hincha because of something else. Not because of its history, the relegation, the idols, but rather about how I feel. I always felt like a La U hincha, and I express that blue sentiment by being sincere with myself: I'm not a man, and that I'm not an hincha since I was a little girl precisely because I was a woman.

The prevailing narrative that fan values are transmitted exclusively from fathers to sons excludes female hinchas, as they have seldom received this patriarchal education. The fact that women attend games in significantly smaller numbers than men further exacerbates their sense of alienation. In response, Las Bulla aimed to cultivate a sense of stranger intimacy among women through their feminist aguante. Andrea elaborates:

> Women sound louder than men. It's what I told you about changing the gender of the lyrics. In general, women have a higher pitch. When a woman projects her voice, men sound softer. If men and women are singing at the same volume, women are louder. Especially if she's saying "soy bullanguera de pendeja" [I'm a bullanguera since I was a little girl]. It happened to me once at the Bar de Jorge [a dive bar where Los de Abajo usually gather]. I came with Juana. Juana has a deadly resonating voice. And Juana is a reveler and started singing a La U song—I can't remember which one. And there was another woman. I started following Juana in singing very passionately. All the men started, too. The other girl also started. And the three of us started to set the tone. I can't explain it musically, but we were the ones who made the volume go higher. The men tried to sing at our volume, and they couldn't. We responded by singing even louder. And they sang louder. It was madness. I think I'm respected because I was singing like that with Juana. When men see me singing and shouting, the

> way I look when I sing, people believe that I'm a La U hincha. That I'm not posing, following a trend, or anything.

In line with Judith Butler's (2007) constructivist gender theory, Las Bulla performed a feminine manifestation of aguante through the "stylized repetition of acts" (191). Yet their sonic performance also encompassed a choreographic dimension (Miller 2017). Susan Foster (1998) argues that the construction and transmission of gender norms not only occur in the repetition but also relationality of acts—that is, in the intersection of performance and choreography. Through their affective labor, Las Bulla were able to publicly perform gendered bodies while simultaneously practicing female modes of politics and sociality.

Sections of Los de Abajo overtly targeted the sonic performativity of Las Bulla. Sexism ranged from critiques of how women sing to their practice of changing lyrics. Andrea explains: "It happened to me once that we were singing one [chant] that we liked a lot which is 'Somos las hinchas más anarquistas' ["we're the most anarchist hinchas," but gendered feminine] because we change the lyrics entirely. Someone behind us—a man, who was one of those who say 'Zorramental' [Whoremental, in reference to Colo-Colo's Monumental Stadium], 'vamos a culiar al indio' [we'll fuck the Indian]—shouted at us, 'Sing the song as it is.'" Misogyny escalated into material violence when a faction of the barra threatened Las Bulla on the eve of International Women's Day in 2019. The female hinchas had intended to organize a fiesta where they would display two banners. One would read "Against patriarchy and the company," while the other would say, "We're the roar of those women who no longer have a voice." They planned to enhance the impact of the banners with pyrotechnics. However, they were unable to fully execute their plans due to intimidation from Los de Abajo. Andrea explains:

> There was a rumor that morning that people from the barra said that they were going to kick the asses of whoever used pyrotechnics. And who was going to use pyrotechnics in the stadium on March 8? And what does that "whoever" mean? Well, I got scared. I went to [Gate] 17 with Juana, and when we got there someone—I can't remember who, but a woman—said that Ferroazul was going to send their girls to bring down our banners with knives if we used pyrotechnics. I looked at Juana, and she had the same look in her face. I looked at her horrified because I imagined the Ferroazul girls [coming at us]. I know them because I've played football with them. They're tough. I'm afraid of them but

> I respect them. There's one with whom I got along once. And I imagined her coming to stab me. That's the biggest fear I've had in my life. Finally, a bunch of men surrounded us, and we turned on one flare. I don't know who turned it on, and you couldn't see her face, only her hand and the flare in the air. The adrenaline was brutal.

While the barra officially claimed that only the frontline should organize fiestas, some members unofficially acknowledged that the censorship was also influenced by the fact that it was women who were challenging their control over the stadium's soundscape, politics, and sociality. The assault on Las Bulla's fiesta carried materials and symbolic significance. By suppressing their gendered performativity, Los de Abajo aimed to erase their public existence as female hinchas.

As time passed, the relationship between Las Bulla and Los de Abajo deteriorated progressively. Some female hinchas, fearing further reprisals, chose to withdraw their participation from the hinchada. While certain members continued collaborating with Las Bulla, others persisted in terrorizing and boycotting their activities. These persecutions created tensions within Las Bulla itself. One faction wanted to continue working and organizing fiestas alongside Los de Abajo, aiming to disseminate feminist values within the hinchada. The other camp preferred to start collaborating with feminist organizations of rival teams—a departure from the conflict-oriented logic of aguante. Unable to reconcile these internal discrepancies, the female collective eventually decided to dissolve the group.

Andrea argues that the tensions enacted by the International Women's Day fiesta were also exacerbated by members of Las Bulla themselves:

> That was the tension: the barra against the academia [i.e., the faction within Las Bulla that did not want to work with Los de Abajo]. And these scholarly girls were stubborn because they didn't want to understand the context in which they were situated and what it meant. I mean, if you made them work with the barra, they wouldn't survive, because they didn't understand the logic. The codes. And that created tensions, that stubbornness of not wanting to let go of a rigid discourse and not working with comrades because they were *machitos* ["little machos," a term used in feminist circles to call sexist men]. They had no issues with working with Colo-Colo girls and with girls of other barras because [they believed that they were] "friends not rivals." They wanted to create a new understanding of football fandom, which was uprooted from where it was born.

> And some girls said that "I'm not going to work with Colo-Colo girls, because they are part of groups who have killed our people."

Andrea offers a class critique of the female hinchas who sought to bypass their peers and establish connections with rival groups. She criticizes their disregard for aguante norms, emphasizing the importance of upholding these principles within the hinchada:

> These girls were college students. They weren't able to empathize with other contexts, with people who used violence as capital because they didn't have anything else, because that's what they learned, it was their way of living. They never thought about feminism, because they never got the chance to think about it, because the girls with whom they hung out weren't that different. I can't ask them to think and live like me, because they haven't received the tools I've had, and I didn't grow up in a context of violence. And La U wasn't either such a strong way of living [for me] as it was for them. They are La U hinchas, and there's nothing more important in their lives for them. And they raise their kids like that and all their friends are like that. These girls didn't want to see that, they didn't want to understand it, they didn't want to work with them.

Andrea concludes that it is within aguante that misogyny needs to be redressed: "Las Bulla was a beautiful project that reached a lot of people, and we did a lot of things, and many girls found a space, but what kind of feminismo bullanguero can be created without understanding the barra's code?"

The diverging politics within Las Bulla foreground the necropolitical nature of the norms governing aguante relations. Affective labor serves as a means of social control. Sonic affect, whether representing or acting as violence, has emerged as a source and expression of power, leading to the establishment of asymmetrical and often unjust relations within fanbases. This necropolitical devaluation of relationality ultimately restricts their political struggle and limits their ability to transcend the existing power structures within the hyper-commodified realm of football.

CONCLUSION

Julio Barroso scored in the final seconds of the game, sealing yet another victory for Colo-Colo over U. de Chile. For the first time all match, the roughly

FIGURE 3.2 Los de Abajo at Colo-Colo's Monumental Stadium.

one thousand U. de Chile hinchas who had managed to secure tickets fell silent. Meanwhile, the rest of Monumental Stadium erupted in celebration. We had endured projectiles, threats, police repression, scorching sun, and dehydration—made worse by the stadium's bathroom water supply being cut off at halftime—but the last-minute goal delivered a particularly bitter sting. The police showed us no mercy, forcing us to vacate the stands immediately, while the Colo-Colo supporters organized a celebration for their idol, Esteban Paredes, who had just become the all-time top scorer in Chilean football. With seven games left in the tournament, U. de Chile remained in the relegation zone.

"What did we do to deserve this?" Miguel lamented as we left the stadium. "The club is destroyed. Socially too. We had two separate banderazos yesterday. We must recover the club."

A couple of weeks later, following a pause in the tournament due to the FIFA International Match Calendar, the competition resumed. U. de Chile was going to face the match against Deportes Iquique as the lowest-ranked team in the league. The significance of the game was emphasized by players, coaches, and club directors, who referred to it as "the first of seven finals."

Although the game was scheduled for a Thursday afternoon, the stadium was completely sold out. The day before, high school students had begun protesting against an increase in subway fare by evading the payment and jumping turnstiles at subway stations. The protests escalated to the point where some stations had to be temporarily closed by the police to prevent further collective evasions. Taking advantage of the mobilization, U. de Chile hinchas took to social media and called on their peers to participate in the subway evasion as they made their way to the stadium: "We're tired of this mercantile system that exploits us and steals from us in every aspect of our lives. We're tired of this terrible company that has kidnapped our beloved club. We invite you to adhere to the different massive evasions or individually. Let's make the discontent strong and evident." Despite concerns that the police might close the subway stations near the National Stadium, I did not encounter any issues while making my way to the stadium.

The game was tense. U. de Chile was struggling to play well, and Iquique was fiercely defending the tie, which kept them three points ahead in the standings. The entire stadium resounded with loud vocalizations, as the crowd tried to motivate the players to continue attacking. In the eighty-fourth minute, the stadium erupted when midfielder Jimmy Martínez's shot was deflected by an Iquique defender, crossing the goal line after making a strange parabola. After the frenzied celebrations, Los de Abajo raised their hands in the air and clapped in sync with the drums while chanting (video 3.5):

Lo más importante	The most important thing
En la vida es	In life is
Alentar al Bulla	To cheer for Bulla
Con optimismo y fe	With optimism and faith

As the bass drums began playing steady quarter notes, the entire crowd leaped into the air while singing in unison:

Salta cuando todos estén tristes	Jump when everyone is sad
Salta solamente por la U	Jump just for La U
Si un mal paso das	If you stumble
No me importará	I won't care
Porque soy de abajo	Because I'm an underdog
Y te vengo a alentar	And I'm here to cheer for you
Dale, dale, Bulla	Go, go, Bulla
Dale, dale, oh	Go, go, oh

The entire stadium was a cohesive mass moving and sounding along. The players held the result, and U. de Chile managed to escape the relegation zone. The stadium kept singing until the players left the field. Meanwhile, on WhatsApp, a video went viral showing Captain Johnny Herrera during the post-game interview, his voice trembling and eyes brimming with tears. The loud chanting coming from the stands forced them to speak loudly:

TV: Look at the people, Johnny. I imagine that this touches you. The first of seven finals. The objective was achieved. How're you? Good night.

JH: This is La U, my friend, this is La U [pauses and looks at the people singing]. Fuck, it's hard to express what I'm feeling. We came onto the field as the worst-ranked team, and the stadium was sold out. I just want to congratulate the hinchas and the players. We all did our best. We won the first final. We have six remaining.

TV: Johnny, why are you so emotional?

JH: Because that's how we're here in La U.

This was the last game of U. de Chile in the 2019 tournament. The next day, the biggest social uprising since the end of the dictatorship erupted in the country. The active and sometimes violent participation of hinchas in the events forced the authorities to terminate the tournament. Alongside structural changes in society, hinchas demanded more participation in their clubs.

Miguel once told me that "the recovery of the club is a work moved by emotions." This resonates with the contention that "any social project that is not imposed through force alone must be affective in order to be effective" (Mazzarella 2009, 299). U. de Chile hinchas value their affective labor as an exertion of stranger intimacy—a challenge to the neoliberal commodification of fan relations.

This chapter has demonstrated the limitations of this claim. Corporate agents can easily co-opt affective labor to serve capitalist production, rendering it incapable of generating immanent multitudes capable of breaking free from neoliberalism. As Shannon Garland (2020) points out, interventions that focus on "the affective constitution of the world, but not the material stratum that *affects* that constitution," fail to abolish "the contradiction which itself produces the imbalance" (292; emphasis in the original). While affective violence may possess the capacity to incite insurrection against the forces that have hyper-commodified football, it risks becoming regressive when directed not only toward structures of domination but also oppressed communities themselves. Necropolitics has further intensified relationalities and subjectivities, to the extent that sounded aguante has now become an immersive, omnidirectional means to engage in conflicts, exert social control, and establish hierarchical asymmetries within hinchadas. In regimes of value where enmity and dominance outweigh solidarity and relationality, affective labor takes on an ambiguous role, oscillating between biopolitical and necropolitical production. Indeed, affect not only holds the potential of "producing and reproducing social life" (Hardt and Negri 2017, 37) but also "destroying persons and creating *death-worlds*" (Mbembe 2019, 92; emphasis in the original).

Readers may have noticed the centrality of the voice within aguante. The next chapter explores hinchas' necropolitics of voice in connection to the social uprising. It showcases how they perceive the destruction of their material voices as a moral expression of agency and dignity.

FOUR
Vocal Damage

On October 24, 2019, a week after the *estallido social* (roughly, "social uprising") shook Chile, I attended Los de Abajo's second call to demonstrate in Plaza Italia—later renamed colloquially Plaza de la Dignidad (Square of Dignity) as it became the epicenter of the protests. Earlier that morning, U. de Chile hinchas posted a text on social media demanding the end of the state of emergency and more transparency regarding the tortures, deaths, and illegal detentions that human rights organizations had been denouncing. "You will not silence us," the statement concluded, "now more than ever we tell you that you won't intimidate us with your police state and that we'll shout aloud that Chile tortures, murders, and violates human rights."

Hundreds of U. de Chile hinchas singing around La Banda de la Chile crammed the terrace between Plaza Italia and the Universidad de Chile Theater. A banner stating "We're the People, We're the Carnival" covered the hall's sign. I could not recognize anyone, but I joined the congregation nonetheless. Many shirtless hinchas donned their jerseys on their heads in such a way that only their mouths and eyes were visible. Dozens waved blue-and-red flags and umbrellas while singing the following over the melody of Fito Páez "Y dale alegría a mi corazón" (And Give Happiness to My Heart):

Ay, policía, qué vida elegiste vos	Ow, cop, what a life you've chosen
Pegarle a la gente humilde es tu vocación	Hitting humble people is your vocation
Matar a la gente pobre es tu profesión	Killing poor people is your profession
Y así brindarles a los ricos la protección	And so provide protection to the rich

Ya van a ver
Las balas que nos tiraron van a volver

They will see
The bullets they shot at us will come back

Although they mostly sang the same chants they vocalize in stadiums, they also created some contingent contrafacta to blast the police and military. They also adapted some of their chants to the current context, attacking law enforcement instead of rival hinchas (video 4.1).

I eventually ran into Miguel and stayed with him. When Los de Abajo launched fireworks and turned on smoke flares, an hincha enthusiastically yelled "¡Aguante La U, conch'e su mar'e! ¡Somos Chile! ¡De menores de La U!" (roughly, "Let's go, La U, motherfuckers! We're Chile! A U. de Chile hincha since juvenile prison!"). Other protesters joined them when they began singing "Oh, Chile despertó" (Oh, Chile woke up), the social uprising's unofficial anthem.

Unlike Los de Abajo, however, I was concerned about the pyrotechnics, fearing a violent reaction from the cops and troops supervising Plaza Italia. My anxiety was well founded as, a couple of minutes later, the place was saturated with tear

FIGURE 4.1 U. de Chile hinchas in Plaza Italia.

gas. The police launched it right behind us, so Miguel and I tried to move toward the other side of the terrace. But as most of Los de Abajo did not move, the few of us who were trying to leave the space created a bottleneck in the corridor between the theater and the subway entrance. The gas began to affect us, and the people with children began to become anxious. My face began to sting, and I could not open my eyes anymore. I got nauseous and my nose started bleeding. "My head is killing me!" Miguel shouted while we tried to go through the people. Despite the gas, a shirtless hincha on top of the bars of the subway entrance angrily yelled at us: "¡Aguanten!" (endure it). His cry was loud yet throaty. After screaming at us, he kept singing loudly with a round yet rather hoarse voice.

Miguel and I eventually managed to leave the place. A woman gave me some water spiked with bicarbonate to ease the pain and clean the blood from my nose and beard. Once I could see better, I realize that a bus filled with cops was coming directly toward the terrace. While I ran away from the imminent clash, Los de Abajo kept singing under a dense cloud of tear gas:

Que lo escuchen los milicos	Listen, military
Que lo escuche la SA	Listen, company
Esta barra no se vende	This barra won't sell out
Esta barra es de verdad	This barra is for real

On my way back to my dad's apartment, the cry and subsequent vocalizations of the hincha kept ringing in my ear, reminding me of the often-repeated expression among U. de Chile hinchas: "cantar hasta romper la voz" (roughly, to sing until the point of destroying the voice).

Hinchas unanimously define vocalizing as aguante's fundamental sonic practice (Achondo 2021). Its vocality is characterized by the production of deep, round, and amplified sounds that emphasize open vowels. As Andrés Recasens (1999) aptly describes: "I listen again to that verse that 'breaks your heart' because of its content, because of the way they sang it, in which the vowels were sung *rallentando*, the 'o' was intubated turning into an 'o' mixed with a 'u'; and the mournful tone coming from inside, from the guts" (55). Yet the husky vocalizations of the aforementioned hincha are also fairly common. When asked about forcing their vocal organs by singing nonstop during games, U. de Chile hinchas often reply that they must sing until they completely lose their voice. Although their dedication to out-singing rival hinchadas may explain the intensity, my conversations with hinchas have shed light on a deeper moral aspect behind this extreme use of the material voice. This realization became even more apparent during the unrest of 2019.

With the social uprising as the backdrop, this chapter examines the politics of voice among Chilean hinchas. I argue that they conceptualize the destruction of their material voices as indexing working-class *dignidad* (dignity)—a moral category with social and political implications in proletarian Chile. Understanding their voices in moral terms, hinchas vocalize not only to cheer for their teams but also to amplify their deprived social conditions, defying silencing, inaudibility, criminalization, and dehumanization. Their desperate urgency to produce deep, round, and loud vocal sounds often leads them to vocalize until the point of complete hoarseness. This vocal damage is not an accident but rather an intended outcome as they conceptualize the destruction of the material voice as an exertion of agency and dignity. The emphasis on the destruction of vocal organs in order to produce loud vocalizations makes audible a necropolitics of the body in which morality is exerted through bodily destruction.

AGUANTE AND THE PHONOSONIC NEXUS

Aguante scholars have amply discussed the idea of "poner el cuerpo" (roughly, "to put the body on the line"), illustrating that hinchas purposely and systematically expose their bodies to pain and damage (Alabarces 2012; Alabarces and Garriga 2007, 2008; Garriga 2005, 2007, 2010). The endurance of adverse weather conditions, encounters with police brutality, confrontations with rival groups, and the consumption of drugs and alcohol are all expressions of aguante. Through tropes of monstrosity, hinchas also prove their aguante by displaying scars, bruises, lacerations, and damaged body parts. María Verónica Moreira (2007, 2008) notes that, in aguante's necropolitics, pain and damage become deeply moral categories as hinchas willingly put their bodies on the line to defend the honor and prestige of their clubs and peers.

But amid the precarity stirred by the Chilean neoliberal model, this corporeal morality exceeds the sports realm. Through thanatopolitics, the Pinochet regime introduced a series of reforms that trumped the state's welfare functions and subsidized free markets and the exercise of individualism, competition, and ownership (Ahumada 2019; Han 2012; Moulian 1997; Paley 2001; Pérez 2022; Richards 1997). The post-dictatorial state sought to maintain the country's macroeconomic success in the global economy by reinforcing this model while avoiding the social investments that characterize social democracies. As Clara

Han (2012) notes, the Chilean state has "displaced the responsibilities for care onto families and individuals, divesting the state of crucial responsibilities for the well-being of the population" (5). In response to this structural disregard for care, the poor have adopted the term *dignity* to generate deeply moral ways of living (Pérez 2022). This working-class morality extends beyond mere discourse, finding expression through the physical body as performative struggles against precarity. As Butler (2015) points out, when infrastructures are being decimated, "demands made in the name of the body (its protection, shelter, nourishment, mobility, expression) sometimes must take place with and through the body and its technical and infrastructural dimensions" (128–29). In a context in which aguante necropolitics intersects with a systemic disregard for care, hinchas performatively enact dignity through the destruction of the material body—a corporeal necropolitics they make audible through their voices.

Anthropologists of voice have amply analyzed how subjects rely on vocal practice to navigate spaces of social deterioration (Fox 2004; Meintjes 2017; Pilzer 2022; Tatro 2022). For instance, Aaron Fox (2004) has contended that Texan country music has been largely "shaped in response to the commodification of human agency in industrialized capitalist society" (310). Presenting the country bar as a refuge for citizens beaten down by political elites, dominant ideas of social worth, and the alienating organization of the labor system, Fox illustrates how country musicians and listeners have incorporated and repurposed popular culture as a means to interpret and comment on their social pressures. In this context, the voice functions as an expression of "dignity and agency" (108). In this chapter, I similarly show that hinchas understand vocalizing until the point of damaging the vocal organs as an expression of agency and audibility—a necropolitics of the voice that has been shaped by and in response to the Chilean neoliberal model.

This chapter thus contributes to studies of voice. A material embodiment of social ideology and experience, the voice can both embody particular qualities and index specific social identities and subject positions (Feld et al. 2004; Weidman 2006, 2014, 2015, 2021). Building on this semiotic model, Nicholas Harkness (2014) employs the term *phonosonic nexus* to foreground the fact that voicing phenomena occur in the intersection of the phonic and the sonic, the material and the sonorous: "The scalar relationship between the voice, as phonosonic nexus, and voicing, as semiotic alignment to perspective within an immanent narrative structure, is made evident by the way the phonosonic nexus facilitates the inhabitance of roles within a culturally framed social world of discursive interaction" (19). Dignity is voiced not only through vocal sounds but also through their physical, material exertion. In contrast to professional singers, who perceive a loss of control over their voice as a threat to their agency (Meizel 2020), hinchas interpret vocal strain as a manifestation of necropower. This chapter thus shows that destructive understandings of the phonosonic nexus can voice moral categories in contexts of structural silencing and inaudibility.

THE OASIS OF LATIN AMERICA

On October 8, 2019, ten days before the social uprising, President Sebastián Piñera stated that "within a convoluted Latin America, we see Chile . . . as a real oasis, with a stable democracy, a growing [economy], we're creating 176,000 jobs per year, [and] the wages are getting better" (quoted in Baeza 2019a). Piñera's statement was not unusual as countless citizens, scholars, politicians, and organizations had systematically celebrated Chile's perceived economic, political, and social stability vis-à-vis other South American countries (Ahumada 2019; Richards 1997). Chilean exceptionalism collapsed violently on October 18, when bewildered analysts struggled to explain the social uprising, resorting to the statement that "nobody saw this crisis coming." Political pundits justified their inability to anticipate the social uprising through tropes of sensory impairment. This chapter takes this convergence of failed anticipation and diminished perception seriously.

The Pinochet regime dramatically transfigured the country's social, political, and economic structures. A triumvirate of military, neoliberal intellectuals, and businesspeople executed a "capitalist revolution" (Moulian 1997, 18) that imposed privatization, deregulation, extractivism, and a more distant relationship between the citizenry and state as the country's new organizing principles. The constitution that Pinochet imposed in 1980 tied the state to these doctrines, providing the ideological and structural framework for a neoliberal mode of governmentality. Conceptualized "as the structuring principle of life itself," Han (2012) notes, "the market became the primary mode of governance, and the social became a terrain in which economic rational actors made choices in their own self-interest" (7). This significantly limited the poor's access to health, education, pensions, and housing, which were reframed as commodities rather than social rights. Even conservative economists have recognized that the Chilean liberalization "went too far" in "the push toward greater reliance on market solutions" (Richard 1997, 150).

Nevertheless, local and foreign commentators disseminated a discourse that portrayed Chile as a resilient, competitive, and successful nation that was rapidly advancing toward development—an example of neoliberalism's developmental capacities. The foreign forces that shaped the country's new social and economic conditions helped support and validate this argument. For instance, Milton Friedman—who, alongside Arnold Harberger and their Chilean advisees at the University of Chicago, used the country as a laboratory for neoliberal policies (Ganti 2014; Han 2012; Valdés 1995)—famously called the country's neoliberal turn the "Miracle of Chile" (Ahumada 2019; Richards 1997).

Post-dictatorship Chile not only inherited but also perpetuated the regime's economic, political, and epistemic structures (Ahumada 2019; Han 2012; Moulian 1997; Paley 2001; Richards 1997). Often called a *transición pactada* (agreed-upon transition), the country's unique reconstruction of democracy was characterized by the pursuit of political consensus between the center-left and the right—compromises constantly scrutinized by Pinochet's looming presence first as commander-in-chief and later as a nonelected senator. The progressive disappearance of state functions and the quieting of social movement activity also marked the transition to democracy. The post-dictatorial governments strategically marketed a discourse of democracy in order to politically legitimize the subsidization and intensification of the country's neoliberal economic reforms. As social mobilizations were absorbed by the state under promises of electoral participation, "many of the crucial decisions that affected people's lives were not accessible to the influence of citizens," thereby limiting "the scope and meaning of democracy" (Paley 2001, 100). With traditional forms of citizenship no longer mediating the social, credit and consumption became the primary modes of social integration and access to modernity in postauthoritarian Chile. As Han (2012) puts it, "social policies to address poverty have posed citizens as 'clients' or 'consumers' of public goods, women as 'mothers' to be civilized, and the consumer credit system [as providing] possibilities for advancement in perceived class status" (11).

The post-dictatorial governments also kept promoting an imaginary of Chile as a politically modern, fiscally responsible, and economically stable nation. Tomás Moulian (1997) contends that the statements that accompanied these campaigns had both internal and external purposes: "The semantic exaggerations used in this advertising campaign (Chile as a jaguar, Chile as a puma, Chile as a leader, Chile as developed) are not random. They are part of a strategy of exaltation aimed to incite 'patriotic pride'—the idea that we are winners. [It] seeks the internal consolidation of the model and identification with it via the idea 'the admired Chile'" (98). In establishing parallels with the so-called *Asian Tigers*, these discourses helped present Chile as an attractive place for the production of transnational capital and wealth. These economic dynamics were also understood as the material base for the country's perceived social and political stability (Ahumada 2019).

Despite these rhetorical strategies, the Chilean neoliberal model has lacked dynamic sources for long-term development (Richards 1997). This has embedded the economy into short-term booms followed by periods of stagnation. After forty years of economic liberalization, Chile remains an extractive economy whose productive structure and patterns of specialization are not radically different from those of regional peers (Ahumada 2019). Promarket doctrines dominate the country's labor laws, unionization is heavily constrained, and most jobs are informal and low-skilled. Economists have linked this kind of peripheral growth not only with economic fluctuation but also with wealth and income inequality.

Indeed, this neoliberal governmentality has exacerbated local inequity. Despite the myth that neoliberalism has reduced socioeconomic disparity, "local inequality has been increasing over the past two decades," placing Chile "among the most unequal Latin American and developed countries" (Atria et al. 2018, 4). This is partly explained by the subsidiary nature of the Chilean state, which both ideologically and institutionally refuses to equitably redistribute capital (Ahumada 2019). Additionally, the privatization of health, pensions, education, and public services has ensnared the working class in debt, scarcity, and precarity (Han 2012). Poverty in Chile is not necessarily manifested in the lack of material goods, but rather in the inability to secure stable jobs, adequate housing, or proper healthcare, "a kind of living that they construe as undignified and degrading" (Pérez 2018, 513). Amid systematic attacks on the dignity and agency of the poor, "dignity (or at least a dignified life) as a moral category" has emerged as a political tool "from which to grow and at the same time become ethical subjects" (Márquez 2020, 671–72).

A glimpse into the life of Riva, an U. de Chile hincha, will exemplify this reality. Born and raised in a typical proletarian household in Puente Alto, his father—who abandoned them for years—worked as a construction worker until a stroke and subsequent complications prostrated him. His mother has had several sporadic jobs including housekeeping, cleaning services, and security guarding. With an absent father during his upbringing and with a Colo-Colo hincha as an older brother, he explains his U. de Chile loyalty as follows:

> I don't know if it's a long story, but it's a kind of personal. At that time, my old man, when I was—how old was I? In '94 to '96, my parents were divorced. And [my brother] Tomás was already a Colo-Colo hincha. I was brought to the Colo-Colo stadium, but I wasn't aware that I was in the stadium or that I had to follow the team. Nothing like that. So, at that time, everyone who lived in my neighborhood was a La U hincha. On top of that, I had a neighbor who invited me to his house to watch La U games. And he gave me an entire La U outfit: shorts, socks, and jersey. And that's when I became a La U hincha. And then I started attending games. And I identified with the team even further. People tend to follow successful teams. But not this team—it was different. Even if it was doing poorly, you felt more passion, more love. You suffered, but you lived the joys more intensely. That's why I became a La U hincha.

As a teenager, Riva found in aguante a space for intimacy and dignity: "When we went to the stadium, we had to protect ourselves—together. At the stadium, when someone brought water bottles, you drank half of it and gave the rest to another one. Little things like that. If you had some extra money after the stadium, you bought some ham, soda, and everyone ate. That was the camaraderie. If there was a fight, you had to fight."

Today, Riva wakes up at 5 a.m. and travels about two hours on the public system to get to his job in a meat shop in northeastern Santiago. At 6 p.m., he travels back to the house of his partner's parents in the city's northwest where he lives in a room with his spouse and toddler. Riva cannot afford a house for his family. On top of the forty thousand pesos (approximately forty US dollars) he spends per month on public transportation, he has to spend a significant portion of the four hundred thousand pesos (approximately four hundred US dollars) he receives every month on pensions and health insurance. Whatever surplus is left over, Riva gives it to his partner's parents. The four hours he spends daily on the uncomfortable public buses, and the fact that arriving at his house late at night has become increasingly dangerous due to nearby narco activity, have moved him to consider asking for a loan to buy a car. Although this would alleviate his everyday problems, it would simultaneously embed him and his family in the tensions of debt, scarcity, and precarity that mar poor households in Santiago (Han 2012).

Riva illustrates the "mirages of the miracle" (Ahumada 2019, 229). The astonishment expressed by commentators toward the social uprising only demonstrates the silencing and inaudibility of the realities of those who have experienced the other side of the coin of the Chilean neoliberal model (Márquez 2020). Those who did not see the unrest coming were actually not seeing—nor listening.

CHILE WOKE UP

I celebrated U. de Chile's victory against Iquique until dawn, so I woke up late on October 18. My phone was exploding with WhatsApp messages. The police had started to heavily repress the high school students who were evading the subway tolls. Images of the police tear-gassing high schools while students sought refuge went viral. The repression enraged adults, who joined the evasions and sought to protect the underage protesters from the police. By the afternoon, people were gathering outside almost every subway station in Santiago while blocking the transit with barricades. The police's use of tear gas and water cannons radicalized the demonstrators, leading to riots and the setting of buses, subway stations, and even government buildings on fire. Santiago burned while *cacerolazos* (pot-banging), honking, and anti-government chants filled the city's soundscape. By night, impoverished neighborhoods had turned into war zones, and different organizations began to join the emerging social uprising. Los de Abajo, for instance, stated on social media:

> The Chilean people have reached their limit with the abuses they've endured. The ongoing social uprising is a testament to this exhaustion. Today, Chile's police force—those who have tear-gassed our children in stadiums and schools, those implicated in the largest corruption scandal in Chilean history, those responsible for the death of Camilo Catrillanca, and those who evade paying for public transportation—stand as defenders of the unjust system plaguing Chile.[1] Our water is being stolen. Public transportation treats us like cattle. Sacrifice zones remain neglected. Our grandparents receive meager pensions. Grassroots activists are met with suspicious deaths. Higher education is only attainable through debt. We call upon the hinchas of Los de Abajo to take to the streets, to join the protests, cacerolazos, and mobilizations in the coming days. . . . Only through a united struggle can we bring about substantial change!

At midnight, Piñera addressed the nation. Defining the protests as expressions of violence, he declared a state of emergency in Santiago, sending out the military to seize control of the city. It was the first implementation not associated with a natural catastrophe since the return to democracy.

Although Piñera froze the subway fare increase on Saturday, the state of emergency only radicalized the protests. The thirty pesos began to symbolize "*everything* that has happened during the last three decades" (Villalobos-Ruminott 2020, 10; emphasis in the original). Several supermarkets were looted and set on fire while protesters clashed with the police and military. The demonstrations rapidly expanded throughout the country, and the government declared curfews for the three major regions. The subway system was shut down and major events—football included—were suspended. The riots and protests continued the entire week, ending with a gigantic 1.2-million-person demonstration in Santiago on Friday. Although the government tried to label this demonstration as the end of the social uprising, the country remained paralyzed for months. In fact, from that week until the start of the COVID-19 crisis in March, every Friday was marked by a massive demonstration in Plaza Italia.

Although the demonstrations did not subside, they never converged on a unified set of demands. Some protesters explicitly tied the social uprising to anti-neoliberal politics, carrying signs stating that "neoliberalism was born and will die in Chile" or that "Chile will be the tomb of neoliberalism." Others simply expressed a vague frustration with an unequal system that had constrained social mobility and impeded equal access to the basic rights of citizenship. And while polls showed that the support for the social uprising fluctuated between 70 and 90 percent, they also illustrated that the main demands were divided evenly between pensions, health, education, and jobs and wages. This cornucopia of claims eventually coalesced around the call for "a life with dignity"—a vague yet telling moral critique and demand for changes in the country's political, social, and economic structures (Pérez 2022).

Although most of the protesters did not engage in violent practices, many saw them as required to shake up the system. This led to a celebration among some protesters of the *primera línea* (front line): a group of protesters who clashed with the police and military so that others could occupy the public space. When the life stories of these protesters began to circulate, it became clear that many were young people coming from impoverished spaces. When asked by a journalist why they put their bodies on the line, they said:

> I'm fighting for my mother. Her pension isn't enough for anything: $60,000 [per month; approximately, 60 USD]. But I fight for the entire people so that we have real justice and have the same opportunities as the rich. . . . We're not afraid anymore. I fight for my mother and grandmother, whose pension and salary . . . combined are not enough for a month . . . even if they cut our tongues,

> we'll keep screaming, we'll keep bleeding for our country. Even if our veins dry out. Even if we all bleed to death. (Quoted in Andonie 2020)

Members of the working class argue that their daily struggles with scarcity, hard labor, and inadequate health care have taken a toll on their physical well-being, leading them to view physical resistance as a means of asserting agency and maintaining dignity. For them, "resistance and self-destruction are largely synonymous" (Mbembe 2019, 88). The bodily damage and public destruction enacted by frontline protesters and state forces brought discussions regarding the political implications of violence to the forefront of public discourse.

Indeed, the emergence of the front line coincided with the thanatopolitical radicalization of state repression. The subsequent end of the state of emergency did not ease state violence. Although troops were no longer in the streets, the police intensified their actions. Videos of brutal beatings, police cars running over protesters, shootings at health workers assisting the injured, and cops consuming cocaine before attacking demonstrators began to flood social media. Cases of people losing their eyes after being shot directly in the face with riot weapons skyrocketed. Although the use of riot shotguns was suspended in mid-November, reports of police shooting tear gas grenades directly at protesters' faces increased. By March 2020 the National Institute for Human Rights had registered 3,838 people wounded, 406 ocular injuries, 257 cases of sexual abuse, 617 cases of torture, and 34 deaths.

Within this atmosphere of violence, a wide range of musical productions emerged (Spencer and Bieletto-Bueno 2020). In addition to the sounds resonating within the protests (Domingo 2020), feminist collectives vocalized against gendered violence (Bieletto-Bueno 2020; Jordán 2023), live performances of Mozart's Requiem took to the streets (Fugellie 2020), impromptu sing-alongs fostered conflict resolution (Party 2023), and new protest songs were created (Spencer 2020). The aural public sphere became a contested site, with sound serving as a means for individuals across the entire political spectrum to audibly engage in public deliberation during the unrest.

Politicians began to recognize that a major compromise was needed to subside the social unrest. The idea of amending the country's structures through a new constitution began to gain traction across the entire political spectrum. In the dawn of November 15, almost every political party signed an agreement that initiated the process of writing a new constitution. The pact was accompanied by the idea of coming back to "normalidad" (normalcy). But as the agreement was reached without the participation of grassroots movements, many distrusted it, arguing that demonstrations should continue in order to secure the transparency of the constitutional process. In addition, many believed that some structural changes, such as the pension system, could not wait. Although the protests diminished slightly during the summer, they only definitely stopped in March when COVID-19 reached the country.

The constitutional agreement gave rise to conflicting interpretations of political praxis, leading to the opposing narratives of *octubrismo* and *noviembrismo*. Conservative pundits characterized Octubrism—named after the tumultuous month of the social uprising—as a juvenile and irrational impulse that prioritized violence over peaceful deliberation. In contrast, Novembrism—named after the month when the constitutional agreement was reached—was seen as a revival of liberal democracy, celebrating consensus, elections, and the silent majority. Critics on the left argued that Octubrism's violent indexicality distorted the peaceful expression of corporeal politics by a significant majority of society. They portrayed the social uprising as the multitude's reclamation of the public sphere—a pacifist response to the political inertia imposed by the post-dictatorial state. I contend that these positions simplify and fail to capture the complexities and ambiguities of the social uprising.

On the one hand, the negative connotation of Octubrism represents a resurgence of the tactics employed by post-dictatorial authorities to legitimize neoliberalism (Paley 2001). The social uprising can be seen as a response to the dominance of electoral politics at the expense of other forms of political engagement in neoliberal Chile. As noted by Judith Butler (2015), the body itself is a political entity, expressing dissent and asserting its right to exist amid precarity: "it exercises a right that is being actively contested and destroyed by military force and that, in its resistance to force, articulates its way of living, showing both its precarity and its right to persist" (83). Indeed, the exaltation of the silent majority and electoral processes has inadvertently silenced the voices and demands of marginalized communities within Chilean society (Achondo 2023).

On the other hand, the left's romanticized portrayal of the social uprising as purely peaceful and detached from any form of violent disruption ends up depoliticizing violence, obscuring its role in social struggles within contexts of precarity. Positions that completely deny the use of violence as a political tool overshadow its potential for insurrection in justified social struggles for legitimate rights. However, as pointed out by Mbembe (2019), the productivity of violence, if "caught in a sterile repetition, could degenerate at any moment" (6). Understanding the simultaneously productive and destructive potential of violence is essential for comprehending the necropolitical and sometimes contradictory pursuit of a life with dignity by hinchas.

NINETY MINUTES WON'T COVER UP THIRTY YEARS

Although the barras of all teams participated in the social uprising, those of U. de Chile, U. Católica, and Colo-Colo, the biggest in the country, received larger attention as they brought the sounds of aguante more loudly to the protests. Alongside the two chants mentioned in the introduction to this chapter, Los de Abajo created another chant over the melody of singer-songwriter León Gieco's "Solo le pido a Dios" (I Only Ask God):

Solo le pido a Dios	I only ask God
Que se mueran todos los milicos	For all the military to die
Que se mueran para siempre	That they die forever
Para la alegría de toda la gente	For the people's joy

This is a re-versioning of a chant that had circulated widely in aguante networks. While Los de Abajo used to call for the demise of Garra Blanca, Argentines used to call for the death of all Chileans. U. de Chile hinchas also changed some of their chants against Colo-Colo to attack the police and military instead. As discussed later, however, this does not mean that hinchas no longer engaged in the aguante conflict during the social uprising.

The presence of hinchadas in the streets caught both protesters and media commentators by surprise. With hinchas singing, playing murga porteña, and clashing with the police, protesters began to question the imaginary of hinchadas as senselessly alienated (Villalobos-Ruminott 2020). As hinchas tended to defend protesters from the police, many felt safer with their presence. Los de Abajo, in particular, were grateful for the protesters' support, as they stated on social media on October 24: "Long live the Chilean people! Today was a historical day for Los de Abajo as we once again were present in the demonstrations in Plaza Italia. It was honestly a pleasure to make everyone sing with our instruments and with chants that today everyone found appropriate because of the current context. We appreciate the space we're given as hinchada, and especially people's reception today." As discussed later, nonetheless, the media and the government managed to resignify the participation of hinchas through tropes of criminality—maneuvers that hinchas themselves inadvertently reinforced.

Hinchas not only participated in the social uprising through sound practice. While many joined the front line, others deployed fireworks, Molotov cocktails, and firearms to clash with the police every night in impoverished neighborhoods. Weeks before the social uprising, Riva had prophetically told me that "if there was another coup, they wouldn't have it so easy, because barras have tons of firearms." Yet it was the riots in stadiums—which eventually led to the termination of the 2019 tournament—that received larger media attention.

Amid governmental pressure to reinstall a sense of normalcy, the ANFP (the football federation) sought to resume the tournament after the constitutional agreement. Organizations of hinchas quickly decried this situation. On November 11 Los de Abajo stated on social media:

> For years, we have experienced injustices in every stadium in the country. They repress us. The ticket prices are excessive, and nobody intervenes. Nobody does anything to make the situation better. They ask the families to attend the stadium, but they systematically drive them away. The fiesta and fandom don't kill, they give life! Safe Stadium Plan never worked—we've been saying this for a long time. Today, the country woke up and Los de Abajo, combative hinchada, adheres to the people's demands, and we took over the streets to be heard. They are failing here, too. Your system of sports spectacles never worked, and you won't cover up the blood with football! Pay for your crimes! We call every blue hincha and all the organizations from every [stadium] gate to adhere to a human chain around [the National Stadium], everyone together holding hands in honor of the fallen. Balloons and shredded paper for the spilled blood. For our parents, our children, and the entire country. Los de Abajo won't enter the stadium for respect to the fallen ones. The struggle continues!

On November 19 they employed similar tropes of vocal agency and bodily destruction to challenge the structures of silencing and inaudibility that led to the social uprising: "You won't cover up thirty years with ninety minutes. Los de Abajo are the people and we want to be heard. The guilty should be punished. We ask all the blue people to not attend the game. We categorically reject the restart of the tournament. They are taking our eyes out and want us to watch football." Fiestas acquired new meanings in this context. They became populist expressions of dignity within a larger outcry against neoliberal precarity and state abandonment.

Football was resumed that weekend, but only a single game could be completed. The match between Unión La Calera and Deportes Iquique was ambushed by Garra Blanca, forcing its suspension. Outside the stadium, Colo-Colo hinchas kept clashing with the police for hours. The tournament was suspended one more time and, weeks later, was finally terminated. ANFP declared U. Católica as champion and suspended relegation, meaning U. de Chile would not compete in the second division the following year.

The ambush had a broader impact on Latin American football programming. Santiago was initially chosen as the host city for the Copa Libertadores final, scheduled for November 23. However, due to the social unrest, the South American football federation decided to relocate the final to Lima, Peru. Prior to this decision, hinchadas had issued threats to disrupt the event. U. de Chile hinchas, for example, posted this statement on social media on November 4: "To have the Copa Libertadores in Chile would mean covering up everything that's happening in the country. It would mean to cover up the human rights violations as they did it in the '73 [coup]. . . . If you want to play [the final here], you must know that we'll boycott it." Later that month, the players of the men's national team decided not to play friendly matches against Peru and Bolivia in support of the social demands. As captain Gary Medel expressed: "Today, Chile has more important priorities than Tuesday's game. There's a more important game, which is about equality, about changing many things so that all Chileans can live in a more just country" (quoted in Ramos and Leira 2019).

While some viewed the ambush as an expression of commitment, consciousness, and solidarity, sports media interpreted it as sheer vandalism. To support their analysis, football journalists tied the actions of hinchadas with the well-documented acts of violence and corruption associated with aguante. Media commentators ultimately suggested that hinchas were motivated by personal gain rather than a genuine pursuit of social justice through their acts of dissent.

Juan Cristóbal Guarello, a prominent figure in Chilean journalism, has played a significant role in shaping perceptions of aguante in the country. He has consistently portrayed hinchas as violent subjects distinct from "regular fans" (Guarello 2021). His well-written, scholarly grounded texts present hinchas as social anomalies: grotesque and fascist entities whose lumpenproletariat nature confines them to expressing themselves solely through acts of destruction and corruption (Améstica 2017).

Guarello has concurrently become an influential political commentator. The son of a human rights lawyer, he rose to prominence by discussing the intersection of politics and sports across books, newspapers, magazines, radio, and television. By the time of the social uprising, he had gained significant media fame and was frequently invited to morning shows and other media platforms to discuss politics. During the social unrest, he consistently separated hinchas from the peaceful protesters demanding a "life with dignity," asserting that hinchas were in search of power and influence through their actions.

Albeit long, the column he published after Garra Blanca ambushed the game between Unión La Calera and Iquique is worth quoting at length as it encapsulates how hegemonic discourses ended up framing the participation of barras in the social uprising:

> Barras are companies—a legitimate product of savage neoliberalism. They are always looking for new business opportunities, efficiently employing extortion, threats, and direct violence, which they disguise as a hypocritical "unbounded" passion for their teams. One day they demand money from players' salaries; the next, they ask for tickets; and then they request buses and funds to attend games abroad. . . . It's unnecessary to clarify that these are profoundly antidemocratic organizations—racist, xenophobic, with different rival factions whose hierarchies are established through sticks, staves, and shots.
>
> It's thus not credible that these groups, with no ideology, law, or god, have magically turned into conscious social fighters advocating for justice, equality, and dignity in less than a month. Those who were recently fighting in the stands over a simple banner, threatening to sodomize and shoot anyone in their path, are now supposedly the democratic, inclusive, and popular avant-garde, with touches of veganism and feminism.
>
> Even more suspicious is their insistence on suspending football "until all social demands are fulfilled and Chile becomes a more just country." . . . What's at stake here, and I bring the idealistic and romantic back to reality, is a power struggle. If barras have already conditioned Chilean football, why not go for the entire prize? That is, to play when they decide and thus surpass the ANFP and the clubs, grabbing hold of football's neck—total control.
>
> From there, everything is possible: seats in the directory, a percentage of players' salaries and transfers, and, why not, part of the football channel's money. I'm sorry to end your fantasy: there's no social demand here, just an opportunity for business and power—to move the fence one more time and obtain more money. (Guarello 2019)

Although Guarello suggests in this text that protests should be ethically and aesthetically conducted within the stadium through the amplification of the collective voice of hinchadas, he has systematically criticized the sounds of aguante elsewhere, labeling as narcissistic and monstrous (see Guarello 2021). In his analysis, the practices of aguante emerge as anomalies both within football and liberal democracy.

Sports journalism took Guarello's analysis as an axiom, repeating it almost verbatim in editorials and television and radio shows. The following day, the Piñera administration echoed Guarello's column and argued that hinchas were responsible for the rioting and looting. Government spokesperson Karla Rubilar articulated this stance, stating: "There are very tough delinquent sectors—take note, I want to make a distinction—made up of members of barras, not football fans, who are associated with drug trafficking and the harsher delinquency and are taking advantage of this circumstance" (quoted in Baeza 2019b). Guarello ultimately provided the framework for a transversal condemnation of hinchas and their practices of dissent.

Garra Blanca promptly replied to Guarello's column on social media. Given that the post contains crucial elements of their necropolitics of the material body, I quote it at length:

> As Garra Blanca, we have been protagonists in the street during the social uprising, expressing discontent and supporting the popular demands that clamor for a more just Chile.
>
> We understood how much we can help as a social organization as well as the power we have if we act together for a greater goal. The struggle has led us to put aside our legitimate differences.
>
> This phenomenon has made the authorities uncomfortable and has also unsettled sports journalism. They lack critical analysis and can't understand what's happening in the streets. What do they have left? To rely on criminalization and demonize hinchadas' organized actions.
>
> For example, listening to the simplistic and biased opinions of journalists such as Juan Cristóbal Guarello, it is clear that they aren't capable of making a detailed and rigorous analysis of what's happening, trying to impose an uneducated vision that lacks total objectivity and is therefore erroneous.
>
> It's impossible to make a proper analysis without considering the genesis of barras. [Guarello] signals that they're a product of neoliberalism when in reality we're an *engendro* ["offspring," but it typically means "monstrosity"] of the severity of the dictatorship in poor neighborhoods; youths with no spaces for amusement, expression, or sense of belonging to something. Garra Blanca's origin is completely social and rebellious.

> Guarello overlooks several political actions that we, as barra, have carried out during the dictatorship and the transition [to democracy]. His analysis rather discusses what barras were when they were polluted by club directors and [Garra Blanca's previous] disastrous administrations, who only sought personal profit.
>
> Garra Blanca has long recovered the role it should never have lost: an active and combative one. You can ask any protesters in the street about the role and relevance we've had in the protests. Many even feel safer with us than the police.
>
> While the press and club directors think about the money of CDF and advertisers, we have in our minds and hearts all of those who died, were tortured, and mutilated. For them, and every Chilean, we'll keep raising our voice!
>
> With hate and revenge, Garra Blanca move forward!

The statement establishes a moral contrast between the current Garra Blanca and the previous administration. They question the idea that hinchas are alienated subjects, presenting hinchadas as spaces for political participation and community cohesion. The post also validates violence as a means to safeguard others, express deep-seated anger, seek revenge against the state and corporations, and ultimately bring about social transformation within the framework of class struggle.

The statement is also a window into aguante's necropolitics of the material body. Garra Blanca angrily and revengefully perceive their bodies and politics as offsprings of state terror and savage neoliberalism. The monstrous meanings of the word *engendro* point to an understanding of the body as abject material whose immolation indexes agency and dignity. This necropolitics of the material body took on a profound sense of martyrdom during the social uprising as hinchas framed their violent clashes with law enforcement as sacrifices for a dignified life for the elderly and children—a conceptualization sensorially and ideologically amplified by the voice.

THE POLITICS OF VOCAL AGUANTE

Aguante has a unique sonic voice. Raising their soft palates, hinchas place sound in the back of their heads instead of their chests or throats, thus producing a deep, round sound. Hinchas tend to emphasize and sustain open vowels (i.e., *a*, *o*, and *u*) when vocalizing. In so doing, they disregard the Spanish elocution of open vowels: instead of voicing *a* as *ah*, *o* as *oh*, and *u* as *oo*, hinchas tend to use the *schwa* sound (i.e., *uh*) for open vowels. This practice makes aguante's vocality more loudly distinguishable in between verses. Scooby explains: "There's an element that characterizes South American barras: the vowels generate an echo. Each vowel produces an echo. The songs used to produce an echo in [National Stadium's gate] 14 that spread to [the] Andes [middle section] and reached the other side [of the stadium]. From far away it seemed like a war cry that came from the other side of the hill." The emphasis on volume and participation makes pitch precision irrelevant in aguante's vocality (Achondo 2021). Although timbre—understood as "everything about the sound of the voice except duration and pitch" (Eidsheim 2019, 10)—is important, an hincha's individual color becomes secondary to the hinchada's collective timbral sonority. As Herrera (2018) notes, "the high density of texture and timbre provides ideal cloaking of individual contributions that might not be too close to the expected pitches" (482).

Aguante intensity turns singing into a viscerally immediate practice. In the center of stands, hinchas cannot hear their own voices while vocalizing. Their sensory perception of the voice comes from the bodily vibrations generated by their vocalizations. Voice scholars have foregrounded the multisensory nature of vocal practice (Eidsheim 2015), noting that ideologies of personhood often emerge from the sonic co-resonance of the body and the vocal muscles (Cavarero 2005). As Adriana Cavarero (2005) puts it, "when the human voice vibrates, there is someone in flesh and bone who emits it" (4). Since hinchas experience their voices through their bodies, they tend to perceive the vocality of aguante as a pure visceral phenomenon.

Unsurprisingly, they contrast the immediacy of the voice with mediated practices of aguante. See, for instance, figure 4.2 where the statement "always destroying the voice" accompanies an image of a person holding a crossed-out phone. The screenshot points to a common concern among Los de Abajo: the growing preference among young hinchas for recording over singing. Tuto explains: "We fight against the cell phone shit. We fight against that in the barra. One time in the barra, we saw a guy in the drum area like this [imitates a person taking a selfie] and that shit pisses you off, man, you know? It can't be like that. Do you know what would've happened in the '90s? A slap and spit in the face, you know? And that was it. If you don't sing, you leave." Los de Abajo sharply distinguish between vocalizing and recording in the stands, imbuing them with moral connotations. While media platforms play a significant role in the reflective dissemination of

FIGURE 4.2 "Siempre rompiendo la voz." Screenshot taken from Los de Abajo's Facebook page.

aguante (the image was, in fact, uploaded to social media), virtuality functions as an antonym of vocal viscerality among hinchas.

But the picture also illustrates that aguante's phonosonic nexus involves a more destructive dimension as hinchas push their vocal organs to the point of hoarseness. This does not imply that they are unable to sustain extended periods of loud and vigorous singing. On the contrary, they argue that repeated vocalization strengthens the resilience of their voices over time. Riva explains: "You need to learn how to use the energy you have in your throat. At that time, we didn't have any money. We didn't have money to buy a soda. We went to the bathroom to try to wet the throat a little bit. Then, we came back to sing again. I believe that your vocal cords and the throat get stronger." Nevertheless, although they believe that forcing the vocal organs develops physical resistance, they also recognize that these constant exertions have short and long-term consequences. For example, Tuto explains the husky grain that currently characterizes his voice in the following way: "With the passing of time, my voice is now completely destroyed. Sometimes, as a side note, I sing for ten minutes and my voice doesn't come out anymore, but I have to keep going. I always keep destroying it. It's already destroyed."

Vocal damage is indeed a common occurrence among singers who lack proper vocal training. Apart from exerting excessive tension on the vocal muscles, the repetitive opening and closing of the vocal folds during loud and intense vocalizations can be particularly harmful. "Similar to the ways in which the skin will blister and swell more easily with repeated vigorous contact," Kelley Tatro (2014) writes, "the vocal folds are more susceptible to injury when vocalists use such force, which causes the vocal folds to crash together in a potentially harmful way" (439). While it is possible to learn techniques that minimize damage while producing extreme vocalizations, singers who engage in prolonged and frequent periods of loud and intense singing commonly experience symptoms such as hoarseness, breathiness, sore throat, and vocal fatigue.

Yet the destruction of the phonic is necropolitically pursued and morally valued among hinchas. Riva explains:

> It's pure adrenaline. The noise is deafening. There, the most important thing is to destroy the voice and feel the passion that everyone who's there is feeling. Because everyone sings there—unlike [other sections of the stadium] where people participate when everyone sings or when someone scores. No, it's exhausting there. You destroy your voice. You feel the passion of everyone who is there, [of those] who are singing nonstop, living and feeling it. There, you sing, you quiver. It's everything. It's the barra itself—the center of the hinchas' emotion. I'm waiting for my kid to grow up a bit more and will start bringing him to the stadium. [For him to have] what I missed: my dad bringing me to the stadium. I want him to see my passion. I'm sure that if he comes with me, he'll support the team. [He'll see me] chanting a lot, destroying the voice. Singing a lot, all the time. [That makes you] visible—a kid or a normal person. [You're] not a *flaite* [derogatory class slur], but a person of the barra, a normal citizen, a Chilean.

Riva's vocal morality resonates with Cavarero's (2005) insight that "the voice belongs to the living; it communicates the presence of an existent in flesh and bone; it signals a throat, a particular body" (177). Riva also connects political audibility and visibility to vocal damage. Singing to the point of destroying the voice interweaves production and destruction for him. He ties vocal damage to the ideals of responsible fatherhood and being a normal citizen—that is, someone who is neither a mere consumer nor a social anomaly.

This moralized vocal necropolitics is thus rooted in a broader context of structural silencing and inaudibility within Chilean society. The act of destroying the vocal organs becomes a means to assert dignity and demand political attention. Tuto expresses:

> In today's corporate football model, we are only valued as things that increase the profits of a company. Our right is, after paying, to enjoy the spectacle. Before the public limited sports companies, that right was real. You had a voice [and] you could raise that voice and suggest ideas to help society. [Now] they want to silence our voice. We have all those kinds of situations where everything that defines us as humans is trampled and corrupted. And that's what scares me: that that dehumanization becomes normal. [So] we must leave the voice in the stands and the life in singing, we must destroy the voice. We [must make] audible the voice of a lot of people who otherwise can't make it audible. The dignity of these people can't be sold.

By pushing the limits of the phonosonic nexus, hinchas not only demonstrate their loyalty to their clubs but also assert their own value within a precarious neoliberal structure. In a society where proletarian voices are systematically ignored or suppressed, the act of forcefully vocalizing to the point of vocal damage becomes an expression of resilience and a refusal to be silenced. By challenging liberal-democratic ethics and aesthetics, hinchas adopt monstrous tropes to vocally and self-destructively confront the violences and precarities they see as direct catalysts of the social uprising. It is a necropolitical way to reclaim agency and demand recognition—a statement of defiance and existence in a context of dehumanization.

This insight became evident during the social uprising as U. de Chile hinchas began to repeatedly signify the destruction of the phonosonic nexus as voicing dignity. Los de Abajo, for instance, shared the following message on social media while urging people to participate in the demonstration on October 24: "For those who are no longer here and those who are not born yet! For our grandparents and our children! For no more repression in stadiums! For no more Safe Stadium Plan! Los de Abajo, the revolution, brave and combative! We're the voice of those who got tired of screaming for a life with dignity." Amid social unrest fueled by deeply ingrained disparities, hinchas recognized that the persistent dismissal and suppression of their voices extended beyond their individual experiences, perpetuating the exclusion of the proletariat as a whole from public discourse. The act of singing until the point of destroying the voice became a corporeal expression of solidarity and empathy, redefining aguante's necropolitics as a collective struggle for social justice. Through vocal damage, hinchas symbolically and materially rebelled against forces that sought to silence and marginalize them. In the face of systemic inequality, commodified human relations, state abandonment, and structural silencing and inaudibility, this moral act of destructive vocalization began to signify a collective pursuit for a life with dignity—a necropolitical defense of the dignity of a broader impoverished community.

THE LIMITS OF MORAL AGUANTE

Despite the moral emphasis on solidarity, aguante's warfare did not recede during the social uprising—quite the contrary. Being viewed as more revolutionary, combative, and martyr-like than rivals emerged as new assets within the aguante conflict. These moral struggles were not merely symbolic as hinchas began to compete over public spaces so as to be seen and heard destroying their material voices. This led to numerous clashes between U. de Chile, U. Católica, and Colo-Colo hinchas. Miguel narrates a particular event to illustrate these hostilities:

> Yesterday, [I saw] two stupid kids with an Indian banner while another drunk asshole was starting fights. When it was over, and we were leaving, two kids came up celebrating that they had stolen a Colo-Colo banner and a jersey. Another guy couldn't accept that Colo-Colo flags were in the square while we were there and started a fight, all by himself, but when the Indians replied, his entire group got involved. In the end, the [peaceful protesters] kicked us out while booing us. I personally told an Indian, who was literally ten feet away from [La Banda de la Chile's] instruments, to leave. I noticed that many were looking at him with anger, but I was quick enough to ask him to leave.

I personally experienced these tensions in late November, when walking toward Plaza Italia while wearing a T-shirt that said "Volveremos" (We'll Come Back) with La U's symbol. I saw two people walking toward me with a flag, but I did not pay attention as I was checking my phone. When I raised my head, I realized that they were Colo-Colo hinchas. One of them defiantly snapped at me: "Qué vay a volver, madre conch'e tu ma're" (roughly, "returning to what, motherfucking mommy" [misogynistic nickname given to U. de Chile hinchas]). I was taken aback and froze in the moment, but they kept walking.

In January 2020, necropolitical tensions reached their peak when Garra Blanca ambushed Los de Abajo at the National Stadium. The latter were gathering donations for the victims of a massive wildfire in Valparaíso. During the ambush, Colo-Colo hinchas stole one of Los de Abajo's official banners. Some U. de Chile hinchas retaliated swiftly, stealing almost all of Garra Blanca's official banners, along with some items from the barra's front line. I was told that an hincha died during the confrontation.

During the social crisis, hinchas' behavior both challenged and reinforced hegemonic discourses portraying them as bodily embodiments of neoliberal alienation, thereby illustrating the political constraints of aguante's necropolitics. The performative moralities of aguante and dignidad form a double-bladed sword within hinchadas, embedding and constraining their bodies, voices, and forms of life within a framework of irreconcilable enmity. In underscoring the morality of aguante, then, I have not sought to romanticize it but rather to foreground the productive centrality of symbolic and material destruction in the political praxis of hinchadas—a conceptualization of violence informed by and responsive to the social conditions that ignited the social uprising. In addition to recapitulating the arguments presented in this chapter, the conclusion asserts that the sounds of aguante were prophetic of social unrest.

CONCLUSION

On October 24, shortly after the demonstration described at the beginning of this chapter, I met up with my friend Kanito at Plaza Ñuñoa, the heart of the privileged neighborhood where I was staying. The festive atmosphere, which was prevalent among the upper middle class in the preceding days, had grown even more intense: Demonstrators were drinking beer, smoking marijuana, playing music, singing along, and dancing to salsa and electronic dance music. I could not help but compare this party-like setting to the image of Los de Abajo singing under tear gas. Eventually, Kanito asked me if I intended to write about the social unrest. I mentioned that I was considering writing a chapter exploring aguante in relation to the social uprising. "That makes sense," he reflected, "in a way, football has long been shedding light on the underlying problems that lie at the heart of this crisis." I added that it made them not only visible but also audible.

Jacques Attali (2017) is well known for using music as a means to explore "the possibility of a superstructure to *anticipate* historical developments, to foreshadow new social formations in a prophetic and annunciatory way" (Jameson 2017, xi;

emphasis in the original). According to Attali, in the Repetition regime that has prevailed in the West since the nineteenth century, the culture industries have taken music away from communities, silencing individuals and erasing their ability to participate in social negotiations. Despite this rather bleak depiction, Attali also identifies an underground form of insurrection in the collective creation of content—a nascent regime he refers to as Composition: "Composition thus appears as a negation of the division of roles and labor as constructed by the old codes . . . beyond the realm of music, [it] calls into question the distinction between worker and consumer, between doing and destroying, a fundamental division of roles in all societies in which usage is defined by the code; to compose is to take pleasure in the instruments, the tools of communication, in use-time and exchange-time as lived and no longer as stockpiled" (2017, 135). Music studies has emphasized the utopian potential of Composition, arguing that by reclaiming "the means of producing art," it could democratize musical practice "for all members of society" (McClary 2017, 156).

However, some scholars have noted the sociopolitical shortcomings of Composition. Eric Drott (2015) argues that Attali's inversion of the base-superstructure relation ends up valorizing mental over manual, elite over proletarian, labor. In glorifying neoliberal notions of freedom, Attali makes "an apologia for measures that would make an already precarious economic lifeworld even more so" (753). Robin James (2019) offers a similar critique, suggesting that Composition transforms subjects into "entrepreneurs, disruptors, and the like" (49), portraying these roles as agents of liberation while concealing underlying mechanisms of alienation.

Despite Jacques Attali's generally optimistic tone, he acknowledges Composition's ambiguous potentials for liberation. He writes:

> Should we read this emergence as the herald of a liberation from exchange-value, or only of the emplacement of a new trap for music and its consumers, that of auto-manipulation? The answer to these questions, I think, depends on the radicality of the experiment. Inducing people to compose using predefined instruments cannot lead to a mode of production different from that authorized by those instruments.
>
> That is the trap. The trap of false liberation through the distribution to each individual of the instruments of his own alienation, tools for self-sacrifice, both monitoring and monitored. (141)

Although he is not necessarily recognizing the aforementioned critiques, this caveat permits a more nuanced approach to the suggestive promotion of music as an anticipatory force. As Fredric Jameson (2017) points out, "both dystopia and utopia are thus contained in the new forms as possibilities whose realization only political praxis can decide" (xiii).

I contend that the vocal necropolitics of Chilean hinchas were prophetic of the deployment of violence and the destruction of the body as a means of insurrection during the social uprising. These vocalizations, in parceling out the "visible and invisible" (Rancière 2004, 19) and amplifying the violence entrenched within impoverished neighborhoods, foreshadowed the self-destructive yet morally charged response of marginalized citizens to neoliberal precarity. Both the tropes of sensory impairment employed by hegemonic commentators and the frustration expressed by hinchas underline the systemic muting of proletarian precarity under neoliberalism. The monstrous vocalizations of aguante rendered audible modes of relationality, political action, and body politics shaped by and in response to the commodification of human care and relations in neoliberal Chile. These abject vocal sounds anticipated the use of violence as a necropolitical tool during the social uprising—a scenario in which subjects immolated their bodies as an expression of dignity while simultaneously engaging in confrontations with fellow protesters to exert social control and create asymmetrical hierarchies.

To a certain extent, then, Guarello's critique of barras as products of savage neoliberalism holds some validity. Hinchas themselves tend to embrace this characterization when they define themselves as engendros—monstrosities emerged and cultivated by neoliberal violence and precarity. By appropriating the monstrous trope, hinchas create an abject phonosonic nexus. However, their self-awareness and active participation in the social uprising demonstrate the limitations of Guarello's analysis. The fact that some citizens have exploited opportunities presented by neoliberal deregulation to engage in criminality should not be misconstrued as contentment with this reality. Hinchas' emphasis on achieving a life with dignity for future generations indicates their yearning, if not outright hope, for a life that transcends the confines of necropolitics. Describing human life under neoliberalism solely in utilitarian or oppressive terms reflects a form of "ethnographic refusal" (Ortner 1995). It is crucial to adopt more nuanced approaches that acknowledge the diverse meanings, effects, and political dimensions of life within neoliberalism. Such approaches should consider the varied ways individuals navigate and respond to their economic and political circumstances.

Vocal aguante foregrounds both symbolic and material interpretations of destruction within neoliberal contexts. Neoliberalism has forged precarious bodies stripped of fundamental rights, positioning hinchas as emblematic embodiments of this precarity. Their torn voices are not merely cries of dissent but living testimonies to the devastating impact of neoliberal policies on their bodies. In the face of inequality and a lack of recognition, individuals destroy the phonosonic nexus to assert their agency and preserve their dignity. This chapter has thus showcased how necropolitical deployments of the voice can serve to express agency, demand audibility, and affirm the worth of human life. It has demonstrated that the destruction of vocal organs can voice highly moralized ideologies about life and death, peace and violence, utopia and dystopia.

Epilogue

The scenes that unfolded at Mexico's Corregidor Stadium on March 5, 2022, sent necrotic shockwaves across the Americas. The cacophony of war cries and calls for help provided a horrifying soundtrack to the images of brutalized Atlas fans. The violent acts committed by Querétaro hinchas shattered the conventional perception of Mexican football fandom, previously characterized as anti-systemic yet still agonistic (Magazine 2007). Commentators from various South American countries expressed dismay, suggesting that aguante had finally made its way to Mexico. I was not fully surprised by the tragedy, as I had been hearing bombos con platillo and aguante chants in broadcasts of Mexican matches for years. The sounds of aguante seemed to foreshadow the violence that unfolded at Corregidor Stadium.

This book has contended that aguante has forged a transnational public assembly in which geographically distant proletarians engage in immediate and mediated dialogues and conflicts. By emphasizing the significance of fan practice on par with the sport itself, this multisited formation challenges conventional views of sports audiences as passive consumers while making audible the effects of the hyper-commodification of football and social life in the Southern Cone. Yet this does not mean that aguante functions as "an open and expansive network," a multitude "in which all differences can be expressed freely and equally, a network that provides the means of encounter so that we can work and live in common" (Hardt and Negri 2004, xiii–xiv). Aguante also amplifies the necropolitical overtones of remediation. Circulation and interconnection can lead to publics marked by degeneration and self-destruction. While aguante provides hinchas a (trans)local platform to amplify their deprived social conditions and voice their ideological positions, it also facilitates the emergence of unjust, asymmetrical, and even deadly forms of politics and governance.

In addition to underscoring the necropolitics of aguante circulation, the events at the Corregidor Stadium demonstrate that my argument regarding the (trans)locality of aguante has fallen short. This cosmopolitan public assembly can no longer be confined to the Southern Cone alone. Rather, it has extended its influence throughout all of Latin America. Hinchas in Brazil, Colombia, Peru, Bolivia, Ecuador, Venezuela, and even Mexico actively participate in (trans)local feedback loops, competing among themselves to determine which hinchada possesses more aguante.[1]

The continental circulation of aguante raises questions about the material and symbolic configuration of Latin America. While the concept of Latin America tends to homogenize cultural difference by promoting specific forms of Latin Americanism, it also underscores that these cultural projects hold significant meaning for many Latin Americans. As Pablo Palomino (2020) writes, "Latin America is not a historically rigorous delimitation, but neither it is just a romantic invocation or a melancholic lamentation of a racial and therefore radical sociocultural difference from the United States" (212). Transcontinental phenomena like aguante highlight that the region transcends mere cultural constructivism, emphasizing the material conditions that inform this imagined community. The resonance of an originally Argentine soundworld among hinchas from Santiago to Querétaro illustrates that some Latin American subalterns share common concerns, desires, and realities. Recent studies argue that vulnerability and marginalization have fostered the development of post-national imaginaries across the Americas (Chávez 2017; Corona and Madrid 2007; Minks and Ochoa Gautier 2021). Aguante has become a meaningful and appealing imaginary for geographically distant subjects, allowing them to participate in a broader cosmopolitan public where they can challenge dominant politics and narratives.

The transcontinental expansion of aguante has coincided with the densification of the fandom's circuits and modes of remediation. Seeking to replicate the success of "Brasil, decime qué se siente," Argentines endeavored to compose and promote viral chants in support of their national team during subsequent World Cups. The viral failure of the 2018 chants starkly contrasts with the success of "Muchachos, ahora nos volvimos a ilusionar" (Boys, Now Let's Dream Again), the anthem that saturated stadiums in Qatar during 2022. Composed by Fernando Romero, a millennial schoolteacher, this piece continues the trend of re-versioning aguante contrafacta to create sanitized chants to rally behind the national team. The lyrics address traumatic events in the Argentine collective memory—the Falklands War, lost finals, and Maradona's death—contrasting them with the current football scenario, filled with optimism following Argentina's victory against Brazil in the 2021 Copa América final. If the 2014 World Cup final had infused "Brasil, decime qué se siente" with traumatic overtones, "Muchachos, ahora nos volvimos a ilusionar" became intertwined with the world championship (video 5.1):

En Argentina nací
Tierra del Diego y Lionel
De los pibes de Malvinas
Que jamás olvidaré
No te lo puedo explicar
Porque no vas a entender
Las finales que perdimos
Cuantos años las lloré
Pero eso se terminó
Porque en el Maracaná
La final con los brazucas
La volvió a ganar papá
Muchachos
Ahora nos volvimos a ilusionar
Quiero ganar la tercera
Quiero ser campeón mundial
Y al Diego
Desde el cielo lo podemos ver
Con Don Diego y con La Tota
Alentándolo a Lionel
Y ser campeones otra vez

In Argentina, I was born
Land of Diego and Lionel
From the kids of the Malvinas
That I will never forget
I can't explain it
Because you'll never understand it
The finals we lost
How much I cried for them
But that's over
Because in the Maracaná
The final with the Brazilians
Was, again, won by your daddy
Boys
Now let's dream again
I want to win the third one
I want to be world champions
And Diego
From the sky we can see him
With Don Diego and Tota
[Maradona's parents]
Cheering Lionel on
And to be champions again

Recognizing the viral potential of the chant, La Mosca Tsé-Tsé, the composers of the original melody, reached out to Romero to collaborate on a music video (video 5.2). The re-versioned song, which incorporated a surdo drum and a bombo con platillo playing murga porteña, led to Romero being registered as a coauthor. With fifty-five million views, it is currently the second most popular video on YouTube for La Mosca Tsé-Tsé.[2] The highly produced video of a rock band performing aguante contrafacta only confirmed the transmedia ties between football, aguante, and popular music in the Southern Cone.

But "Muchachos, ahora nos volvimos a ilusionar" was not the only chant reversioned during the 2022 World Cup. In July 2024 an Instagram livestream by Enzo Fernández, a player for Chelsea and the Argentine national team, ignited a controversy that reached the highest levels of government. The video, which captured the Argentine squad celebrating their victory over Colombia in the 2024 Copa América final, showed several players singing a contentious chant that had been originally composed for the 2022 World Cup (video 5.3):

Escuchen, corran la bola	Listen, pass the ball
Juegan en Francia	They play for France
Pero son todos de Angola	But they're all from Angola
Qué lindo es	So cute
Van a correr	They'll run away
Son cometravas	They're cometravas [transphobic slur]
Como el puto de Mbappé	Like that puto [Kylian] Mbappé
Su vieja es nigeriana	Their old lady is from Cameroon
Su viejo camerunés	Their old man from Nigeria
Pero en el documento	But in their passports
Nacionalidad francés	French nationality

The chant, aimed at intensifying the rivalry sparked by Argentina's victory over France in the World Cup final, included discriminatory comments about French star Kylian Mbappé, who had been in a relationship with the transgender model Ines Rau. The lyrics also contained racist remarks about Africa and people of African descent, conflating nations colonized by France, Portugal, and the United Kingdom into a single colonial whole. The chant's racism, homophobia, and transphobia were sharply criticized by Black athletes, including Fernández's Chelsea teammates. The situation escalated when Argentina's president, Javier Milei, defended the player, tweeting: "No colonialist country will intimidate us over a stadium chant or for speaking the truths that no one wants to admit. Enough with feigned indignation, hypocrites. . . . Argentines, always hold your heads high! Long live Argentine-ness!" (quoted in BBC *News Mundo* 2024). While "Muchachos, ahora nos volvimos a ilusionar" exemplifies new, sanitized practices, "Escuchen, corran la bola" illustrates the deep cultural roots of violence within aguante. The chant underscores how necropolitics shapes aguante's soundworld, embodying an understanding of sound and music as tools for engaging in both local and transnational conflicts.

Indeed, in this book, I have amplified the cultural and political outcomes of violence. My aim has been to provide an ethical yet morally volatile representation of a necropolitical formation by avoiding the framing of destruction and production as opposing binaries. I have presented violence as an everyday, atmospheric force capable of constructing cultures and forging subjectivities. In doing so, I have highlighted how varied deployments of violence can simultaneously fight and enact injustice and inequality. This approach has led me to avoid portraying aguante as populated by heroes and villains. Instead, I have argued that we are all somewhat complicit in the emergence and reproduction of this death-world. Necropolitics forces us to embrace the messiness and ambiguities of neoliberalism in the Global South.

This alternative public assembly, facilitated through the creation of feedback loops involving immediate and mediated violence, has given rise to a necropolitical acoustemology. Aguante necropolitics, as a world-making force, has transformed understandings and deployments of sound and music, reframing practices of voicing, silencing, sounding, listening, and musicking in terms of conflict and violence. Sound, as a source and expression of necropower, possesses the capacity to disrupt bodies and minds, enabling hinchas to influence players, peers, rivals, and the outcomes of games. However, sound also empowers hinchas to assert agency within larger, asymmetrical dynamics in the realms of sports and society. Whether representing or acting as violence, the sounds of aguante have evolved into tools for inciting rebellion, exercising social control, and engaging in radicalized conflicts, both within and between hinchadas. By overwhelming subjectivities and relationalities, aguante's necropolitical acoustemology has played a central role in shaping its vivid death-world. Aguante serves as an example of the generative, creative, and transformative potential of sonic violence.

I have also approached sound as an object with fluid analytical boundaries. One of the key theoretical contributions of Feld's acoustemology is its epistemological break from analyses exclusively centered on finite manifestations of expressive culture, such as music. But approaching aguante acoustemologically does not imply rejecting musical forms and practices, which are significantly covered in this book. Rather, it means situating music within a broader soundworld, foregrounding the holistic and contingent processes involved in the production, perception, and conceptualization of sound. Comprehending aguante as a way of thinking and being in the world requires paying equal attention to the various sonic expressions and practices of listening mediating it, understanding them as interconnected sources of acoustic knowledge and sonic expression. Highlighting "music's sounded-ness" (Sakakeeny 2015, 122) entails underscoring the porous boundaries between chants, songs, fireworks, whistling, drumming, and other sonic practices of fandom performed by hinchas.

In illustrating the contingent acoustemological knowledge developed within necropolitical formations shaped by global inequalities, I have sought to contribute to recent critiques of the predominance of Global North phenomena, ontologies, and epistemologies in sound studies. Scholarship on sound and listening has predominantly focused on Euro-American practices, dynamics, and experiences, leading to problematic generalizations about listening subjects and sound relations (Feld 2012; Kane 2015; Novak and Sakakeeny 2015; Steingo 2019; Steingo and Sykes 2019; Sterne 2015; Ochoa Gautier 2014, 2019). As Gavin Steingo and Jim Sykes (2019) point out, decolonizing sound studies does not mean remapping northern-centered themes and theories onto the Global South. Rather, it involves developing a cartography for sound studies that recognizes subaltern formations as active mediators of global life, not merely as conduits for knowledge and expressions from the Global North. In their own words, it means "taking seriously the existence of multiple ontologies" (18).

Beyond its contributions to music and sound studies, this book has also provided a critical examination of the concreteness and contingency of neoliberalism. Critics argue that neoliberalism has become a catchall term used to discuss a wide array of issues, from socioeconomic structures and forms of governance to contemporary subjectivities (Ganti 2014), asserting that its vague and all-encompassing nature renders it theoretically useless (Dunn 2017). However, neoliberalism is far from an abstract concept in the Global South. The Southern Cone has been a crucial testing ground for neoliberal policies since the 1970s, making the term a concrete and prominent topic in regional public discourse. Nevertheless, in emphasizing the concreteness of neoliberalism, I have not promoted a homogenizing view of late capitalism. Instead, I have underscored the contextual nature of neoliberal formations—social, political, and economic realities characterized by contingent dynamics and structures. My intention has been to foster a more nuanced discussion of neoliberalism, highlighting its plurality. By foregrounding the diverse manifestations of late capitalism, I have challenged the sweeping analyses offered by scholars like Hardt and Negri (2000, 2004, 2009, 2017), who portray the contemporary neoliberal world as a uniform social, economic, and political entity. While interconnected, neoliberal spaces also display distinct characteristics in the Global South—capitalist frictions that are vividly illustrated through sports.

Football, one of the most hyper-commodified phenomena in the contemporary world, vividly illustrates the contingent materiality of neoliberalism. A central mediator of South American urban realities, it is unsurprising that neoliberal actors and forces have sought to engulf the sport. Investors have fetishized the passion surrounding football—intensities paradoxically created by the hinchas themselves—while simultaneously attempting to transform stadium practices and behaviors into experiences marked by peaceful observation and active consumption. Reflecting the increasing commodification of human relations in the Southern Cone, hinchas perceive the liberalization of the sport as an existential threat to their way of being and thinking. Yet hinchas also exhibit an ambiguous relationship with neoliberalism. While they lament their reduction to mere consumers, they also embrace transactional and accumulative approaches to the material and symbolic resources of football. The crystallization and evolution of aguante have paralleled broader societal shifts toward privatized approaches to violence, resulting in a messy, contradictory formation that both emerges from and reacts to neoliberalism.

In this context, sound and music emerge as arenas for navigating a radicalized, conflict-based reality. Collectives and individuals who refrain from participating in deadly confrontations have sought to develop creative ways to navigate aguante. Nevertheless, nonviolent exertions of sonic power have normally been silenced or overshadowed by the sonorous expressions of those who govern hinchadas. In the aguante world, necropower supersedes biopower.

Recent scholarship has challenged the notion of sound as an unbounded biopolitical force, demonstrating how it can echo and reinforce the constraints of social movements in late capitalism (James 2019; Tausig 2019). While sound can foster communities, radicalize actors, and amplify messages, it can also reveal "how agency caroms and fractures, how political actors often find themselves bouncing off walls rather than passing frictionlessly through them" (Tausig 2019, 8). Sound is mediated by networks, structures, and relations of power from which it cannot easily escape or effect change independently. While I have portrayed sound as a source and exertion of power, I have also emphasized its social and political limitations. Sonic aguante, while insurgent, can also be regressive, simultaneously challenging and perpetuating injustice and inequality.

However, aguante's constraints and contradictions do not diminish its essence as a political project. Necropolitics is politics, even if readers find it objectionable on moral, ethical, or political grounds. Aguante embodies a distinct ideology and positionality—an alternative political stance that deliberately incorporates violence as a tool in the hyper-commodified arenas of sports and society. In a context marked by radicalized conflicts and limited political avenues, violence becomes a mode of insurrection against neoliberal structures and a way to navigate hostile dynamics within and between hinchadas. Violence, as the most significant material and symbolic resource within fandom, manifests in both direct and mediated forms, challenging conventional ethics and aesthetics. Aguante thus represents a radical and confrontational form of politics, disrupting the status quo.

Ultimately, as a modest witness, I have sought to narrate the effects of violence within a specific soundworld of the Global South, underscoring the necrotic dynamics that decades of neoliberalism have imposed on South America's most precarious spaces. The sense of pessimism this book may evoke has been intentional. Presenting a sanitized, optimistic view of aguante would have been disingenuous. Achieving a more utopian future requires systemic changes in the global and local circulation and distribution of capital—the very dynamics that have produced and reproduced aguante's necropolitics and that have also facilitated the research and publication of this book. Only through structural transformation can a true "fiesta culture" (Alabarces 2012, 132) emerge: a fandom where conflict remains as a symbolic competition between adversaries rather than enemies, overcoming its degenerative aspects while continuing to produce subaltern politics and expressions.

GLOSSARY

AHA: Asociación de Hinchas Azules (Association of Blue Hinchas), political organization of U. Chile hinchas

Azul Azul: Public Limited Sports Company controlling Universidad de Chile

Barra: An organization of hinchas

Boca Juniors: Argentine football club

Colo-Colo: Chilean football club

Corfuch: Nonprofit that controlled Universidad de Chile before Azul Azul

Escuela de Tablones: A collective of San Lorenzo hinchas

Hincha: A football fan or supporter

Hinchada: Roughly, a club's fanbase

Huracán: Argentine football club

Independiente: Argentine football club

La Banda de la Chile: Los de Abajo's music ensemble

La Gloriosa Butteler: The San Lorenzo barra

Las Bulla: Collective of female hinchas of Universidad de Chile

Los de Abajo: The Universidad de Chile barra

Racing Club: Argentine football club

River Plate: Argentine football club

San Lorenzo: Argentine football club

U. de Chile: Chilean football club (do not confuse with the university)

U. Católica: Chilean football club (do not confuse with the university)

NOTES

Introduction

1. Football scholars typically classify fanbases into three distinct groups (Archetti 1984). They label *barrabravas* (hooligans) those who engage in violent and criminal behavior, *hinchas militantes* (militant supporters) those who participate in nonviolent fan practices, and *espectadores* (spectators) those who merely attend games. I have chosen to omit these classifications for two reasons: They are not emic terms and also blur the inherent fluidity of these social spaces. Instead, I refer to these individuals as hinchas—a term my collaborators employ to define themselves—and examine ethnographically how they partake in the conflicts and organizations discussed within this book.

2. To distinguish between the club and the university, I will refer to the former as U. de Chile (as is customary in football jargon) and the latter as Universidad de Chile.

3. All quotations in Spanish were translated by me.

4. The terms *barra* and *hinchada* are subjects of debate. While some individuals employ them interchangeably, others argue that the latter signifies the entirety of a fanbase, whereas the former refers to the most radical section within an hinchada. In this instance, for instance, Los de Abajo is the barra within the U. de Chile hinchada. This book will adopt this distinction, thus distinguishing between barras and hinchadas.

5. Corfuch stands for "Corporación de fútbol de la Universidad de Chile" (football Corporation of the University of Chile).

6. Bulla (Noise) is a nickname for both U. de Chile and its fanbase, conflating the two. It implies that the club and its hinchada are one construct. Pedrero is the location of Colo-Colo's Monumental Stadium. Zorra (fox) is a misogynist nickname for Colo-Colo hinchas. Although it can be translated as "whore," I have chosen not to translate it because the everyday use of such utterances does not carry the same meanings and implications in Latin America as it does in the United States. I have followed this approach for most of the sexist and homophobic slurs present in this book.

7. *Indio* (Indian) is a word used to call Colo-Colo hinchas. Named after a colonial-era Indigenous warrior, this club uses Indigenous words and images as part of their celebra-

tion of *mestizaje*—an ideology that contends that Latin America is the product of the positive biological and cultural mixture of Indigenous, African, and European people. Here, Indio does not necessarily carry a pejorative connotation.

8. Aguante research has predominantly focused on male embodiments. While the male domination of aguante persists, women do participate in the fan culture, especially in Chile. Tapia and Vergara (2017) have explored notions of aguante among female hinchas of Santiago Wanderers, foregrounding their assimilation of "masculine schemes of perception and valorization" (282). Although I have observed analogous dynamics among certain female hinchas of U. de Chile, I have also encountered women who reject these frameworks, framing aguante as a font and manifestation of feminist empowerment.

9. While Chile and Uruguay do not track data on football-related deaths, 339 Argentines have died, according to the NGO Salvemos el Fútbol (Let's Save Football). However, this count only includes individuals who have died in or near stadiums. The number of hinchas who continue to die in other settings remains silently unaccounted for.

10. Some words about class are necessary here. In South America, "clase media" and "clase trabajadora" ("middle class" and "working class," respectively) do not signify the same as in Anglophone spaces. Although middle-class citizens are perceived to be located "below the elite yet above the poor and working masses" (Parker 2013, 3), demarcations are hazy and unstable in the Southern Cone. In fact, substantial segments of the middle class are frequently associated with traits typically linked to the working class in the Global North: frugality, scarcity, and reliance on state services. Individuals deemed middle class are those who, while not impoverished, "struggle to make ends meet," as one hincha once told me. This comparison does not seek to equate the experiences of the working and middle classes but rather to emphasize that, despite varying degrees of precarity and disenfranchisement, they share a subaltern condition. As underscored by Pablo Alabarces, aguante's constituents are "the middle, lower-middle, and lower classes, in other words, the subaltern classes of every society" (Alabarces 2012, 123).

11. For readers familiar with South American cultures, societies, and relations, this designation may appear arbitrary, given the region's porous borders. Furthermore, those knowledgeable about South American football cultures may argue that the entire region, including southern Brazil, shares a common fandom. My definition of the Southern Cone as a space constituted by Chile, Argentina, and Uruguay is driven by conceptual and methodological considerations. First, it has emerged as a native term to discuss cultural, social, and economic exchanges among these three countries. Second, I limit my focus to these three countries to provide a certain degree of feasibility to my multisited ethnography. Including additional countries in the research would have posed significant methodological challenges.

12. The stylistic and semiotic heterogeneity of aguante demands analyses that depart from the Argentine exceptionalism dominating scholarly and public conversations about

South American football—statements positing that everything that is productive and destructive in the Southern Cone is Argentina's fault.

13. In addition to San Lorenzo, the Big Five is made up of River Plate, Boca Juniors, Independiente, and Racing, teams that will be referenced throughout the book. Huracán, San Lorenzo's archrival, also comes up in this book.

14. U. de Chile is one of the big three of Chilean football alongside Colo-Colo and Universidad Católica. Like the Universidad de Chile, the Pontificia Universidad Católica (Pontifical Catholic University, PUC), the country's leading private academic institution, also created a team in the 1930s.

15. Clásico Universitario refers to matches between U. de Chile and U. Católica. Throughout this book, the term *clásico* will be used continuously. It signifies a heated historical rivalry between two teams. In the United Kingdom, such matches are known as derbies (e.g., Manchester United versus Liverpool in England and Rangers versus Celtic in Scotland). The rivalries between the Boston Red Sox and the New York Yankees, and the Boston Celtics and the Los Angeles Lakers would be considered clásicos in South America. These matches often receive a nickname.

ONE *(Trans)local Feedbacks*

1. While Cachila is correct in noting that aguante has influenced fans in Rio Grande do Sul, there are still torcidas in Southern Brazil.

2. Porteño and porteña (masculine and feminine, respectively) mean "from the port" and signify anything or anyone from Buenos Aires.

3. Neighborhoods of Independiente and Racing Club, and Boca Juniors, respectively.

4. As discussed later, La Gloriosa Butteler takes its name from the square where its members gather.

5. Tango, developed in the *arrabales* (outskirts) of Buenos Aires, initially revolved around male experiences within the underworld. This is evident in tango's celebration of the *compadrito*, a tough, street-smart, and manipulative outlaw. As tango transformed into a mainstream urban popular genre, its emphasis on unruliness diminished, but its lyrics retained their intense bitterness and ill-humored tone, often portraying love and everyday life in notably pessimistic, if not fatalistic, terms. The bruised dignity of the poor, extensively explored in tango, eventually became the prevailing experience of Argentine working-class male subjects.

6. The origins of the melody remain somewhat ambiguous. The tune was reportedly sung in various settings, including carnivals, football clubs, and a graphic workers union, even before its formal recording (Adamovsky and Buch 2016).

7. Uruguay is the country with the third-highest number of appearances in the tournament's final. As of 2024, Brazil leads the list with forty-one appearances, followed closely

by Argentina with thirty-eight appearances.

8. They also differ in terms of presentation and performance.

9. Despite these associations, it is important to note that murga uruguaya has a longstanding connection with football, commenting on sports events and incorporating elements of its lexicon to signify its practices (Kirschstein 2007).

10. Rafael Di Zeo, the leader of La 12, once said that they were the Harvard University of barras.

11. This changed in the 2020s as ESPN and Fox Sports moved away from this transnational approach, creating national channels, establishing local headquarters, and hiring local journalists and commentators.

12. Their two most viewed YouTube videos—5.3 and 2.3 million views, respectively—are edited versions of previas.

TWO *Attribution and Creativity*

1. This emphasis on stadium materiality is a common theme among sports fans. Remember, for instance, how Americans talk about Fenway Park, Wrigley Field, or Madison Square Garden.

2. River Plate hinchas set their stadium on fire when they were relegated to the second division in 2011.

3. Puto literally means "male-whore" and functions as a homophobic slur.

4. In 2013 the Argentine football federation prohibited the attendance of away hinchas, arguing that it would stop aguante violence.

5. Huracán hinchas make similar connections when they assert that Parque Patricios is a "barrio de guapos" (a neighborhood of tough guys) (Garriga 2007). At the turn of the century, this place used to be an arrabal. Huracán hinchas tend to establish imaginary connections with the compadrito.

6. It is ironic that Creedence Clearwater Revival was at the center of one of the most notorious copyright lawsuits in Intellectual Property history. Fantasy Records, the label owning the rights for Creedence Clearwater Revival's songs, accused John Fogerty of plagiarizing himself in a solo album recorded after the band broke up.

7. An intersection two blocks away from Butteler Square.

THREE *Affect and Labor*

1. The bill was introduced by Sebastián Piñera, who later served as Chile's president for two nonconsecutive terms (2010–2014 and 2018–2022). Piñera, a fan of U. Católica, acquired 13.7 percent of the stocks of the sports corporation overseeing Colo-Colo (Matamala 2015). Notably, two major shareholders of Azul Azul were Carlos Heller, a member

of the billionaire Solari family, owner of the multinational chain Falabella, among other businesses, and José Yuraszeck, a former member of the Pinochet regime who was infamously convicted of fraud during the privatization of Chilectra, the country's former state-owned electrical energy company.

2. In Spanish, most nouns and adjectives are gendered. The masculine form is typically marked by ending with the letter "o," while the feminine form ends with the letter "a."

FOUR *Vocal Damage*

1. The police had been involved in one of the biggest corruption cases in the country's history. Additionally, they do not pay for public transportation. Camilo Catrillanca, a Mapuche farmer, was murdered by the police.

Epilogue

1. In fact, it can be argued that aguante has generated feedback loops that transcend the Americas. Jack (2024) foregrounds that the Ultra movement has evolved into a transnational phenomenon, noting that while supporters in Ireland and Germany have largely adopted stylistic and rhetorical elements from Italian fans, they have also drawn inspiration from Argentina, impacting musicking and performance styles. These transatlantic exchanges highlight the (trans)local frictions sparked by football, which have intensified with the rise of digital media. Rather than leading to homogenization, these cycles of influence are characterized by disjunctions and variations. Although football has facilitated the development of transnational imaginaries and interactions, these interconnected (trans)local publics remain profoundly diverse and compounded, shaped by distinct local dynamics.

2. "Muchachos, Esta Noche Me Emborracho," with its prominent visual and sonic references to tango, the compadrito, and the arrabal, has eleven million views.

BIBLIOGRAPHY

Achondo, Luis. 2021. "A Cry for Palestine: Vocal Practice and Imaginaries of Palestinianness among Chilean Football Supporters of Club Deportivo Palestino." *Ethnomusicology Forum* 30 (2): 302–23.

———. 2022. "Musical Messaging: The Social and Anti-Social Affordances of WhatsApp in the Football Culture of the Latin American Southern Cone." *Twentieth-Century Music* 19 (3): 517–36.

———. 2023. "The Silent Majority: Social and Aural Silence in the Games of Chile Men's National Football Team." *Soccer & Society* 24 (2): 158–71.

Adamovsky, Ezequiel, and Esteban Buch. 2016. *La Marchita, El Escudo y El Bombo: Una Historia Cultural de Los Emblemas Del Peronismo, de Perón a Cristina Kirchner*. Buenos Aires: Planeta.

Ahmed, Sara. 2014. *The Cultural Politics of Emotion*. Edinburgh: Edinburgh University Press.

Ahumada, José Miguel. 2019. *The Political Economy of Peripheral Growth: Chile in the Global Economy*. London: Palgrave Macmillan.

Alabarces, Pablo. 2007. *Fútbol y Patria*. Buenos Aires: Prometeo Libros.

———. 2012. *Crónicas Del Aguante. Fútbol, Violencia y Política*. Buenos Aires: Capital Intelectual.

———. 2014. *Héroes, Machos y Patriotas: El Fútbol entre la Violencia y los Medios*. Buenos Aires: Aguilar.

———. 2015. "Fútbol, Música y Narcisismo: Algunas Conjeturas Sobre 'Brasil, Decime Qué Se Siente.'" *El Oído Pensante* 3 (1).

———. 2018. *Historia Mínima del Futbol en América Latina*. Mexico City: Colegio de Mexico.

Alabarces, Pablo, and José Garriga. 2007. "Identidades Corporales: Entre El Relato y El Aguante." *Campos* 8 (1): 145–65.

———. 2008. "El 'Aguante': Una Identidad Corporal y Popular." *Intersecciones En Antropología* 9: 275–89.

Alabarces, Pablo, and María Graciela Rodríguez, eds. 1996. *Cuestión de Pelotas: Fútbol, Deporte, Sociedad, Cultura*. Buenos Aires: Atuel.

Améstica, Camilo. 2017. "El Aparato Seccionador: Discursos Hegemónicos y 'Barra-bravas.'" In *¿Quién Raya La Cancha?*, edited by Rodrigo Soto and Omar Fernández, 89–108. Buenos Aires: CLACSO.

Andonie, María Elena. 2020. "La 'Primera Línea': ¿Individualistas o Filántropos?" *El Mostrador*, February 24, 2020.

Appadurai, Arjun. 1996. *Modernity at Large: Cultural Dimensions of Globalization*. Minneapolis: University of Minnesota Press.

———. 2013. *The Social Life of Things: Commodities in Cultural Perspective*. Cambridge: Cambridge University Press.

Araujo, Samuel M. 1988. "Brega: Music and Conflict in Urban Brazil." *Latin American Music Review* 9 (1): 50.

Archetti, Eduardo. 1984. "Fútbol y Ethos." *Monografías e Informes de Investigación* 1 (7): 1–38.

———. 1999. *Masculinities: Football, Polo and the Tango in Argentina*. New York: Berg.

Artl, Roberto. 2002. "Football and Popular Joy." In *The Argentina Reader: History, Culture, and Society*, edited by Gabriela Nouzeilles and Graciela R. Montaldo, 263–65. Durham, NC: Duke University Press.

Atria, Jorge, Ignacio Flores, Claudia Sanhueza, and Ricardo Meyer. 2018. "Top Incomes in Chile: A Historical Perspective of Income Inequality (1964–2015)." *Wid.World Working Paper Series* 11 (2018): 1–31.

Attali, Jacques. 2017. *Noise: The Political Economy of Music*. University of Minnesota Press.

Baeza, Angélica. 2019a. "Piñera Asegura Que 'En Medio de Esta América Latina Convulsionada, Chile Es Un Verdadero Oasis Con Una Democracia Estable.'" *La Tercera*, October 8, 2019.

———. 2019b. "Vocera de Gobierno Responsabiliza de Violencia a 'Barras Bravas Relacionadas Con Narcotráfico y Delincuencia Más Dura.'" *La Tercera*, November 22, 2019.

Baker, Geoffrey. 2015. "'Digital Indigestion': Cumbia, Class and a Post-Digital Ethos in Buenos Aires." *Popular Music* 34 (2): 175–96.

Baym, Nancy, and danah boyd. 2012. "Socially Mediated Publicness." *Journal of Broadcasting & Electronic Media* 56 (3): 320–29.

BBC News Mundo. 2024. "'Ningún País Colonialista Nos va a Amedrentar': El Gobierno de Milei Defiende a Los Jugadores de La Selección Argentina En Medio Del Escándalo Por Los Cánticos Racistas." July 18, 2024.

Benjamin, Walter. 2021. *Toward the Critique of Violence*. Edited by Peter Fenves and Julia Ng. Stanford, CA: Stanford University Press.

Bieletto-Bueno, Natalia. 2020. "Sonido, Vocalidad y El Espacio de Audibilidad Pública. El Caso de La Performance «Un Violador En Tu Camino» Por Las Tesis Senior En El Estadio Nacional de Chile." *Boletín Música* 54: 71.

Birenbaum Quintero, Michael. 2006. "La Música Pacifica al Pacífico Violento: Música, Multiculturalismo y Marginalización En El Pacífico Negro Colombiano." *Trans* 10.

———. 2019. *Rites, Rights and Rhythms: A Genealogy of Musical Meaning in Colombia's Black Pacific*. New York: Oxford University Press.

Blesser, Barry, and Linda Salter. 2006. *Spaces Speak, Are You Listening?: Experiencing Aural Architecture*. Cambridge, MA: MIT Press.

Bollier, David. 2008. *Viral Spiral: How the Commoners Built a Digital Republic of Their Own*. New York: New Press.

Bolter, J. David, and Richard Grusin. 1999. *Remediation: Understanding New Media*. Cambridge, MA: MIT Press.

Bourdieu, Pierre. 1999. *The Weight of the World: Social Suffering in Contemporary Society*. Stanford, CA: Stanford University Press.

Bourgois, Philippe. 2001. "The Power of Violence in War and Peace: Post–Cold War Lessons from El Salvador." *Ethnography* 2 (1): 5–34.

boyd, danah. 2011. "Social Network Sites as Networked Publics: Affordances, Dynamics, and Implications." In *A Networked Self: Identity, Community, and Culture on Social Network Sites*, edited by Zizi Papacharissi, 39–58. London: Routledge.

Brown, Matthew. 2014. *From Frontiers to Football: An Alternative History of Latin America since 1800*. London: Reaktion Books.

Bundio, Javier Sebastián. 2020. *La Identidad se Forja en el Tablón: Masculinidad, Etnicidad y Discriminación en los Cantos de las Hinchadas Argentinas*. Buenos Aires: CLACSO.

Butterworth, James. 2017. "Framing Culture: VCD Music Videos and the Politics of Genre in the Peruvian Andes." *Ethnomusicology Forum* 26 (3): 331–48.

Buarque de Hollanda, Bernardo, and Thomas Busset, eds. 2023. *Football Fandom in Europe and Latin America: Culture, Politics, and Violence in the 21st Century*. Cham: Springer International Publishing.

Butler, Judith. 2007. *Gender Trouble: Feminism and the Subversion of Identity*. London: Routledge Classics.

———. 2015. *Notes toward a Performative Theory of Assembly*. Cambridge, MA: Harvard University Press.

Campomar, Andreas. 2014. *Golazo! A History of Latin American Football*. New York: Riverhead Books.

Carrión, Fernando, and María José Rodríguez, eds. 2014. *Luchas Urbanas Alrededor del Fútbol*. Quito: FES.

Castells, Manuel. 2007. "Communication, Power and Counter-power in the Network Society." *International Journal of Communication* 1: 238–66.

Cavarero, Adriana. 2005. *For More than One Voice: Toward a Philosophy of Vocal Expression*. Stanford, CA: Stanford University Press.

Chávez, Alex E. 2017. *Sounds of Crossing: Music, Migration, and the Aural Poetics of Huapango Arribeño*. Durham, NC: Duke University Press.

Chornik, Katia. 2013. "Music and Torture in Chilean Detention Centers: Conversations with an Ex-Agent of Pinochet's Secret Police." *The World of Music* 2 (1): 51–65.

Clastres, Pierre. 1994. *Archeology of Violence*. New York: Scmiotext(e).

Cloonan, Martin, and Bruce Johnson. 2009. *Dark Side of the Tune: Popular Music and Violence*. Burlington: Ashgate.

Cook, Nicholas. 2018. *Music as Creative Practice*. New York: Oxford University Press.

Corona, Ignacio, and Alejandro L. Madrid. 2007. *Postnational Musical Identities: Cultural Production, Distribution and Consumption in a Globalized Scenario*. Lanham: Lexington.

Costa, Carlos, and Luiz Henrique De Toledo. 2022. "Transformações do Torcer: Esportividades do Olhar e Olhares sobre a Esportificação." *Ilha Revista de Antropologia* 24 (3).

Crawford, Kate. 2012. "Following You: Disciplines of Listening in Social Media." In *The Sound Studies Reader*, edited by Jonathan Sterne, 79–90. New York: Routledge.

Crook, Larry N. 1993. "Black Consciousness, Samba Reggae, and the Re-Africanization of Bahian Carnival Music in Brazil." *The World of Music* 35 (2): 90–108.

Cusick, Suzanne G. 2006. "Music as Torture / Music as Weapon." *Trans* 10.

———. 2013. "Towards an Acoustemology of Detention in the 'Global War on Terror.'" In *Music, Sound and Space*, edited by Georgina Born, 275–91. Cambridge: Cambridge University Press.

Darling, Kate, and Aaron Perzanowski, eds. 2017. *Creativity without Law: Challenging the Assumptions of Intellectual Property*. New York: New York University Press.

Das, Veena. 2007. *Life and Words: Violence and the Descent into the Ordinary*. Berkeley: University of California Press.

———. 2008. "Violence, Gender, and Subjectivity." *Annual Review of Anthropology* 37 (1): 283–99.

Daughtry, J. Martin. 2015. *Listening to War: Sound, Music, Trauma, and Survival in Wartime Iraq*. New York: Oxford University Press.

Daughtry, J. Martin, and Jonathan Ritter, eds. 2007. *Music in the Post-9/11 World*. New York: Routledge.

Dent, Alexander. 2012. "Piracy, Circulatory Legitimacy, and Neoliberal Subjectivity in Brazil." *Cultural Anthropology* 27 (1): 28–49.

———. 2020. *Digital Pirates: Policing Intellectual Property in Brazil*. Stanford, CA: Stanford University Press.

Desai-Stephens, Anaar, and Nicole Reisnour. 2020. "Musical Feelings and Affective Politics." *Culture, Theory and Critique* 61 (2–3): 99–111.

Domingo, Daniel. 2020. "No era Paz, era Silencio. El Sonido en el Paisaje Sociosemiótico

Urbano del 'Estallido social' Chileno desde los ECDM." *Arboles y Rizomas. Revista de Estudios Lingüísticos y Literarios* 2 (2): 44–68.

Drott, Eric. 2015. "Rereading Jacques Attali's Bruits." *Critical Inquiry* 41 (4): 721–56.

Dueck, Byron. 2013. *Musical Intimacies and Indigenous Imaginaries: Aboriginal Music and Dance in Public Performance*. New York: Oxford University Press.

Dunn, Bill. 2017. "Against Neoliberalism as a Concept." *Capital & Class* 41 (3): 435–54.

Eidsheim, Nina Sun. 2015. *Sensing Sound: Singing and Listening as Vibrational Practice*. Durham, NC: Duke University Press.

———. 2019. *The Race of Sound: Listening, Timbre, and Vocality in African American Music*. Durham, NC: Duke University Press.

Elsey, Brenda. 2011. *Citizens and Sportsmen: Fútbol and Politics in Twentieth-Century Chile*. Austin: University of Texas Press.

———. 2017. "Introduction: Marking the Field." In *Football and the Boundaries of History: Critical Studies in football*, edited by Brenda Elsey and Stanislao G. Pugliese, 1–10. New York: Palgrave Macmillan.

Emerson, R. Guy. 2019. *Necropolitics: Living Death in Mexico*. London: Palgrave Macmillan.

Elyachar, Julia. 2010. "Phatic Labor, Infrastructure, and the Question of Empowerment in Cairo." *American Ethnologist* 37 (3): 452–64.

Esposito, Roberto. 2008. *Bíos: Biopolitics and Philosophy*. Minneapolis: University of Minnesota Press.

Fanon, Frantz. 2004. *The Wretched of the Earth*. New York: Grove Press.

Farmer, Paul. 2004. "An Anthropology of Structural Violence." *Current Anthropology* 45 (3): 305–25.

Fast, Susan, and Kip Pegley. 2012. "Introduction." In *Music, Politics, and Violence*, edited by Susan Fast and Kip Pegley, 1–33. Middletown, CT: Wesleyan University Press.

Feld, Steven. 1994. "From Schizophonia to Schismogenesis: On the Discourses and Commodification Practices of 'World Music' and 'World Beat.'" In *Music Grooves: Essays and Dialogues*, edited by Charles Keil and Steven Feld, 257–89. Chicago: University of Chicago Press.

———. 1996. "Waterfalls of Song: An Acoustemology of Place Resounding in Bosavi, Papua New Guinea." In *Senses of Place*, edited by Steven Feld and Keith Basso, 91–136. Santa Fe: School of American Research Press.

———. 2003. "A Rainforest Acoustemology." In *The Auditory Culture Reader*, edited by Michael Bull and Les Back, 223–39. New York: Berg.

———. 2012. *Sound and Sentiment: Birds, Weeping, Poetics, and Song in Kaluli Expression*. Durham, NC: Duke University Press.

———. 2015. "Acoustemology." In *Keywords in Sound*, edited by David Novak and Matt Sakakeeny, 12–21. Durham, NC: Duke University Press.

Feld, Steven, Aaron A. Fox, and Thomas Porcello. 2004. "Vocal Anthropology: From the

Music of Language to the Language of Song." In *A Companion to Linguistic Anthropology*, edited by Alessandro Duranti, 321–45. Malden: Blackwell.

Fernández, José Tomás. 2019. "Doctor Orozco: 'No Quiero Que Descienda, Pero Si Desciende, Nos van a Ayudar a Recuperar a La U.'" *Radio La Clave*, October 2, 2019.

Figueroa, Michael A. 2022. "Post-Tarab: Music and Affective Politics in the US SWANA Diaspora." *Ethnomusicology* 66 (2): 236–63.

Forment, C. A. 2007. "The Democratic Dribbler: Football Clubs, Neoliberal Globalization, and Buenos Aires' Municipal Election of 2003." *Public Culture* 19 (1): 85–116.

Foucault, Michel. 1990. *The History of Sexuality, Volume 1: An Introduction*. New York: Vintage Books.

Fossum, David. 2025. *Copyright Consciousness: Musical Creativity and Intellectual Property in Turkey*. Middletown, CT: Wesleyean University Press.

Foster, Susan. 1998. "Choreographies of Gender." *Sign* 1: 1–33.

Fox, Aaron A. 2004. *Real Country: Music and Language in Working-Class Culture*. Durham, NC: Duke University Press.

Frydenberg, Julio. 2011. *Historia Social Del Fútbol: Del Amateurismo a La Profesionalización*. Buenos Aires: Siglo XXI.

Fugellie, Daniela. 2020. "Resignificando El Canon: El Requiem de Mozart En El Estallido Social Chileno." *Boletín Música* 54: 93–109.

Gaffney, Chris. 2008. *Temples of the Earthbound Gods: Stadiums in the Cultural Landscapes of Rio de Janeiro and Buenos Aires*. Austin: University of Texas Press.

Galeano, Eduardo. 1998. *Football in Sun and Shadow*. New York: Verso.

Gallo, Bruno del. 2017. "Los Ingeniosos Del Tablón." *Olé*, May 19, 2017.

Galloway, Kate. 2015. "Materiality and Aural Memory in the Harbour Symphony (St. John's, Newfoundland)." *Sound Studies* 1 (1): 118–43.

Ganti, Tejaswini. 2014. "Neoliberalism." *Annual Review of Anthropology* 43 (1): 89–104.

García Canclini, Néstor. 2001. *Consumers and Citizens: Globalization and Multicultural Conflicts*. Minneapolis: University of Minnesota Press.

Garcia, Luis-Manuel. 2015. "Beats, Flesh, and Grain: Sonic Tactility and Affect in Electronic Dance Music." *Sound Studies* 1 (1): 59–76.

———. 2020. "Feeling the Vibe: Sound, Vibration, and Affective Attunement in Electronic Dance Music Scenes." *Ethnomusicology Forum*, 1–19.

———. 2023. *Together, Somehow: Music, Affect, and Intimacy on the Dancefloor*. Durham, NC: Duke University Press.

Garland, Shannon. 2020. "No Love without Conflict: Rights to the City, Cultural Activism, and the 'Irony of Affect' in São Paulo, Brazil." *Culture, Theory and Critique* 61 (2–3): 283–302.

———. 2024. "Music, Phones and Bank Loans: The Unproductive Labor of Branded Spotify Playlists and the Limits of 'Affective Labor.'" *Journal of Extreme Anthropology* 7 (2): 1–24.

Garriga, José. 2005. "Lomo de Macho: Cuerpo, Masculinidad y Violencia de Un Grupo de Simpatizantes Del Fútbol." *Cuadernos de Antropología Social* 22: 201–16.

———. 2007. *Haciendo Amigos a Las Piñas: Violencia y Redes Sociales de Una Hinchada de Fútbol*. Buenos Aires: Prometeo Libros.

———. 2010. *Nosotros Nos Peleamos: Violencia e Identidad de Una Hinchada de Fútbol*. Buenos Aires: Prometeo Libros.

Gavira, Mariano. 2016. "Nuevos Poetas Del Tablón: Las Canciones de Cancha Ahora Se Escriben Por WhatsApp." *Clarín*, October 2016.

Gill, Denise. 2017. *Melancholic Modalities: Affect, Islam, and Turkish Classical Musicians*. New York: Oxford University Press.

Gillespie, Tarleton. 2010. "The Politics of 'Platforms.'" *New Media & Society* 12 (3): 347–64.

Giulianotti, Richard. 2002. "Supporters, Followers, Fans, and Flaneurs." *Journal of Sport & Social Issues* 26 (1): 25–46.

Giulianotti, Richard, and Roland Robertson. 2009. *Globalization & Football*. London: Sage.

Goldschmitt, K. E. 2011. "'Joga Bonito Pelo Mundo, Guerreiro': Music, Transmedia Advertising, and Brasilidade in the 2006 World Cup." *Popular Music and Society* 34 (4): 417–36.

Goodman, Steve. 2010. *Sonic Warfare: Sound, Affect, and the Ecology of Fear*. Cambridge, MA: MIT Press.

Graeber, David. 2001. *Toward an Anthropological Theory of Value: The False Coin of Our Own Dreams*. New York: Palgrave.

———. 2005. "Value: Anthropological Theories of Value." In *A Handbook of Economic Anthropology*, edited by James Carrier, 439–54. Northampton: Edward Elgar.

Gray, Lila Ellen. 2013. *Fado Resounding: Affective Politics and Urban Life*. Durham, NC: Duke University Press.

Gregg, Melissa, and Gregory Seigworth, eds. 2010. "An Inventory of Shimmers." In *The Affect Theory Reader*, 1–25. Durham, NC: Duke University Press.

Grimson, Alejandro. 2005. *On Argentina and the Southern Cone: Neoliberalism and National Imaginations*. New York: Routledge.

Grumann, Andres. 2013. *Anfiteatro Estadio Nacional*. Santiago de Chile: Cuarto Propio.

Guarello, Juan Cristóbal. 2019. "Los Emprendedores." *La Tercera*, November 21, 2019.

———. 2021. *País Barrabrava*. Santiago de Chile: Debate.

Gutmann, Matthew C. 2006. *The Meanings of Macho: Being a Man in Mexico City*. Berkeley: University of California Press.

Hale, Charles R. 2006. "Activist Research v. Cultural Critique: Indigenous Land Rights and the Contradictions of Politically Engaged Anthropology." *Cultural Anthropology* 21 (1): 96–120.

———. 2008. "Introduction." In *Engaging Contradictions: Theory, Politics, and Method of Activist Scholarship*, edited by Charles R. Hale, 1–30. Los Angeles: University of California Press.

Han, Clara. 2012. *Life in Debt Times of Care and Violence in Neoliberal Chile*. Berkeley: University of California Press.

Hardt, Michael, and Antonio Negri. 2000. *Empire*. Cambridge, MA: Harvard University Press.

———. 2004. *Multitude: War and Democracy in the Age of Empire*. New York: Penguin Press.

———. 2009. *Commonwealth*. Cambridge, MA: Belknap Press.

———. 2017. *Assembly*. New York: Oxford University Press.

Harvey, David. 2005. *A Brief History of Neoliberalism*. New York: Oxford University Press.

———. 2007. "Neoliberalism as Creative Destruction." *The ANNALS of the American Academy of Political and Social Science* 610 (1): 21–44.

Harkness, Nicholas. 2014. *Songs of Seoul: An Ethnography of Voice and Voicing in Christian South Korea*. Berkeley: University of California Press.

Hawkins, Matthew. 2017. "'This Is Boedo': Stories of a Lost Football Stadium, a Buenos Aires Barrio, and How the Hinchas of San Lorenzo Fought to Return." PhD diss., Carleton University.

Henriques, Julian. 2011. *Sonic Bodies: Reggae Sound Systems, Performance Techniques, and Ways of Knowing*. New York: Continuum.

Herrera, Eduardo. 2018. "Masculinity, Violence, and Deindividuation in Argentine Football Chants: The Sonic Potentials of Participatory Sounding in Synchrony." *Ethnomusicology* 62 (3): 470–99.

Hobsbawm, Eric J. 1990. *Nations and Nationalism since 1780: Programme, Myth, Reality*. Cambridge: Cambridge University Press.

Hofman, Ana. 2015. "Music (as) Labour: Professional Musicianship, Affective Labour and Gender in Socialist Yugoslavia." *Ethnomusicology Forum* 24 (1): 28–50.

———. 2020a. "Disobedient: Activist Choirs, Radical Amateurism, and the Politics of the Past after Yugoslavia." *Ethnomusicology* 64 (1): 89.

———. 2020b. "The Romance with Affect: Sonic Politics in a Time of Political Exhaustion." *Culture, Theory and Critique* 61 (2–3): 303–18.

Hollanda, Bernardo Borges Buarque de. 2011. "O Futebol como Alegoria Antropofágica: Modernismo, Música popular e a Descoberta da 'Brasilidade' Esportiva." *Artelogie* 1.

Hollanda, Bernardo Borges Buarque de, and Thomas Busset, eds. 2023. *Football Fandom in Europe and Latin America: Culture, Politics, and Violence in the 21st Century*. Cham: Springer International Publishing.

Holzmeister, Antonio. 2014. "A Brief History of Football Stadiums in Brazil." *Soccer & Society* 15 (1): 65–80.

Ito, Mizuko. 2008. "Introduction." In *Networked Publics*, edited by Kazys Varnelis, 1–14. Cambridge, MA: MIT Press.

Jack, Max. 2021a. "The Crowd in Flux: Atmosphere and the Governance of Public Affects at FC Union Berlin." *Ethnomusicology* 65 (3): 497–518.

———. 2021b. "'You Call This Democracy?' FC Saint Pauli Supporters, Football Chants, and the Police." In *Football and Popular Culture: Singing Out from the Stands*, edited by Stephen Millar, Martin Power, Paul Widdop, Daniel Parnell, and James Carr. London: Routledge.

———. 2022. "What's the Crowd Got to Do with It?: On Fandom and Antifascist Action at Eis Hockey Club Dynamo Berlin." *TDR: The Drama Review* 66 (3): 133–48.

———. 2024. *Insurgent Fandom: An Ethnography of Crowds and Unruly Sounds*. New York: Oxford University Press.

James, Daniel. 1988. "October 17th and 18th, 1945: Mass Protest, Peronism and the Argentine Working Class Author." *Journal of Social History* 21 (3): 441–61.

James, Robin. 2019. *The Sonic Episteme: Acoustic Resonance, Neoliberalism, and Biopolitics*. Durham, NC: Duke University Press.

Jameson, Fredric. 2017. "Foreword." In *Noise: The Political Economy of Music*, vii–xiv. Minneapolis: University of Minnesota Press.

Jordán, Laura. 2023. "Feminist Performance as Challenging Voice-Body Regimentation." *Studies in Latin American Popular Culture* 41: 130–49.

Kane, Brian. 2015. "Sound Studies without Auditory Culture: A Critique of the Ontological Turn." *Sound Studies* 1 (1): 2–21.

Karush, Matthew B. 2003. "National Identity in the Sports Pages: Football and the Mass Media in 1920s Buenos Aires." *The Americas* 60 (1): 11–32.

———. 2007. "The Melodramatic Nation: Integration and Polarization in the Argentine Cinema of the 1930s." *Hispanic American Historical Review* 87 (2): 293–326.

———. 2010. "Populism, Melodrama, and the Market: The Mass Cultural Origins of Peronism." In *The New Cultural History of Peronism: Power and Identity in Mid-Twentieth-Century Argentina*, edited by Matthew B. Karush and Oscar Chamosa, 21–51. Durham, NC: Duke University Press.

———. 2012. *Culture of Class: Radio and Cinema in the Making of a Divided Argentina, 1920–1946*. Durham, NC: Duke University Press.

———. 2017. *Musicians in Transit: Argentina and the Globalization of Popular Music*. Durham, NC: Duke University Press.

Karush, Matthew B., and Oscar Chamosa, eds. 2010. *The New Cultural History of Peronism: Power and Identity in Mid-Twentieth-Century Argentina*. Durham, NC: Duke University Press.

Katzenbach, Christian. 2018. "There Is Always More Than Law! From Low IP Regimes to a Governance Perspective in Copyright Research." *Journal of Technology Law and Policy* 22 (1–26).

Kirschstein, Natalie. 2007. "Reclaiming the Future: Communal Space, Collective Memory, and Political Narrative Uruguay's Murga Stage." PhD diss., Harvard University.

Kunz, Marco. 2001. "Épica y Picaresca del Fútbol en la Narrativa de Osvaldo Soriano." *Versants* 40: 261–79.

Laing, Dave, and Andy Linehan. 2015. "Football Sounds: Popular Music and Football in Britain." *Popular Music History* 8 (3): 307–25.

Leys, Ruth. 2011. "The Turn to Affect: A Critique." *Critical Inquiry* 37 (3): 434–72.

Lipsitz, George. 2008. "Breaking the Chains and Steering the Ship: How Activism Can Help Change Teaching and Scholarship." In *Engaging Contradictions: Theory, Politics, and Methods of Activist Scholarship*, edited by Charles R. Hale, 88–111. Los Angeles: University of California Press.

Long, Nicholas J., and Henrietta L. Moore. 2012. "Sociality Revisited: Setting a New Agenda." *The Cambridge Journal of Anthropology* 30 (1).

Lopes, Felipe Tavares Paes. 2013. "Dimensões Ideológicas do Debate Público acerca da Violência no Futebol Brasileiro." *Revista Brasileira de Educação Física e Esporte* 27 (4): 597–612.

Lopes, Felipe Tavares Paes, and Bernardo Borges Buarque De Hollanda. 2018. "'Ódio Eterno ao Futebol Moderno': Poder, Dominação e Resistência nas Arquibancadas dos Estádios da Cidade de São Paulo." *Tempo* 24 (2): 206–32.

Lopes, Felipe Tavares Paes, and Heloisa Helena Baldy Dos Reis. 2017. "Ideologia, Futebol e Violência: Uma Análise do Relatório 'Preservar o Espetáculo, Garantindo a Segurança e o Direito à Cidadania.'" *Arquivos Brasileiros de Psicologia* 69 (3): 36–51.

Louie, Kam. 2002. *Chinese Masculinity: Society and Gender in China*. Cambridge: Cambridge University Press.

———. 2003. "Chinese, Japanese and Global Masculine Identities." In *Asian Masculinities: The Meaning and Practice of Manhood in China and Japan*, edited by Kam Louie and Morris Low, 1–16. London: Routledge.

Luker, Morgan. 2016. *The Tango Machine: Musical Culture in the Age of Expediency*. Chicago: University of Chicago Press.

Lutz, Catherine. 2017. "What Matters." *Cultural Anthropology* 32 (2): 181–91.

MacMillen, Ian. 2020. "Affective Block and the Musical Racialisation of Romani Sincerity." *Ethnomusicology Forum* 29 (1): 81–106.

Magazine, Roger. 2007. *Golden and Blue like My Heart: Masculinity, Youth, and Power among Football Fans in Mexico City*. Tucson: University of Arizona Press.

Mahmood, Saba. 2011. *Politics of Piety: The Islamic Revival and the Feminist Subject*. Princeton, NJ: Princeton University Press.

Manuel, Peter. 1993. *Cassette Culture: Popular Music and Technology in North India*. Chicago: University of Chicago Press.

———. 2006. "The Saga of a Song: Authorship and Ownership in the Case of 'Guantanamera.'" *Latin American Music Review* 27 (2): 121–47.

Manuel, Peter, and Wayne Marshall. 2006. "The Riddim Method: Aesthetics, Practice, and Ownership in Jamaican Dancehall." *Popular Music* 25 (3): 447–70.

Márquez, Francisca. 2020. "Por una Antropología de los Escombros. El Estallido Social en Plaza Dignidad, Santiago de Chile." *Revista 180*, no. 45.

Marra, Pedro. 2009. "Paisagens Sonoras do Futebol: Som e Esporte em uma Metrópole Latinoamericana." *Razón y palabra* 69.

———. 2012. "'Vou Ficar de Arquibancada Pra Sentir Mais Emocao' - As Sonoridades Nas Dinamicas de Producao Da Torcida de Futebol Do Clube Atlético Mineiro." *Contemporanea* 10 (1).

———. 2014. "Unfair Players, ou 'Da Copa eu Abro Mão, Quero Dinheiro pra Saúde e Educação.'" *Logos* 1 (24).

———. 2017. "'Ei, Juiz, Vai Tomar no Cu': Políticas Torcedoras e do Futebol e Sonoridades de Xingamentos em Performances Masculinas." *FuLiA* 2 (2): 56–79.

———. 2018. "Acceleration, Deceleration, Sonic Torture and Inertia: Temporalities of a Football Match." 5 (1).

———. 2021. "Sound, Violence and Gender Performances in Brazilian Football." In *Football and Popular Culture: Singing Out from the Stands*, edited by Stephen Millar, Martin Power, Paul Widdop, Daniel Parnell, and James Carr, 38–50. London: Routledge.

Marra, Pedro, and Felipe Trotta. 2019. "Sound, Music and Magic in Football Stadiums." *Popular Music* 38 (1): 73–89.

Martín, Alicia. 1997. *Fiesta En La Calle: Carnaval, Murgas e Identidad En El Folklore de Buenos Aires*. Buenos Aires: Ediciones Colihue.

Marwick, Alice, and danah boyd. 2010. "I Tweet Honestly, I Tweet Passionately: Twitter Users, Context Collapse, and the Imagined Audience." *New Media & Society* 7: 1–20.

Mason, Tony. 1995. *Passion of the People?: Football in South America*. New York: Verso.

Massumi, Brian. 2002. *Parables for the Virtual: Movement, Affect, Sensation*. Durham, NC: Duke University Press.

Matamala, Daniel. 2015. *Goles y Autogoles: Historia Política del Fútbol Chileno*. Santiago de Chile: Patagonia.

Mazzarella, William. 2004. "Culture, Globalization, Mediation." *Annual Review of Anthropology* 33 (1): 345–67.

———. 2009. "Affect: What Is It Good For?" In *Enchantments of Modernity: Empire, Nation, Globalization*, edited by Saurabh Dube, 291–309. New York: Routledge.

Mbembe, Achille. 2003. "Necropolitics." Translated by Libby Meintjes. *Public Culture* 15 (1): 11–40.

———. 2019. *Necropolitics*. Durham, NC: Duke University Press.

McCann, Anthony. 2001. "All That Is Not Given Is Lost: Irish Traditional Music, Copyright, and Common Property." *Ethnomusicology* 45 (1): 89–106.

McClary, Susan. 2017. "Afterword." In *Noise: The Political Economy of Music*, 149–60. Minneapolis: University of Minnesota Press.

McDaniel, Byrd. 2024. *Spectacular Listening: Music and Disability in the Digital Age*. New York: Oxford University Press.

McDonald, David A. 2013. *My Voice Is My Weapon: Music, Nationalism, and the Poetics of Palestinian Resistance*. Durham, NC: Duke University Press.

Meintjes, Louise. 2003. *Sound of Africa!: Making Music Zulu in a South African Studio*. Durham, NC: Duke University Press.

———. 2017. *Dust of the Zulu: Ngoma Aesthetics after Apartheid*. Durham, NC: Duke University Press.

Meizel, Katherine. 2020. *Multivocality: Singing on the Borders of Identity*. New York: Oxford University Press.

Millar, Stephen R. 2020. *Sounding Dissent: Rebel Songs, Resistance, and Irish Republicanism*. Ann Arbor: University of Michigan Press.

Miller, Kiri. 2017. *Playable Bodies: Dance Games and Intimate Media*. New York: Oxford University Press.

Minks, Amanda, and Ana María Ochoa Gautier. 2021. "Music, Language, Aurality: Latin American and Caribbean Resoundings." *Annual Review of Anthropology* 50 (1): 23–39.

Moreira, María Verónica. 2007. "Etnografía Sobre El Honor y La Violencia de Una Hinchada de Fútbol En Argentina." *Revista Austral de Ciencias Sociales* 13: 5–19.

———. 2008. "Aguante, Generosidad y Política En Una Hinchada de Fútbol Argentina." *Avá* 12: 79–94.

Moreira, María Verónica, David Quitián, and Rodrigo Soto, eds. 2018. *Los Días Del Mundial: Miradas Críticas Desde América Latina Sobre Rusia 2018*. Buenos Aires: CLACSO.

Mouffe, Chantal. 2013. *Agonistics: Thinking the World Politically*. New York: Verso.

Moulian, Tomás. 1997. *Chile Actual: Anatomía de Un Mito*. Santiago de Chile: LOM.

Nadel, Joshua H. 2014. *Fútbol!: Why Football Matters in Latin America*. Gainesville: University Press of Florida.

Navaro-Yashin, Yael. 2009. "Affective Spaces, Melancholic Objects: Ruination and the Production of Anthropological Knowledge." *The Journal of the Royal Anthropological Institute* 15 (1): 1–18.

Nordstrom, Carolyn. 2004. *Shadows of War: Violence, Power, and International Profiteering in the Twenty-First Century*. Berkeley: University of California Press.

Nouzeilles, Gabriela, and Graciela R. Montaldo, eds. 2002. *The Argentina Reader: History, Culture, and Society*. Durham, NC: Duke University Press.

Novak, David. 2010. "Cosmopolitanism, Remediation, and the Ghost World of Bollywood." *Cultural Anthropology* 25 (1): 40–72.

———. 2013. *Japanoise: Music at the Edge of Circulation*. Durham, NC: Duke University Press.

Novak, David, and Matt Sakakeeny, eds. 2015. "Introduction." In *Keywords in Sound*, edited by David Novak and Matt Sakakeeny, 1–11. Durham, NC: Duke University Press.

O'Brien, Michael. 2016. "El Corso Sigue. Apuntes Sobre Murga, Tango, y Lo Carnavalesco." In *Tango: Ventanas Del Presente II: De La Gesta a La Historia Musical Reciente*, edited by Mercedes Liska and Soledad Venegas, 113–32. Buenos Aires: Ediciones del IMFC.

———. 2018. "El Bombo Loco: Sounding Alterity and Populism in Buenos Aires." *Ethnomusicology* 62 (3): 439–69.

Ochoa Gautier, Ana María. 2006a. "A Manera de Introducción: La Materialidad de Lo Musical y Su Relación Con La Violencia." *Trans* 10.

———. 2006b. "Sonic Transculturation, Epistemologies of Purification and the Aural Public Sphere in Latin America." *Social Identities* 12 (6): 803–25.

———. 2014. *Aurality: Listening and Knowledge in Nineteenth-Century Colombia*. Durham, NC: Duke University Press.

———. 2017. "El Silencio como Armamento Sonoro." In *Los Silencios de la Guerra*, edited by Camila de Gamboa and María Victoria Uribe, 117–58. Bogotá: Universidad del Rosario.

———. 2019. "Afterword: Sonic Cartographies." In *Remapping Sound Studies*, edited by Jim Sykes and Gavin Steingo, 261–74. Durham, NC: Duke University Press.

Ortner, Sherry B. 1995. "Resistance and the Problem of Ethnographic Refusal." *Comparative Studies in Society and History* 37 (1): 173–93.

Orton, Mark. 2023. *Football and National Identity in Twentieth-Century Argentina: La Nuestra*. Cham: Springer International Publishing.

Osorio, Javier. 2023. "El Entusiasmo Bullicioso de los Hinchas: Sonido, Espacio y Sensaciones en los Espectáculos Deportivos en Chile, 1910–1949." *Autoctonia Revista de Ciencias Sociales e Historia* 7 (2): 796–831.

Paley, Julia. 2001. *Marketing Democracy: Power and Social Movements in Post-Dictatorship Chile*. Berkeley: University of California Press.

Palomino, Pablo. 2020. *The Invention of Latin American Music: A Transnational History*. New York: Oxford University Press.

Papacharissi, Zizi. 2015. *Affective Publics: Sentiment, Technology, and Politics*. New York: Oxford University Press.

Parker, David. 2013. "Introduction: The Making and Endless Remaking of the Middle Class." In *Latin America's Middle Class: Unsettled Debates and New Histories*, edited by Louise Walker and David Parker. Lanham: Lexington Books.

Parrish, Charles T., and John Nauright. 2013. "Fútbol Cantitos: Negotiating Masculinity in Argentina." *Soccer & Society* 14 (1): 1–19.

Party, Daniel. 2023. "The Right to Live in Peace: Musical Responses to Violence in the 2019 Chilean Uprising." *Latin American Perspectives* 50 (3): 37–52.

Paulich, Diego. 2016. "Música Clásica." *Olé*, June 11, 2016.

Pérez, Miguel. 2018. "Toward a Life with Dignity: Housing Struggles and New Political Horizons in Urban Chile." *American Ethnologist* 45 (4): 508–20.

———. 2022. *The Right to Dignity: Housing Struggles, City Making, and Citizenship in Urban Chile*. Stanford, CA: Stanford University Press.

Perlman, Marc. 2004. "Golden Ears and Meter Readers: The Contest for Epistemic Authority in Audiophilia." *Social Studies of Science* 34 (5): 783–807.

———. 2019. "Meta-Ideologies of Textuality: Authorship, Plagiarism, Copyright." *Signs and Society* 7 (2): 245–87.

Pettan, Svanibor, ed. 1998. *Music, Politics, and War: Views from Croatia*. Zagreb: Institute of Ethnology and Folklore Research.

Pieslak, Jonathan. 2009. *Sound Targets: American Soldiers and Music in the Iraq War*. Bloomington: Indiana University Press.

Pilzer, Joshua D. 2022. *Quietude: A Musical Anthropology of "Korea's Hiroshima."* New York: Oxford University Press.

Porcello, Thomas. 2004. "Speaking of Sound: Language and the Professionalization of Sound-Recording Engineers." *Social Studies of Science* 34 (5): 733–58.

Rabi, Roberto, and Gustavo Villafranca. 2017. *Toda La Historia de La U: El Fútbol, La Hinchada, La Insttución*. Santiago de Chile: RIL Editores.

Ramos, Natalia, and Javiera Leira. 2019. "Futbolistas Selección Chilena Deciden No Jugar Amistoso Con Perú En Medio de Revuelta Social." *Reuters*, November 13, 2019.

Rancière, Jacques. 2006. *The Politics of Aesthetics*. London: A&C Black.

Recasens, Andrés. 1999. *Diagnóstico Antropológico de Las Barras Bravas y de La Violencia Ligada al Fútbol*. Santiago de Chile: FACSO Universidad de Chile.

Reis, Heloisa Helena Baldy Dos, and Felipe Tavares Paes Lopes. 2016. "O Torcedor por Detrás do Rótulo: Caracterização e Percepção da Violência de Jovens Torcedores Organizados." *Movimento* 22 (3): 693.

Rein, Raanan. 2014. *Fútbol, Jews, and the Making of Argentina*. Stanford, CA: Stanford University Press.

Rein, Raanan, ed. 2015. *La Cancha Peronista: Fútbol y Política (1946–1955)*. Buenos Aires: Unsam Edita.

Richards, Donald G. 1997. "The Political Economy of the Chilean Miracle." *Latin American Research Review* 32 (1).

Rios, Fernando. 2008. "La Flûte Indienne: The Early History of Andean Folkloric-Popular Music in France and Its Impact on Nueva Canción." *Latin American Music Review* 29 (2): 145–81.

———. 2014. "'They're Stealing Our Music': The Argentinísima Controversy, National Culture Boundaries, and the Rise of a Bolivian Nationalist Discourse." *Latin American Music Review* 35 (2): 197–227.

Ritter, Jonathan. 2002. "Siren Songs: Ritual and Revolution in the Peruvian Andes." *British Journal of Ethnomusicology* 11 (1): 9–42.

Rossano, Salvatore. 2009. "Murga y Carnaval, de 'Cosas de Negros' a Patrimonio Ciudadano. Construcción de Identidad En La Murga Porteña." *Etno-Folk* 14–15: 574–95.

———. 2012. "El Espacio Sonoro Del Bombo Con Platillo En Buenos Aires, Entre Música, Ruido e Invisibilidad." *Revista Argentina de Musicología* 12–13: 183–204.

Ruete, Gabriela, Daniela Tapia, Sebastián Díaz, Santiago Rosselot, and Daniel Albornoz. 2021. "Club Universidad de Chile: Recuperar o Clube para os seus Torcedores, Superando o Fracaso das S.A." In *Clube Empresa: Abordagens Críticas Globais às Sociedades Anônimas no Futebol*, edited by Irlan Simões. Brazil: Editora Na Bancada.

Sakakeeny, Matt. 2015. "Music." In *Keywords in Sound*, edited by Matt Sakakeeny and David Novak. Durham, NC: Duke University Press.

Salazar, Gabriel, and Julio Pinto, eds. 1999. *Historia Contemporánea de Chile V: Niñez y Juventud*. Santiago de Chile: LOM Ediciones.

Salerno, Daniel. 2006. "Apología, Estigma y Represión. Los Hinchas Televisados de Fútbol." In *Hinchadas*, edited by Pablo Alabarces, 129–60. Buenos Aires: Prometeo Libros.

Samuels, David. 2004. *Putting a Song on Top of It: Expression and Identity on the San Carlos Apache Reservation*. Tucson: University of Arizona Press.

Santos, Irlan Simões. 2016. "Mercantilização do Futebol e Movimentos de Resistência dos Torcedores: Histórico, Abordagens e Experiências Brasileiras." *Esporte e Sociedade* 11 (27).

Schafer, Murray R. 1994. *The Soundscape: Our Sonic Environment and the Tuning of the World*. Rochester, VT: Destiny Books.

Scheper-Hughes, Nancy. 1992. *Death without Weeping: The Violence of Everyday Life in Brazil*. Berkeley: University of California Press.

———. 1995. "The Primacy of the Ethical: Propositions for a Militant Anthropology." *Current Anthropology* 36 (3): 409–40.

Scheper-Hughes, Nancy, and Philippe Bourgois. 2003. "Introduction: Making Sense of Violence." In *Violence in War and Peace: An Anthology*, edited by Nancy Scheper-Hughes and Philippe Bourgois. Malden: Blackwell.

Schneider, Jane, and Peter Schneider. 2008. "The Anthropology of Crime and Criminalization." *Annual Review of Anthropology* 37 (1): 351–73.

Schmidt, Bettina, and Ingo Schröder, eds. 2001. "Introduction: Violent Imaginaries and Violent Practices." In *Anthropology of Violence and Conflict*, edited by Bettina Schmidt and Ingo Schröder, 1–24. European Association of Social Anthropologists. London: Routledge.

Serna, Miguel, and Franco González. 2017. "Cambios Hasta Cierto Punto: Segregación Residencial y Desigualdades Económicas En Montevideo (1996–2015)." *Latin American Research Review* 52 (4): 571–88.

Sibaja, Rwany, and Charles Parrish. 2014. "Pibes, Cracks and Caudillos: Argentina, the World Cup and Identity Politics." *Soccer & Society* 15 (5): 655–70.

Simonett, Helena. 2001. "Narcocorridos: An Emerging Micromusic of Nuevo L.A." *Ethnomusicology* 45 (2): 315–37.

Sneed, Paul. 2007. "Bandidos de Cristo: Representations of the Power of Criminal Factions in Rio's Proibidão Funk." *Latin American Music Review* 28 (2): 220–41.

Soriano, Osvaldo. 1996. *Artistas, Locos y Criminales*. Barcelona: Grupo Editorial Norma.

Spencer, Christian, and Natalia Bieletto-Bueno. 2020. "Volver a Creer. Crisis Social, Música, Sonido y Escucha En La Revuelta Chilena (2019–2020)." *Buletín Música* 54: 3–27.

Spencer, Christian. 2020. "Hacia Un Nuevo Cancionero Popular: Música, Creación y Política En La Revuelta Social Chilena (2019–2020)." *Boletín Música* 54: 29–51.

Steingo, Gavin. 2019. "Another Resonance: Africa and the Study of Sound." In *Remapping Sound Studies*, edited by Gavin Steingo and Jim Sykes, 39–60. Durham, NC: Duke University Press.

Steingo, Gavin, and Jim Sykes, eds. 2019. "Introduction: Remapping Sound Studies in the Global South." In *Remapping Sound Studies*, edited by Gavin Steingo and Jim Sykes, 1–36. Durham, NC: Duke University Press.

Sterne, Jonathan. 2003. *The Audible Past: Cultural Origins of Sound Reproduction*. Durham, NC: Duke University Press.

———. 2012. *MP3: The Meaning of a Format*. Durham, NC: Duke University Press.

———. 2015. "Hearing." In *Keywords in Sound*, edited by David Novak and Matt Sakakeeny, 65–77. Durham, NC: Duke University Press.

Stobart, Henry. 2010. "Rampant Reproduction and Digital Democracy: Shifting Landscapes of Music Production and 'Piracy' in Bolivia." *Ethnomusicology Forum* 19 (1): 27–56.

———. 2011. "Constructing Community in the Digital Home Studio: Carnival, Creativity and Indigenous Music Video Production in the Bolivian Andes." *Popular Music* 30 (2): 209–26.

Tapia, Yanis, and Carlos Vergara. 2017. "'Mujeres Que van de Frente': Prácticas Sociales y Aguante En Las Hinchas Del Club Santiago Wanderers de Valparaíso." In *¿Quién Raya La Cancha?*, edited by Rodrigo Soto and Omar Fernández, 261–90. Buenos Aires: CLACSO.

Tatro, Kelley. 2014. "The Hard Work of Screaming: Physical Exertion and Affective Labor Among Mexico City's Punk Vocalists." *Ethnomusicology* 58 (3): 431–53.

———. 2022. *Love and Rage: Autonomy in Mexico City's Punk Scene*. Middletown, CT: Wesleyan University Press.

Tausig, Benjamin. 2019. *Bangkok Is Ringing: Sound, Protest, and Constraint*. New York: Oxford University Press.

Taylor, Timothy D. 2016. *Music and Capitalism: A History of the Present*. Big Issues in Music. Chicago: University of Chicago Press.

Teitelbaum, Benjamin. 2017. *Lions of the North: Sounds of the New Nordic Radical Nationalism*. New York: Oxford University Press.

———. 2019. "Collaborating with the Radical Right: Scholar-Informant Solidarity and the Case for an Immoral Anthropology." *Current Anthropology* 60 (3): 414–35.

———. 2022. "Music and the Immorality of Ethnography." In *The Routledge Companion to Ethics and Research in Ethnomusicology*, edited by Jonathan P. J. Stock and Beverley Diamond, 89–99. New York: Routledge.

Teixeira, Rosana Da Câmara. 2016. "Espetáculo Futebolístico e Associativismo Torcedor No Brasil: Desafios e Perspectivas Das Entidades Representativas de Torcidas Organizadas No Futebol Brasileiro Contemporâneo." *Esporte e Sociedade* 28: 1–26.

———. 2018. "A Associação Nacional das Torcidas Organizadas do Brasil na Arena Pública: Desafios de um Movimento Coletivo." *Antípoda. Revista de Antropología y Arqueología* 30: 11–28.

Teubal, Miguel. 2004. "Rise and Collapse of Neoliberalism in Argentina: The Role of Economic Groups." *Journal of Developing Societies* 20 (3–4): 173–88.

Tochka, Nicholas. 2017. "Singing 'with Culture': Popular Musicians and Affective Labour in State-Socialist Albania." *Ethnomusicology Forum* 26 (3): 289–306.

Tsing, Anna Lowenhaupt. 2005. *Friction: An Ethnography of Global Connection*. Princeton, NJ: Princeton University Press.

Tucker, Joshua. 2013. *Gentleman Troubadours and Andean Pop Stars: Huayno Music, Media Work, and Ethnic Imaginaries in Urban Peru*. Chicago: University of Chicago Press.

Turino, Thomas. 2000. *Nationalists, Cosmopolitans, and Popular Music in Zimbabwe*. Chicago: University of Chicago Press.

Valdés, Juan Gabriel. 1995. *Pinochet's Economists: The Chicago School of Economics in Chile*. Cambridge: Cambridge University Press.

Veal, Michael E. 2007. *Dub: Soundscapes & Shattered Songs in Jamaican Reggae*. Middletown, CT: Wesleyan University Press.

Villalobos-Ruminott, Sergio. 2020. "Chilean Revolts and the Crisis of Neoliberal Governance." *Radical Philosophy* 2 (7): 9–16.

Vimieiro, Ana Carolina. 2015. "Football Supporter Cultures in Modern Day Brazil: Hypercommodification, Networked Collectivisms and Digital Productivity." PhD diss., Queensland University of Technology.

Viveiros de Castro, Eduardo. 2004. "Perspectival Anthropology and the Method of Controlled Equivocation." *Tipití: Journal of the Society for the Anthropology of Lowland South America* 2 (1).

Warner, Michael. 2002. *Publics and Counterpublics*. New York: Zone Books.

Weidman, Amanda. 2006. *Singing the Classical, Voicing the Modern: The Postcolonial Politics of Music in South India*. Durham, NC: Duke University Press.

———. 2014. "Anthropology and Voice." *Annual Review of Anthropology* 43 (1): 37–51.

———. 2015. "Voice." In *Keywords in Sound*, edited by David Novak and Matt Sakakeeny, 232–45. Durham, NC: Duke University Press.

———. 2021. *Brought to Life by the Voice: Playback Singing and Cultural Politics in South India*. Berkeley: University of California Press.

Wieviorka, Michel. 2009. *Violence: A New Approach*. London: SAGE.

Žižek, Slavoj. 2008. *Violence: Six Sideways Reflections*. New York: Picador.

INDEX

Page numbers in *italics* refer to illustrations.

MUSIC / CULTURE

A series from Wesleyan University Press
Edited by Deborah Wong, Sherrie Tucker, and Jeremy Wallach

The Music/Culture series has consistently reshaped and redirected music scholarship. Founded in 1993 by George Lipsitz, Susan McClary, and Robert Walser, the series features outstanding critical work on music. Unconstrained by disciplinary divides, the series addresses music and power through a range of times, places, and approaches. Music/Culture strives to integrate a variety of approaches to the study of music, linking analysis of musical significance to larger issues of power—what is permitted and forbidden, who is included and excluded, who speaks and who gets silenced. From ethnographic classics to cutting-edge studies, Music/Culture zeroes in on how musicians articulate social needs, conflicts, coalitions, and hope. Books in the series investigate the cultural work of music in urgent and sometimes experimental ways, from the radical fringe to the quotidian. Music/Culture asks deep and broad questions about music through the framework of the most restless and rigorous critical theory.

FALL 2025

Luis Achondo
The Sounds of Aguante: Politics of Fandom in South American Football

SPRING 2025

Dave Fossum
Copyright Consciousness: Musical Creativity and Intellectual Property in Turkey

FALL 2024

Benjamin Barson
Brassroots Democracy: Maroon Ecologies and the Jazz Commons

Donna Lee Kwon
Stepping in the Madang: Sustaining Expressive Ecologies of Korean Drumming and Dance

Sumarsam
The In-Between in Javanese Performing Arts: History and Myth, Interculturalism and Interreligiosity

A COMPLETE LIST OF SERIES TITLES CAN BE FOUND AT
https://www.weslpress.org/search-results/?series=music-culture

ABOUT THE AUTHOR

Luis Achondo is an Assistant Professor at Memorial University. He holds a PhD in Ethnomusicology from Brown University and has previously held postdoctoral positions at Case Western Reserve University and Pontificia Universidad Católica de Chile. His projects have been generously funded by the Wenner-Gren Foundation for Anthropological Research, the US Fulbright Program, the Tinker Foundation, and Chile's National Agency for Research and Development, and his work has been published in edited volumes, the *Journal of Latin American and Caribbean Anthropology*, *Twentieth-Century Music*, *Ethnomusicology Forum*, *Sound Studies*, *Soccer and Society*, *Journal of the Society for American Music*, *Journal of Musicological Research, and Resonancias*. He was also awarded the Society for Ethnomusicology's James T. Koetting Prize and LACSEM Prize.